Esther C. Hays

Dorothy Parke
621 W. 11th St.
Medford, OR 97501

D0498460

The Hearthstone of My Heart

The Hearthstone of My Heart

Elizabeth Borton de Treviño

Introduction by Margaret Cousins

Doubleday & Company, Inc., Garden City, New York, 1977

Library of Congress Cataloging in Publication Data

Treviño, Elizabeth Borton, 1904–
The hearthstone of my heart.

1. Treviño, Elizabeth Borton, 1904–   —Biography.
2. Authors, American—20th century—Biography.
I. Title.
PS3539.R455Z516   813'.5'2   [B]
ISBN: 0-385-03550-0
Library of Congress Catalog Card Number: 76-18340

Copyright © 1977 by Elizabeth Borton de Treviño
All Rights Reserved
Printed in the United States of America
First Edition

To my sister
Barbara Borton Phillips
and my brother
Judge Paul R. Borton
with love

INTRODUCTION

So much contemporary reading matter is wracked with pain, violence and despair in subject matter and with dissonance and derogation in language, that to read this modest memoir is like coming out of a storm into a sunlit garden. Elizabeth Borton de Treviño writes with affection and insight about times, places and people in the recent American past, and she has mastered her craft. Perhaps her memoir seems modest only because she is a modest person and the book actually has much wider connotations.

Mrs. Treviño writes about a loving family circle, an eclectic but stable community, a demanding but irresistible landscape, enthusiasm for work and achievement, the drive and panache of people operative in a maturing frontier. The early decades of the twentieth century in the United States now seem an idyllic setting for coming of age—a more innocent and hopeful time—but the facts are that the whole population was helpless before the scourge of disease, unable to ameliorate the extremes of the land and climate, limited in communications, slow and ponderous in methods of transportation, largely deprived of the advantages of higher education, and the majority tied to some variety of hard, drudging work. Any comparison with the opportunities and resources of the present would find those days severely wanting.

The quality which does illuminate this period, as indicated in Mrs. Treviño's book, is the character of the people. Profoundly individual, they exhibit basic integrity, a respect for disciplines, willingness to accept responsibility—even to welcome it—to cherish expectations and believe they can accomplish them. And they are happy. While these characteristics could be described as holdovers from a frontier society, there seems to be no real reason why they could not be operative today. They are all the product of personal will. Given the opportunity, surely most people would opt for happy lives. These tools are still available, so the opportunity exists for anyone willing to use them. The minds of many young people are already veering in this direction.

Tolstoy has said, in his oft-misquoted dictum, that all happy families resemble one another. Perhaps they do, for readers who have experienced happy family life (and I am convinced there are more of these than the opposite) will enjoy pleasurable shocks of recognition, regardless of race, creed, color or geography. On the other hand, happy families—like Tolstoy's unhappy ones—are each happy in their own fashion. They harbor myths, traditions, superstitions, legends, proverbs and jokes unique to themselves. They produce poets, romantics, adventurers, eccentrics and rascals, as well as the salt of the earth. They achieve happiness by differing approaches.

Witness Mrs. Borton, who refused for forty years to take off the forty pounds of overweight recommended by the medical profession. She died, buxom, at ninety-three, still buttering her bread. (Mrs. Borton, a matron of irreproachable probity, had one telling maxim: "Always lie to gossips . . . they will be hoist with their own petard!") Lawyer Borton, *pater familias* extraordinary, who deliberately chose the hot, arid climate of Bakersfield, California, as a setting for his life work, had a habit of slipping off alone, embarking on two long train rides and two ferry sails, to spend the day sitting out in the rain in San Francisco whenever a storm at sea was forecast. He did not invite his wife and children.

It seems unlikely that Elizabeth Borton, a sentimental homebody with guileless eyes, schoolgirl braids, and the gentle nature and manners of a sheltered lady, would find happiness as an important reporter on a large metropolitan daily newspaper at a time when women were scarcely permitted to set foot in the City Room. But that is what she did. It seems even more unlikely that she—who always wept copiously at any separation from her family and admits that she had to be ejected forcibly from the nest— should fall in love with a Mexican gentleman, marry and spend the rest of her days in a foreign city a thousand miles away. But of course she did, and she has written books about her happy family life there which have endeared the Mexican domestic scene to more Americans than anything else.

Intrinsic in these revelations is the author's lifelong interest in books, music and the arts, inculcated and encouraged in her upbringing. These interests opened doors for her in her career and remain a continuing joy. There is little gainsaying that such handmaidens of happiness provide a bulwark that never fails. It came naturally to the Bortons to expose their children to such influences when they were young and to encourage them to become performers, not merely spectators.

The author's announced intention in this volume is to conjure the world of her youth, which in the march of progress has virtually disappeared. She hazards the opinion that the time may come when nobody will remember the way it was. This has urged her to set down her memories. There is charming nostalgia here, of course, but there is much that is applicable now to fledglings of every sort. Mrs. Treviño is, as ever, concerned with the human heart, which remains vulnerable and may be the last thing to change.

You will find considerable garnered wisdom, suitable for today or tomorrow, and while it is her deprecating way to credit it largely to other people, it represents a winnowing of personal experience, salted with common sense. She delivers opinions with candor and warmth.

The Hearthstone of My Heart is written with style and spirit and none of the cloying sweetness which has come to be associated with the subject matter of happiness. The reader is likely to be seduced by the flowing narrative and the remarkable characters, but sooner or later it is borne in that—along with the Golden Rule—the formula for a satisfactory life is joy in the human condition and the disposition to be equal to whatever presents itself. This conclusion is not spawned by flimsy optimism or a tendency to ignore outrageous fortune or acts of God, but by the reliance of the individual on himself to cope, welcome experience and find means of enjoying life. This is the testament of one who has.

Margaret Cousins

Friends my soul with joy remembers!
How the quivering flames they start,
When I fan the living embers
On the hearth-stone of my heart!

Henry Wadsworth Longfellow

The Hearthstone of My Heart

Part I

The Hearthstone of My Heart

Backward, turn backward, O Time, in your flight,
Make me a child again just for tonight!

Henry Wadsworth Longfellow

1.

When I was a little girl in Bakersfield, California, it was a favorite game to count the white horses we saw as we trudged our mile to school. When we had counted (and duly stamped spit in our palm and recited an appropriate ritual) one hundred white horses, we could expect to find "our wish" under our pillow next morning. And our parents having been privy to all the counting and its daily progress, and no doubt consulted about "the wish," we usually found it—the ribbon, or the box of pencils—under the pillow.

Now no children play this game. No horses are seen in our streets, so full of automobiles, noise and smog; indeed, few horses are seen anywhere except at riding schools, and races run for the purpose of gambling. Horses have become luxuries, like yachts.

My father owned one of the first automobiles ever to frighten those same horses we counted (and many people) into shying and snorting. But now men walk on the moon, and enormous jets whisk passengers from one side of the continent to the other in less time than it took us to drive eighty miles in our Maxwell.

I have been thinking about the years of my childhood and of my youth—exceptionally happy they were for me—and it occurs to me that unless I, and a few other people who lived in the beginning of this century, tell about those times, they will soon be totally forgotten, for almost nothing of them remains in our present-day culture.

I have seen fantastic discoveries and metamorphoses, many of the most astounding ones within the last decade. In this era of accelerating change, the quiet years before the First World War and the peaceful, hopeful ones after we had "made the world safe for democracy," may well be almost entirely forgotten. But I, at least, remember them with longing, for they offered happiness without introspection and doubt; joy without fear of the future; contentment without cynicism.

In the hope that these recollections may preserve for some of us what we loved, at least in memory, I am encouraged to recall my earliest years. Across my life many wonderful people made their way, many dear and good people have guided and helped me, many—far more than I deserve—have loved me.

I shall stir the living embers on the hearthstone of my heart, before my little flame, too, dies away into ashes.

2.

My father was a lawyer. More, he had loved the law from his earliest childhood. Just as, fifty years later, boys used to play hookey from school to go to the movies, my father played truant to go to court and listen to the great lawyers of his day argue a case. He believed that law and justice were the greatest achievements of civilized man, and he set out to take part in the orderly pattern of what civilization had evolved for the government and protection of men, their rights, and their dignity. He loved the law, and he trusted it.

Papa had chosen Bakersfield, California, as a place to start his law practice because it was a fairly new town and it was growing. The year was 1901. Bakersfield was developing along with industries and business that interested him and that would provide opportunities for him. Oil had been discovered and derricks were springing up everywhere, like a forest of leafless trees. The valley produced cattle, wheat, grapes, cotton. Silver was mined in the fabulous Kelly Rand, and two important railways served the town, the Santa Fe and the Southern Pacific.

Papa was self-made in a way that few men are nowadays. His father, a schoolmaster, had died when Papa was nine, and Grandmother, like so many women of her day, had no way of supporting herself and her little son and daughter, other than by taking in roomers and boarders. She moved from Evergreen, California, to San Jose, took a house near the Normal School, and provided a home for its students (girls). Papa had to help, in countless ways. He did his part—gathering eggs, carrying in wood, making fires, even sweeping—he went to school and learned his lessons, and he spent blissful stolen hours at court, and when he was seventeen he went to San Francisco to study law. In order to support himself he got up every morning at four to deliver the San Francisco *Examiner* to newsstands in the city. He hauled the papers around on a small handcart. What he earned paid his fees and rent for his small attic room, and bills for his sketchy food. Nevertheless, he had wonderful Saturday evenings, which he told us about later around our dinner table. On Saturday evenings he ate at an Italian restaurant for fifty cents, with a bottle of "dago red" thrown in, and for an additional twenty-five cents (making a grand total of what we in the West called "six bits") he sat in the balcony of a theater and watched a vaudeville show.

("Two bits," "four bits," and "six bits" were common terms for twenty-five cents, fifty cents, and seventy-five cents, in my childhood; the expression came from the Spanish *real*, or "bit," which was roughly twelve and a half cents.)

After graduation from law school, and distinguishing himself by having been appointed to the prestigious "Carnot Debate" at the University of California, Papa worked for a San Francisco firm of lawyers. Then one day, the head of the firm called him in and said, "Fred, you are a bright boy, and I am going to give you a piece of advice. Don't stay here. Go out and find a lively, growing small town, and grow with it."

Papa took the advice and spent his last ten dollars on a train ticket to Bakersfield. Before nightfall he had a job as stenographer to Judge Paul R. Bennet, and his career had begun. He grew with Bakersfield, and Bakersfield grew with him.

Bakersfield, in the San Joaquin Valley, had a reputation (it still has) as a hardship post. The early settlers in Bakersfield were proud, in a morbid way, of the horrible summer heat (which often reached 120 degrees). They used to brag that if you dug down a few feet and listened, you could hear voices, so close was Bakersfield to the hot hinges. Also, Bakersfield suffered in the winter from solid weeks of chilling tule fog (miasma above reedy marshes), and malaria was endemic.

When my mother arrived in Bakersfield, on a deadly September day, after her week's honeymoon, she said to my father, "Dear, let's save up our money and get out of here!" But she lived there over sixty years, and though she never loved Bakersfield, as my father did, she came to think of it as "home."

My earliest memories are of the little house in Bakersfield where Mama had come as a bride. There was no air conditioning in those days, and ladies wore many more layers of clothes than they do now. She must have suffered.

My mother had been born and brought up on a lonely ranch in Monterey County, near the town of Soledad (which means solitude). She walked three miles to school every day, along the railroad tracks, and three miles home. The school was a one-room institution, and my mother told me that by the end of the first grade she knew all the lessons, right through eighth grade and could recite them. She had a good memory.

Her life had been comfortable, even pampered, for my grandmother had lost her first little daughter, and when at last, after two boys, my mother was born, Grandma cared for her with desperate, passionate devotion. My mother told me that when visitors appeared on the road leading into the ranch, Grandma took Mama and locked her into the grain bin, with a couple of toys, and ordered her to keep quiet. If Grandma found that the visitors were healthy and had no red-eyed, coughing, or feverish children with them, she might let Mama out. But if she suspected anything like a cold or a rash, Mama was not produced. Thus Mama was preserved throughout her girlhood, and thus too she made use of animals, flowers, books, and her own imagination for companionship, since visits were few and far between, and even at school, Mama was snatched out the moment word came that some plague was raging among the pupils.

The day came when Grandma had to face sending her two sons and Mama off to high school. Grandpa agreed that she must go with them to watch over the children, especially their frail, beautiful little girl. Berkeley was chosen because it was near the sea (for Mama's health), and because the older boys, and later Mama, could continue on there, through the University of California. Grandfather, a European intellectual, insisted that Mama go to college too—an attitude rare in those days. As for Grandpa, he must have been lonely at the ranch with only his books for company. But he was a mysterious, extremely well-educated and wealthy man, and he spent most of his time locked in his library, reading his books in Danish, German, English, Spanish, French and Russian. More of him later, for his enigmatic figure haunted much of my girlhood imagination, and I had the privilege of knowing him for at least ten years.

Away in Berkeley, in high school and later at college, Mama was cared for, protected and preserved from all evil, from within and from without, by Grandma's watchful and loving eyes, her unwearied and loving hands.

Berkeley was cool and fresh, and Mama lived there eight years until her graduation from the University of California, in 1903. Tenderly cared for and looked after like a hothouse flower, she found the brawling, dusty town of Bakersfield, where she went as a bride, a kind of Purgatory.

Besides, she and Papa were poor. Mama learned, to her horror, that my father had borrowed three hundred dollars for their honeymoon, and the money was owing. He had bought a horse and trap, and he had started paying for the little cottage. Young lawyers did not have a steady income, and Mama, who had always been given everything she wanted, started to count pennies.

But she was in love and she was proud.

Mama and Papa had met in high school, and for him, Mama was the only woman in the world from the moment he laid eyes on her coppery hair, green eyes, delicate profile, and slender figure. He fell in love with her and he never fell out, to his dying day. They wished to marry the year my mother began college, but my grandfather took one look at my shabby, penniless young father, with his bony, hungry face and thundered, "Never! That fellow could never support you! No marriage until you have finished college and received your teaching certificate!"

Actually, they married in September, after Mama's June graduation, and she never earned a penny in her life. She quickly learned how to stretch them, however.

I remember the little house. It was a small wooden frame cottage with four rooms—a "front room," bedroom, dining room and kitchen. Shaded in front by umbrella trees, it had a large back yard where Papa grew alfalfa for the horse and Mama raised chickens and planted vegetables. I soon learned that one put seeds into the ground and afterward plants came up and reproduced themselves. Accordingly, I once buried my mother's rings, in the hope of getting a good crop. I must have been about two. Somehow I was persuaded to dig them up before they sprouted.

There were a few neighbors, on each side and nearby, but behind the little house the dusty land stretched away to the horizon and the distant hills; it was alkali land, covered in sagebrush and tumbleweed.

My mother had no baby-sitter. She had to wash (with washtubs and scrubbing board) and cook (on a wood-burning stove) and clean her house (with broom and dustrags), so she was too busy to sit and sing to me or play with me. But she had Star. Star took care of me. Star was a liquid-eyed, loving Irish setter, who mothered any small creature set down beside her. While Star raised me, she also raised Rufus, a little black Clumber spaniel my father brought home in his coat pocket one dark winter evening. We were always a family for animals. Mama never worried about me, because from her kitchen window she could look out into the sagebrush and see Star's red plumy tail waving, and know that I was there, guarded and safe.

When I learned to talk, I became instantly garrulous and a great trial. I was a devoted purveyor of news, to my mother's discomfiture. My father went to his office, on the other side of town, on the local streetcar, and came home on it in the evening.

He left the horse and buggy for my mother's use. I used to wait for him at the corner, where he descended sometime after five, and ride home on his shoulder. In that short block I would rob my mother of all her stored-up conversation for the evening, because when we reached home Papa knew everything that had happened.

On hot summer evenings, we sat out on our front porch as darkness fell, and Papa and I named the toads that came flopping out to eat the insects in the grass. I loved the big velvety-soft-looking ungainly creatures, with their sweet fluting voices, and we gave them beautiful names.

On cold winter evenings, while Mama was baking bread in the kitchen and Papa was studying in the front room, they had great fun with me, perhaps in lieu of Scrabble and anagrams. They sent me back and forth with messages from one to the other—long, difficult messages which I had to repeat over and over to myself as I went, to make sure I got them right: "The ichthyosaurus has absconded with the whiffle tree," and other absurdities. I marvel now at their inventiveness.

But of course they had no radio and no television. Not even movies. So they entertained themselves with what was at hand. And what was at hand was I.

I was induced to lull myself to sleep at night by repeating to myself the names of the neighboring Alexander family's dogs, which were always legion. I would begin: "Paca, and Juana, and Jim Douglas, and Flippy Dog, and Rags and Curly, and Swiff . . ." and on and on.

The sounds of our town were what small towns everywhere in those days were used to: the huffing and puffing of the railroad engines in the roundhouse; the scream and clang of the streetcar every half hour; the wailing of the night train, "The Owl," as it made off for San Francisco every night at midnight; a horizon of dogs, barking in the distance, as Garcia Lorca has it for a town in Spain, but it was true of our town too. There were roosters crowing at first light, the ubiquitous clop-clop of horses along the roads, hauling drays laden with goods or passengers. Plus the occasional howling of a child being chastised, for in those days parents did not spare the rod, and woodsheds were scenes of regular parental rituals.

Jung Sing came every few days with his horses and wagon to sell us fresh vegetables from his garden. I remember him well. He always wore the same kind of blue coat and trousers which have become standard in Mao's China. He was, he told Mama, a "Mission boy." He related that once he and his wife had lost all their six children, from diphtheria, within the space of a week. But, he went on happily, he "had 'em all back now." So Mrs. Jung Sing had produced twelve, all told. He and his wife, he told Mama—filling her dishpan with lettuce, string beans, young onions and fresh corn (all for about twenty cents)—ate rice and drank tea. But the kids were Americans. They wanted bread and coffee.

Mama had ridden all over Grandpa's ranch in Soledad bareback, sitting sideways on the horse, and could drive a team of six, so Papa bought her a pretty frisky little mare, which she could ride or drive, as the mare was broken to the fast two-wheeled trap that dashing young dandies liked to use. I vaguely recall a scene. I remember the atmosphere of mutual recrimination one time when Papa came home and reported accusingly that Mama had been seen out in the trap on Twenty-fourth Street, racing Mexicans. "Well, I won!" shouted Mama, who was all for excellence in every endeavor.

Poor and struggling as they were, they soon found that they had difficulty making ends meet. My mother, with the wisdom of a serpent, suggested that each of them carry a little notebook and jot down all their expenditures in it, then compare them at the end of a week. Papa accepted this as very reasonable and duly noted down his carfare, cigarettes, a new gun, bullets, a fountain pen, and four or five books about American Indians, hunting, or African travels. They compared. Mama had bought flour, soap, chicken feed, meat, tea, coffee, and vegetables.

Papa gave in. From then on, he gave all his money to Mama, and she passed him an allowance for carfare and cigarettes, and so they managed for the rest of their lives.

All this quiet and semirural life came to an end with the advent of the automobile. Papa promptly forgot the notebook and

all his promises and went into debt to buy one. His was one of
the first automobiles in our town.

3.

In a modern household, full of all sorts of appliances and auto-
mation, one could not refer to "the machine" and be instantly
understood. In my childhood, the machine meant the automobile.

Our machine was a Maxwell. It was red, and it was high, and
had no doors, as I knew to my terror, for I went on fast rides (up
to fifteen miles an hour) with my parents, seated on a small folding carpet stool at my mother's feet. To Papa's left was a large
brass horn with a bulbous rubber attachment, like those carried
later in films by the silent Marx brother. My mother clutched the
collar of my dress, my father blasted on his horn, and we traveled in an enfolding cloud of dust, to the dismay of chickens,
horses, and pedestrians.

There was an attire proper for riding in the machine. It
consisted of a long sort of smock, goggles and a cap, though my
father, in his enthusiasm, usually leaped into his machine in
whatever he was wearing at the moment. But Mama and I wore
the regulation uniform: cotton coats to cover one from head to
foot, and hats tied on with voluminous veils.

It was a triumph to own a machine, but hard work to operate
it. There were no garages, no gas stations, and few roads appropriate for leisurely driving. Papa (and every other man who
bought a car) had to take a week off from work in order to study
the diagrams and instructions that came with the machine, to
memorize the maps of its insides and what each part was supposed to do, to master the art of changing tires and vulcanizing
inner tubes, putting on patches, and fastening up the canvas
rain-cover, with its little windows of isinglass. And of course, everyone who ran a machine had to be a good walker. For often
the automobile coughed and died out in the middle of nowhere,
and long weary trudges with buckets, for water or gasoline or

both, had to be undertaken. Farmers with teams of horses made extra money pulling stalled cars out of ditches, getting machines stuck in the mud out onto dry ground, and generally rescuing Maxwells, Overlands and Fords from other unexpected and terrible dangers.

By the time I was five, we had moved from our little house to the other side of the city, because I would soon be in school and had to be near enough to walk. In our new house we were only five blocks from Papa's office in the Producer's Bank Building, and he came home for lunch every day. Our house was on Twentieth Street on the block between C and D streets, a street full of children. (By then I had a little sister, Barbara, and when I was eight and a half, my baby brother Dick arrived.) These friends of my childhood, and of my sister's and brother's, were a whole world to us, and those of us who survive are fast friends to this day.

I believe it was about this time that my father bought his Stanley Steamer. This was a large and powerful machine, demanding infinite respect. Papa attached colored threads to each of its tubes and convolutions and followed them until he had them all memorized, and then there ensued many wonderful Sunday picnics. First Papa would go out to the garage to get up steam. This took about twenty minutes (I never understood the mysterious process). Then, when we were all assembled in front of the house, in our coats and veils, with the picnic hamper ready, Papa would silently slide up to us, the Stanley hissing gently.

It must be that some of these engines got up too much steam and blew up, because people became afraid of them. Or could it be that the makers of gasoline-burning machines produced insinuating propaganda? I don't know. Now that I am old and cynical, I have my suspicions. But Papa loved his Steamer, and many were the anecdotes recounted of him and other heroes who owned the same kind of machine.

One famous story concerns the then notorious White Wolf Grade, a very steep hill, which Steamers usually negotiated like mountain goats while other cars huffed and puffed and died all along the grade, unable to make it to the top. A lawyer friend of my father's, who also owned a Steamer, had bragged all over town about how his car could run right up the White Wolf Grade. He then conveyed a nonbeliever out to the site (just north of Bakersfield) to demonstrate. But he had allowed his steam to decline in some strange way, so his Steamer also stalled on the grade. The lawyer got out, kicked and cursed his car and called it and its manufacturer every name that came to his talented tongue. Whereupon (the steam having built up again, something these cars did) he got in, and the Steamer went right to the top of the grade in admirable style. The nonbeliever was converted and told everyone in town that the Steamer was the best darn car made; it listened and took orders like a darn mule.

A later acquisition of my father's was the Overland. Parents who had automobiles in those days sometimes would use them to get children to sleep on hot summer evenings. Children, fed and bathed and shucked into pajamas, were tossed into the back seat and the automobile was started. The movement created a small hot breeze, the chugging was soporific, and the route most fathers took put us all to sleep. They drove out over Kern River Bridge, where there was usually a wet smell from the reedy shallows; through the oilfields, where the odor of raw oil hung in the hot still air (to this day I love that smell); up China Grade and along the bluffs, where often a cool breeze blew. In my day there was no life along the bluffs but lizards and little cottontails, and if there was air, it swept along the bluff and seemed refreshing. By the time the car and its passengers got home, the children were fast asleep and could be laid out on their little beds.

4.

It seems to me now that our town was remarkably cosmopolitan, considering that it was located in the midst of farming country in the West and counted fewer than twenty thousand inhabitants. We had an Italian colony, a strong and influential Basque colony (people still come from other parts of the state to eat at

Bakersfield's wonderful Basque restaurants), a fair sprinkling of
Irish, a Jewish community that brought a rabbi from Los Angeles or San Francisco for the High Holidays (I used to play the
Kol Nidre and Eli Eli for these services on my violin), many Chinese (who celebrated Chinese New Year with a long cloth
Dragon, manned by twenty or thirty men, and many firecrackers),
and a resident Second Son, from England, who lived like a lord
amongst his roses a little distance out of town. Mostly the inhabitants were American Southerners, and there was a large black
community, with rival churches. Besides, there were several families of blacks who had "passed," a stratagem to which contemporary blacks do not resort, out of admirable pride. Yet these
families—known to all of us as Negro, despite the fact that some
members had light skins and golden hair—were accepted for
what they said they were and were taken into the white community with no questions asked; many became outstanding in the
professions and in community life.

On the block where I lived, we were very cosmopolitan as
well. Next door were the Ikenbergs, German Jews; Hattie (born
Hedwig) and Carrie, my mother (born Karen), became best
friends. My mother spoke German with Hattie, and to this day I
can hear her and Hattie admonishing us: *"Ve sits du,"* and
"Stige." And at household tasks we were sometimes ordered:
"Schnell, schnell!" From Hattie we learned a few wonderful Yiddish words which became part of our family vocabulary: *Me-
shuga, schnorrer, schlumpf, plotz, tiniff,* and *gonaf.* Across the
street, next door to the Lutheran Church, lived the German-born
pastor and his family. He dared to speak out against Hitler in
the early years before the United States entered World War II,
and his proud German congregation haughtily asked him to re-
sign, which he did at once. He moved to Los Angeles and made
a new career for himself, far from whited sepulchers.

On our block was a family in which the father was English
and the mother Irish. Across the street from them was an
English-born mother who believed firmly in not sparing the rod.
We used to hear the bellows of her progeny with regularity,
and if their howls didn't put the fear of God into her own children, they did for the rest of us. Then there was a family whose

father was German; and another headed by an Irishman. The latter was adored by all the children, for his Irish wit was lavished on young and old. On the next block in back lived a family from Virginia, whose voices were soft and slow, and a French lady whose voice was strident. And on another block was a French family whose children would join in our noisy sports until it was time for *mon père* to come home, then would hiss at us, "Cheese it, kids! our papá!"

Around us, too, were all the activities of the town, in the professions of the *pater familias*—from lawyer to harnessmaker, gardener to pharmacist, newspaper editor to wine merchant, grocer to surveyor.

The block was a small community in itself, and my mother and Hattie knew the life and miracles of every person in it. We children all played together in the evenings during the hot summer months, and I recall Crack the Whip, Statues, Prisoner's Base (which our dogs played with us), Tag and many other games. The girls (who predominated) also played jacks and jumprope and hopscotch on the sidewalks, and once in a while we played with dolls. Generally we were active and the dolls were left at home, to be cuddled when we were quarantined with some illness. Or they suffered the fate of Barbara's and my big doll, which we tore apart in order to dress our baby brother in the golden wig and the sashed white dress and blue kid slippers.

One by one, Santa Claus brought us bicycles, and we all became wheel-borne, and yet the roar and screech of roller skates could be heard all year, as well. And when, one summer, the Borton children had the use of Pedro, a subtle and intelligent donkey, there was a good deal of riding around, with regular screams of protest when Pedro bucked someone off. He refused to carry more than three at a time.

I remember those early years on our block with a great feeling of peace and security, and yet I must not give the impression that our town was a specially virtuous one. On the contrary, it was known as a brawling, tough town in the early days. Ladies and children were cautioned not to walk down to the crossing of Chester Avenue and Nineteenth Street, because there was a sa-

loon on each of the four corners, and gentlemen in their cups
were often ejected with the speed of cannonballs, constituting a
real menace to the health of passers-by. Also, there were shots
now and then, and sometimes corpses; also, agitated rushing of
the wounded to emergency rooms or to the nearest doctor's
office.

The fracases at the corner of Nineteenth and Chester gave the
surgeons interesting problems. Papa's special friend, Dr. Sabichi, happened to be in the operating room of Bakersfield hospital
one Saturday evening when a young gangster was brought in,
having been thoroughly shot up. He was covered with blood,
and unconscious. The doctor told Papa he didn't think the young
man had a chance, but he did his best for him. They quickly cut
off his clothes, chloroformed him, and saw that he had fifteen or
sixteen gunshot wounds in the abdomen.

"So I opened him up," reported the doctor, "took his tripes
out into a sterile basin, sewed up every hole I could find, put
them back in him, and stitched him together. He's doing fine."

Besides the gunmen, gamblers and swindlers who came to
Bakersfield to ply their trades or to keep in practice, there were
more sophisticated offenders. I remember hearing of one handsome young man who worked in a bank and took advantage of
his golden opportunities to embezzle a considerable quantity of
money. He was caught, tried and convicted, and sent off to
meditate in what was then called a penitentiary. Having done
his time, he returned to Bakersfield, and his train was met by
loyal friends with a brass band and banners.

From every front porch, news went round about people who
broke the law or disturbed the peace. Comments on miscreants
were embellished with whatever one knew of their ancestors or
previous condition of servitude—the whole thing being rolled up
into great wads of gossip and sent humming along every telephone line. I rather think it was salubrious because the ladies
who sat in their porch rockers and noticed, or at their windows
and observed, were totally feared by everyone in the neighborhood. The husband who rolled home drunk at three in the
morning could never hope to keep it a secret. Lovers who took
ladders to the windows of their sweethearts were cautioned off

at once, not only by neighborhood dogs, but also by the window watchers who had telephones.

Flirtations across marital lines were spotted and scotched in a hurry.

I suppose the life of our town at the turn of the century, having faded now into an old misty daguerreotype, at whose details the young moderns look with wonder and often with amusement, has been idealized in my memory. That would be natural, and I must ask indulgence. Yet this time produced men like my father, who was unique in a way many young people, it seems to me, are trying wistfully to imitate. It may seem hard to believe in this age of novels about life's frustrations and bitterness, the identity crisis, and the need to let go and indulge one's fantasies (in our age a whole profession has grown up around the resolution of personal conflicts, and psychiatrists flourish as the green bay tree), but my father was a perfectly happy man. He was fulfilled, at peace with himself and the world, successful insofar as he wanted to be successful, and he looked at the world and at his family with amazed delight. He enjoyed his life to the fullest, lived by his own code of honor, and was beloved of countless friends.

I think our culture, before the automobile age, produced many such men. But there still were those who were failures, who endured bad marriages, who were hurt and humiliated by difficult children. Only in those years, part of the natural courage of men and women consisted in keeping their mouths shut. Catholics went to confession, Protestants talked things over with their ministers, and women put on starched shirtwaists and served tea and homemade cake, and pretended. It worked very well. The literature of the breast-beater had not come into flower.

5.

Those summers in Bakersfield, before the saint who invented air conditioning, were awful beyond description. Men who worked in stores and offices could slave beneath whirling ceiling fans, some of which were enormous. But women who cooked, scrubbed and cleaned in the small frame houses of wood or brick, stifled. Further, they did their work in corsets, drawers, petticoats, house dresses, aprons and laced shoes (except for a few slatterns, and everybody knew who *they* were). By August, most of the men managed to send their heat-crazy families away, if not to the shore or "the city" (which always meant San Francisco), then at least to cabins in the nearby mountains.

During the summer, mothers never had to worry about their children running away. They merely hid their shoes, as no little foot could bear the heat of the sidewalk, which literally burned. Those who could leap across the sidewalks, walked on the grass and could get from house to house. Hoses and sprinklers were kept going all day so that children and dogs could play in and out of the water, and so keep alive until nightfall.

One wonderful thing about Bakersfield, appreciated in summer, was the cool deep well water which was piped into the houses. One could always refresh oneself at the kitchen tap, and ice wasn't needed. Though we had an iceman. He came by in a truck, drawn by two big horses, and he was always big and brawny. Over his shoulder he wore a piece of leather, which was wet, because on it he rested the cake of ice. Children were sent out to give the family's daily order—twenty pounds, or thirty, or fifty—and the iceman chipped off a square (he never weighed the ice, but he seemed to know by its shape how much it would weigh), and then, with ice tongs, he hoisted it to his shoulder and carried it into the house.

The iceman was much admired, but a more immediate hero to us was John McNally, the ice-cream man. He drove a big old white horse which was speckled all over with light-golden spots. We held many anxious consultations about whether it was fair to count John McNally's horse among our "lucky lucky white horses" because of his freckles. Voting at last decided that John's horse could be counted, but only once a day—that is, when it came down Twentieth Street but not again on the return journey up Twenty-first.

John sold cones. They cost five cents, but he was known to extend credit. Flavors were chocolate, strawberry and vanilla, and sometimes maple nut. If John wasn't late on his route, or annoyed about something, he would permit strange mixtures, and occasionally he even sent a gallant cone of pineapple ice to some mama who had purchased five or six cones of ice cream for the rabble that always followed him.

When allowances were spent and poverty had set in, we had to beg chips of ice from the iceman, and bold boys even stole these chips sometimes. They tasted of straw and were not too satisfactory, but they never seemed to make anybody sick. Anyhow, one never mentioned a stomach ache, unless absolutely doubled up, because the immediate result was always Fletcher's Castoria (for the littlest ones) or castor oil (for those over six). My charge for castor oil was fifty cents, but my sister was a better bargainer and got the price up to a dollar. Papa always solemnly paid when we had to take the nasty stuff.

At the end of school, in the summertime, I trembled with dread, because then my mother would begin to can and preserve. I peeled mounds of peaches and apricots and plums, and Mama canned and made sauce and jam and jelly. Wonderful orchards surrounded Bakersfield. Then the tomatoes came in and I peeled lug after lug of tomatoes, while Mama hovered over the hot stove (and it was always steaming weather) canning them. All these good things were stored in the cellar and appeared on our table all year round. In every household the same hot heavy work was going on.

But one year Mama and her friends on the block all made catsup. I don't know what went wrong, but a few weeks later our block resounded with a noise that sounded like a hundred machine guns. All the catsup bottles blew up and every cellar looked as if creatures had been dismembered in it: walls were bespattered with red and the floors were awash. There ensued a frenzied cleaning up, and vows were taken never to trust that recipe again.

Women's Lib had not reared its head, and while women and girls canned and peeled and sterilized jars, the boys played poker in the cool cellar, with bottle tops for chips.

And then, of course, sometime during the dreadful summer,

we would go to Grandma's, and Grandma lived in Monterey, on the sea.

In the summertime, like all the other little girls, I wore "barefoot" sandals, a Ferris waist, panties and a dress. But our clothes in winter were far different, and worth a description.

First we would put on a shirt, usually long-sleeved, of some finely knitted material, either all wool or with some wool in it. Long drawers were provided next, of the same stuff. These came to the ankles. Over the shirt went the Ferris waist, a garment equipped with many tapes and buttons, onto which the panties were fastened. These went on over the long drawers and were made of white cotton and trimmed with lace or eyelet embroidery. Each pair of panties had three buttonholes in front, fastened to buttons on the Ferris waist, and two at the sides in back. From the Ferris waist depended garters to which long ribbed cotton stockings (black or brown) were attached. In winter, folding the leg of the underdrawers, so that the stocking above looked neat, was a task over which many children wept, while others whimpered or howled as they buttoned up their shoes with an implement called a buttonhook. Then came a petticoat, often knitted from colored wool by loving grandmothers, and sewed onto a little bodice. Then the cotton petticoat went on, and finally, the dress.

In winter I always had two dresses, worn on alternate weeks. I recall, with love, a brown corduroy and a red wool.

In the spring and fall the woolen underwear was banished, but we wore the rest. For parties we all had pink or blue or white cotton stockings (to match the wide ribbon sash on our white embroidered party dresses), and we all wore black velvet strap slippers.

Except for the rich princess or two in our town who had beaver fur hats, most of the girls wore hats made by their mothers. (Boys wore caps.) Our mothers went to the store to buy a frame, which they then covered with whatever material their fancy dictated. One winter I had a hat of brown velvet, high-crowned and trimmed with a bit of fur from an old cape of Grandma's. And one heavenly Easter I had a hat made of seablue maline (a kind of gauze) trimmed with pink roses. I wore it, certain that under my gorgeous hat I was the most elegant and beautiful young woman at the Easter service (of whatever church I was patronizing at the moment).

In the summer we sometimes wore hats made of stitched denim, with an elastic strap under the chin; I had one in gray-blue, which was *de rigueur* for the beach. Also, sometimes, our mothers bought straw shapes and trimmed them with ribbons and flowers. When Milan straw came in, we all stepped forth handsomely protected from the sun (except the girls who preferred the Breton, or off-the-face shape), and there were even, sometimes, lovely leghorn straws, with wide floppy brims, which called for black velvet and a single rose.

Tanned faces and freckles were not fashionable. Though the little arms that emerged from the summer dresses were usually brown as berries from the hot sun, our faces were, by preference, pale.

Little boys had to wear the fearful winter underwear also (known as the union suit), and the long stockings, with shirt and woolen knickerbocker suit over all. Sometimes, in frosty weather, they wore scarves or mufflers (usually hand-knitted), and a few sissies wore mittens. Most of us had chapped hands all winter.

The hair combing was a big production every morning, in every household where there were girls. Boys could slick back their mops with water, but a girl had to kneel down by her seated mother, submit to disentangling, and then have her hair braided and tied to the head in various ways—sometimes with braids crossed in back, or on top of the head, or looped to one side. Big girls could have one braid in back and a wide bow.

I longed for curls, but my straight hair would have been the envy of the young ladies who now iron their hair to make it lank. Once in a while my busy mother would work on me with rags and water, constructing tight cylinders of hair, on the knobby protuberances of which I slept all night in the hope of lovely ringlets in the morning. But alas, when the rags were unwound, I usually had a tight curl partway down, and a long straight wisp at the end, spoiling the whole effect. I suffered, and I bitterly envied Gladys and Helen, whose mamas could make curls by simply winding their hair around their fingers.

Before the advent of the bob, women washed their hair at home. This was a process that involved heating water, filling bowls and leaning over them draped in towels (while somebody rubbed in soap, then sluiced rinse water through the hair), and finally sitting out in the sun for half an hour or more until the hair was thoroughly dry. Beauty shops were rare, and the ladies who couldn't stand their hair used curling tongs, heated on the stove, to achieve what we used to refer to (we straight-haired ones) as "bent hair." Then something called the Marcel hit the country, and everybody went to get one. The beauty shop (and "having your hair done") came in with the bob and the Marcel. Meanwhile, some brave ladies "ratted" their hair, by combing it backward, forming a fine snarl which could be covered with top hair and give an illusion of thickness. Others dropped eggs onto their scalps and rinsed with sage tea, vinegar, or even whiskey.

The day came when I was to enter school. I was to go to what was called "the receiving grade," which antedated the kindergarten. But first I had to be vaccinated, and there were several unforgettable visits to the doctor's office, where I saw awful "bone men" and "meat men" (on charts) and was thoroughly frightened. After several tries, I achieved a good vaccination and a scar. After the first two attempts, which didn't take, my father teased me by suggesting I should have the vaccination on my nose. Even then, I was vain enough to tremble at the idea of such a hideous fate.

At last the big day arrived. I was to go to school. I remember my dress. It was of white voile, printed with tiny pink rosebuds. At the sleeves and waist there was wide embroidery, made so as to allow black velvet ribbon to be threaded through it, and I was brave in my velvet ribbons and velvet shoes. Gene Glenn (later a prominent lawyer in San Diego), two houses away, was delegated to take me to school. He arrived, in knickerbockers and cap, said, "Come on," and stalked ahead of me. At the school-yard he pointed, said, "In there," and in I went.

My teacher was Miss Timmons. I will never forget her, because through her I had the greatest thrill of my life, and something happened which has enriched all my days, and will until I die.

She had a big chart, with leaves that flopped over, and a long-handled pointer. With this she showed us a letter of the alphabet (which we all knew and recognized) and taught us to make appropriate sounds. *Aaaaaa* for A. A stuttering *bbbbbb,* then a sound like K, or *kkkkkk* for C, and so on. This went on for some time, and seemed to have no reason. It was just something teachers made you do.

But one day she showed three letters and we sounded each one. C (*kkkkk*) A (*aaaaa*) T (*ttttt*). And there, on the chart, was a picture of a cat. And we had said it! CAT! The wonderful, radiant light broke over me. This was reading! I never got over it.

After my first glorious day in the rosebud dress and velvet slippers, I wore checked cotton, button shoes, and an apron, like all the other little girls. The apron was white, with upstanding ruffles on the shoulders; it was voluminous and tied in back. Its function was to keep the dress clean. At home the school apron was changed for a stout one of dark cotton, because we had our household tasks to do and were expected to "help Mama." In those days we were told to keep our clothes clean, for there were no washing machines to churr on the back porch, providing clean clothes every day. Mama washed on Monday, and on Tuesday she ironed. Washing was a production. You soaked white things overnight in a big tub—towels and sheets and white underwear—and they were the first things scrubbed out with soap and warm water next morning. Then the colored clothes were done, one by one. Last, the heavy black stockings and socks.

I suppose it was heavy work, but most of the mamas got at it early, and by ten o'clock on Monday mornings clotheslines all over the city were waving sheets and clothes in the breeze and the sun, and no modern rinse ever made towels and underwear and shirts and dresses smell sweeter than the sun and air.

I remember Papa asking Mama, when the washing machine appeared on the market, if she wanted one, and she said no, because she thought she might be expected to operate it all the time, and would then have to iron all week. So, for years, she sent her heavy work out. Ma Toy called for it in his Sam Woo laundry wagon, and he delivered laundry fresh and clean regularly. He also became a great friend of the family, bestowed lilies in a shallow dish on Chinese New Year, and bracelets made of white, pink and green glass for the little girls. Sacks of coconut candy and dried lichee nuts appeared frequently, and he often paused to give advice and dispense philosophy in the kitchen.

One Christmas my father had given my mother what was called a dinner ring; it was shaped like a double triangle and paved with small diamonds. Ma Toy lifted Mama's hand, scrutinized the ring and asked, "Your boss give?"

Bridling somewhat, my mother answered that he had.

"No good," pronounced Ma Toy. "More better one big one."

In all households where there was a modicum of extra money, husbands were being pressured to buy washing machines, mostly (at first) because some pioneer husbands had done so, and eventually all fell into line. But Papa had one friend who thought that the washing machine was the beginning of The End.

"It's this way, Fred," he told Papa in deeply felt oratory: "Right now the women wash on Mondays and on Tuesdays they iron, and they get behind and have to do the rest of the house and the baking on the rest of the days, and they get tired and it's good for them. Keeps them out of mischief and they don't have time to stop and think about their wrongs. Besides, what will this lead to? Next thing you know, they'll want machines to clean with and iron with, and even . . . my gosh, they may even want machines to wash the dishes! Then, Fred, we are lost. With nothing to wear them out and keep them quiet around the house, they'll want to drive the automobiles, and, mark my words, next thing you know they'll want to get into politics and run things! Fred, it's The End."

As for me, I loved Ma Toy and we managed with him and Sam Woo for years. I had to put away clothes when they were delivered, and sweep the front porch and dust the parlor before school, do errands after school, then set the table for supper, clear it afterward, and dry the dishes while Mama washed.

When my little brother Dick came along, I also had to "watch the baby" and take care of him when my mother was busy. Besides, we had a piano, and I had to practice "my hour" every day, and do my school lessons.

Despite all these daily activities, I embroidered, learned to tat and knit and crochet and do some simple sewing, and had time to play jacks on the front sidewalk with Gladdie, Rada, Alice and Ventura. After a few sessions at jacks, our white panties were gray and dusty, and our mothers, as one woman, went to town and bought yards of black sateen, from which they constructed "bloomers" that we had to wear over the white panties, and thus protected, we could scrub around on the sidewalk and play all the varieties of jacks we knew, from "Over the bridge" to "Into the house." Some geniuses were able to play jacks, taking the rubber ball on the fly, but most of us had to let it bounce once.

Sometimes we played mumblety-peg with the boys, on the grass, or marbles. I was no good at marbles, but I was envied for my tops. I had a walker and a plain "girl" top, which had a rounded peg on which to dance and was less dangerous. A thrown top with a sharp peg could bite an ankle or dance into a leg.

By the time I was in fourth grade, I had learned to iron, and from then on, I did all the handkerchiefs, tea towels and pillowcases. On cold days it was nice to iron and keep warm, and I loved the steamy smell.

6.

There were many delights, even in those days before movies and television.

Firstly, there was "the show." We had two theaters, Parra's and Grogg's, and there was an opera house. As far as I know, no opera ever came to Bakersfield, but once, for an enchanted week, we had a road company that performed Gilbert and Sullivan. Papa went right out and bought seats for the entire family, for every performance, and we saw *The Mikado, The Pirates of Penzance, The Gondoliers* and *Trial by Jury*. A genius named Joseph de Angelis played the part of Koko in *The Mikado*, and I have never forgotten his characterization of the oily, obsequious, terrified, yet philosophical and sympathetic Koko, caught in the toils of an ambitious woman. He couldn't sing but he tried, and when he came to a high note he used to signal the tenor to take it, and then stop and say clearly, "Thank you," before going on with his number.

At Grogg's and Parra's, where almost all the people we knew went on Saturday nights, there was always vaudeville, and I remember some of the skits as well as if I had seen them yesterday, especially a droll little man named Jimmy Savo, who danced in time to the music, which went faster and faster, and he with it, until he fell down dead and was carried off stage on a stretcher.

Minstrel shows came to town and we loved them and remembered all the jokes. Also, the University of California Glee Club toured once a year, offering a wonderful evening of songs and entertainment. Once in a while, theatrical companies on their way to San Francisco from Los Angeles, or vice versa, stayed overnight to give a performance. Papa always took Mama to these plays, and we were left with Mammy C., or with Vee, who lived with us after my little brother was born. More about these two people, who influenced much of my youth, later.

One time, when Mammy C. was not available and Vee was not with us, Mama and Papa had tickets for a play, so they left my little sister and me at home, with instructions to phone Mrs. Ikenberg if anything odd seemed to be happening, but not to open the doors to anyone for any reason. They took little Dick, a baby, with them. He was a good quiet baby and made no noise at all, sitting on Mama's lap during the play. But he had just learned to kiss, and there was a lot of kissing going on up there on the stage. Just in front sat a lady wearing a low-cut evening dress, with a good deal of neck and shoulder showing, and little Dick, inspired, leaned forward and kissed her, noisily and wetly, on the back of the neck. She rose three feet in the air with a shrill squeak, and there was a small pandemonium until the shocked lady learned that her admirer was not quite two years old.

Meanwhile, I, with my active imagination, had become frightened at being alone in the house at night for the first time, and in order to foil possible intruders, I set traps for them. I strung pots and pans all over the stairs so that they would make a great racket if anyone got in, and my little sister and I went to bed upstairs, shivering with dread. Mama and Papa got home, with Dick asleep in Mama's arms, and they started up the dark stairs without flipping on the light. Papa fell down, tangled in pots and pans, Dick woke up and yelled, and a very unpleasant scene ensued in which I was the chief attraction. I will not describe it.

Actually, we were quite safe from marauders of any kind in those far-off days. When Mama or her friends Hattie or Grace went to town, they did not lock their doors; they called out to each other where they were going, and so departed. They watched each other's houses. We locked doors when we went away for vacations. And only once in my childhood did I hear of a sex offender—a man called "Mr. Few Clothes" who was said to lurk in Schultz's barn, covered only by an overcoat, which he opened when he thought some passer-by might enjoy the view. A net was dropped over him and he was hurried off to Stockton.

Once Buffalo Bill himself came to town, bringing with him a great spectacle, and the entire population went to see him. Buffalo Bill swept into the arena, dressed all in white fringed leather and riding a white horse. There were Indian riders who mounted bareback and who could slip round to the other side of their steed, or under it and back up again, while the animal was at a flat-out run. My father loved the Old West of his inheritance, collected books about it, and taught us much about the Indian nations. At the Buffalo Bill Wild West Show, he collected us together and said solemnly: "Remember this day. Buffalo Bill is one of our great American heroes; someday you can tell your children that you saw him."

Papa was something of a talent scout, as well as a prophet. Once he had to go to Los Angeles to try a case, and as it had been held over a day, he indulged his love of the sea by going out to Santa Monica on the streetcar. When he came home he was full of enthusiasm for a motion-picture company he had seen working there. Movies were just coming into prominence, and we had occasionally seen parts of a serial called *Who Pays?* and another one called *The Perils of Pauline.*

"This company at Santa Monica was directed by the funniest little man I ever saw in my life," Papa related. "He could play every part, and he did, making the other actors imitate him, and then when they filmed, he played his own part. But he was really doing the whole thing. He's a little, thin fellow with baggy pants, a shock of black hair, a tiny mustache. He wears great big shoes and a tight coat and carries a little cane. If his movie comes here to town, I will take you all. I inquired about his name; it is Charlie Chaplin, and the movie will be called *Tillie's Punctured Romance.*"

In due course we all went, roared with laughter and almost rolled in the aisles, as the ads said people were doing all over California.

But we had unorthodox pleasures, too. One enormous excitement was rain. Five inches of rain is a wet year in Bakersfield; people there love and respect the rain. When rain fell, people took their rockers out to the front porch and sat and enjoyed. When Papa read of a great storm roaring into San Francisco from the Pacific, if he could arrange a day away from the office, he took "The Owl" up to San Francisco, crossed the bay on the ferry and went straight out to the Cliff House. There he sat and watched and thrilled to the wind and rain and crashing waves. He stayed all day, existing on a sandwich and coffee. Then, in the late afternoon, he would go down to the Embarcadero, eat a Hangtown Fry, take the ferry across to the Oakland Mole and ride "The Owl" home again, much refreshed in his spirit.

A gusher was always a wonderful event, and we lived near oilfields where they happened now and again. Whenever the papers reported a gusher, we usually tried to get out to see it. I remember one that sprayed fine black droplets all over my white piqué dress from a mile away. It was a marvelous sight to admire —the great plumes of black oil rushing into the sky with a tremendous noise like an express train. And I felt a kind of cosmic compassion, seeing the earth's black blood gushing up from its wounds.

7.

Close to our hearts and deep in our lives were two black women: Mammy C. and Vee. Later, Lula came to us, and we cherished her too.

Mammy C. deserves a book, but I will tell a little about her here, for she was *sui generis*.

When I first knew her, she was already a very old woman; her hair was almost snow-white, and her very black face was wrinkled like wet silk. She had been a slave. She used to tell us that Old Master, in Tennessee, had chained all his slaves together and had marched them into Texas when he moved there. She was a tot of three at the time, but she walked beside her mother. When Lincoln made her free, she was still a child, but she then went to work for money, and saved it. When she had enough, she bought a ticket on a train going west. She wanted to get to California. "Put me off where there's a lot of niggas," she told the conductor. The black porter enlightened him. "She wants Bakersfield," he said. (Our town, with many acres planted in cotton, attracted black workers.) However, after arriving in Bakersfield, Mammy turned her nose up. "No niggas a-*tall*," she told my mother, with enormous scorn. "Only *cullud* folks!"

Far ahead of her time, Mammy was proud of being black and she had great dignity. She always wore clean light cotton clothes, spotless and starched to within an inch of their lives, and a big starched sunbonnet. Absolutely reliable and honest, she was always in demand to sit with children or watch over a household when the owners were away. Many were the wonderful tales she told.

Once, when she had come to stay the evening with us until Mama and Papa got home from the theater, she took a long look

at me and pronounced sadly, "If you want to be as good-lookin'
as your mama, you better whip up your horses!"

Occasionally, but infrequently, she would call on my father in
his law office. He always received her with pleasure because he
admired her fierce pride and her intelligence. She would sit
down, smooth her skirts and inquire carefully for all the family,
and then at last say the words she had come to say.

"Mr. Borton, I'm scratchin' on the bottom of the barrel!"

Papa would always offer to make her a small loan, which she
accepted with quiet dignity. And as the weeks went by, he
would find that she had come in and left money with his stenographer, paying back her loan in nickels and dimes, to the last
cent. Papa never insulted her by offering to pardon the loan. She
wanted no charity.

The black girl who came to our house to help Mama after the
birth of my little brother, was different, but no less admirable.
We children loved her and she was devoted to us, but she chastised us when we needed it. Her judgment was good, and Mama
left the discipline to her.

Her name was Valeria, but we were told to call her Vee.
Pretty and stylish and trim, she had many admirers, but, we
learned later, Vee had only one great love in her life—her little
son Floyd, who lived in Los Angeles with his grandmother. The
only time we ever saw Vee in tears was when she received a
long-distance call from her mother and little Floyd spoke to his
mother on the telephone. She broke down and sobbed with emotion, and we, who had thought she loved us most of all, felt left
out and jealous for days.

Vee made us "country ice cream" by setting out a pan of
cream to freeze on a cold winter morning. Then she would stir in
sugar and vanilla, and we languished over it.

One day a passing delivery boy left a sample of a dessert in a
little square box. Vee followed directions and made it. We ab-
sorbed it slowly and thoughtfully, like tea tasters. It had a
slightly rubbery texture, very pleasant, and tasted both sweet
and tart like fruit. Mama and Hattie consulted over the phone
and decided it was worth ten cents a package, and we all bought
some. The name of the product was Jello.

When the terrible flu epidemic struck, in 1918, Vee, who was terrified of it, made us all wear little bags of asafetida around our necks; she even made us swallow some of the awful stuff. Perhaps it was effective. Anyhow, although a few of us were very sick, we did not lose anyone in our immediate family. Vee nursed us all, and Mama nursed Vee.

That was a dreadful time, like scenes painted by Brueghel. I will never forget the rows of corpses on the lawns of the funeral parlor, covered with sheets, awaiting the arrival of coffins, and the services of the overworked and decimated staffs.

Dr. Sabichi saved many people—he didn't quite know how. His prescription was eggnog laced heavily with whiskey every three hours. He explained to Papa that this kept them nourished and kept them in bed, and he didn't know what else to do. People who got up too soon had relapses, which were always fatal.

From that awful time of death and trouble came one anecdote which became part of our family language—those special words which recall something to members of a family that makes them all respond immediately with mirth or pity or some other shared emotion.

Two little old ladies—sisters, who were militant members of the Women's Temperance Union and who had tried for years to close some of Bakersfield's saloons—came down with the flu at the same time. Dr. Sabichi, hurrying about the city twenty-four hours a day, dropped in on them and found them in very bad shape. He recommended whiskey and eggnog. Their reaction was horror and adamant refusal. Out of his immense kindness, he worried about them and found another moment to drop in on them, about three days later. When they heard his step, one of the sisters raised her head from the pillow and croaked, "I give up. Gimme the whiskey!"

Those words, whenever we repeat them in our family, mean, "I surrender! Absolutely!"

Our Vee stayed with us several years and then departed for Los Angeles and Floyd. We missed her and looked forward to her infrequent visits. But when I was about twelve, Lula came into our lives. Lula was enormous. As her personal recommendation for a job with us, Lula explained that to clean a room, she had to take everything out of it in order to get in.

Lula came to us for daily work, for she had a nice home and a husband with whom she was on terms of uneasy truce most of the time.

Lula took no orders from anybody. She moved in her orbit, doing what she considered should be done, and she was as immutable as the stars. From Lula (and from my grandmother) I learned what it means to be a lady. My mother soon saw that Lula, with her rigid code of what was fitting for the daughters of a lawyer, would leave no stone unturned to make us behave properly.

"Miss Beth, you planning to go to town in that dress?"

"Yes, I was."

"That dress is wrinkled and it has a smudge. Gimme that dress. You go upstairs and put on your pink."

I went and put on my pink.

"You go back upstairs and put on your hat. Do you want to get freckles all over you?"

I put on my hat.

Woe to the young lady who used bad words or exhibited temper. She felt Lula's wrath, which took the form of terrible scoldings.

I suppose Lula was a snob, in a way. She divided people into ladies and trash. Ladies were not late for lunch, as I learned to my discomfiture one time when I gave a luncheon for a few friends. Lula and I planned a delicious menu (that is, Lula planned it and cooked it), and we used my mother's best table linen and her Haviland china. My guests were invited for one o'clock. But two of my invited friends worked on a newspaper, and they were late. One-fifteen came. One-thirty. One-forty-five. At exactly two o'clock Lula slammed the sliding door of the dining room open, stood there in rage, and said to me, "Miss Beth, I'm serving! I'm not waiting any longer for any trash!"

Lula was part of our family for many years. She had a high development of a quality much more common to her race than mine. She could see and feel the future, and she had flashes of extrasensory perception that were amazing.

Not long after the horrendous news of the kidnaping of the Lindbergh baby appeared in the papers, Lula came to work one day very sad and silent. Finally, she said to my mother, "I dreamed about that baby last night. I saw him, under a tree, not far from home, and he was dead."

In the days when I used to fly home from Boston, where I was working, I never told my mother the exact day or hour of my flight, because I didn't want her to worry. But Lula always knew, announced it, and baked the cake of welcome. "She's coming home," she would carol, "she'll get here about three o'clock today. You better be out at the airport."

And when my brother was in the Army, Lula came one day and did a jig step all over the kitchen, making the house shake. "Mr. Dick is coming home today, and he is bringing a bride!" she announced, and immediately ordered chickens and all the makings of a wonderful bridal cake. He arrived—with the bride!

She was always right.

At one time I was engaged to an American, a young man I had known since childhood. But Lula shook her head.

"She'll never marry him," she told my mother. "She's going to marry some foreigner and go to live far away."

Which I did.

I wish I had Lula near me now. There are so many things I would like to ask her.

Mama had been brought up riding all over Grandpa's ranch, bareback, and Papa had gone to school aboard an old horse. They were never without a few equine pensioners. These were boarded on some one of the Land Company's lots, when it was no longer possible to keep them in town. However, we did keep Pedro, the donkey, in the back yard.

Pedro was a very wise, sly, and calculating burro which had been loaned to Papa "for his little girls" one year. Since I was the oldest, I rode him most of the time. There was no Western saddle small enough for me, so the town saw me on my long-eared steed, using an elegant postage-stamp English saddle as I went about doing my errands. Since I had the use of Pedro, I had to water him, and I also had to saddle him. This was much more of a trick than one might suppose, because when Pedro saw me coming toward him with the saddle, he had a way of inflating himself to about twice his normal size. As soon as the cinch had been fastened, he would heave a great gusty sigh, deflate, and the saddle would slip down and hang beneath his stomach. One had to fight guile with guile. The only way to get the better of him was to attract his attention with his favorite vice, a vanilla ice-cream cone. With his eyes half closed in pleasure as he munched, he would delay inflation, and I could get him saddled up.

Horses seem to like ice cream too. I think it was mostly for the ice cream (but he also accepted cake and cookies) that Murphy, a fast-walking cow pony that Papa brought down from the mountains for our pleasure, joined all children's lawn parties whenever he saw one in progress. He had a hard mouth, and when he decided to attend a party where blindman's buff and pin the tail on the donkey were in progress, he did so, together with his passenger, willy-nilly. We also had Buster—a lovely, sleek, black single-footing creature who had no vices except that he was very imaginative—who saw ghosts and rattlesnakes in every bit of blown paper or pile of dead leaves, and would then shy and roll his eyes and pretend to be nervous as a kitten.

Murphy and Buster were pastured in a lot rented from the Land Company, and were safe, we supposed, when one day somebody told my father that many old horses were being rounded up and sent off by cattle car to a glue factory. Papa tore off to make sure that his old horses were not among them, and he was in the very nick of time. He called Murphy and Buster by name, not seeing them in the milling throng of horses being loaded, but they whinnied with pleasure and, tossing their manes, leaped over fences and obstacles and came to him, hoping for oats or an apple. So they were saved. That was when Papa acquired a ranch up in the hills that is still known among the cognoscenti as Horse Heaven. Papa bought a horse trailer and took his friends up to the ranch, where they would be out of danger. There they grew long in the tooth, capricious and arthritic at their leisure. The Bortons never sold a horse.

It was at Horse Heaven that Papa conducted an experiment in animal psychology that ended by driving a perfectly sound pig into a nervous breakdown. In his boyhood, Papa had learned to slip and grow roses, which he sold to help his mother meet expenses. He had a green thumb, and he liked to set out a vegetable garden now and then. I am told that when slipping roses, it is good luck if half of them "take," but Papa never lost more than six or ten out of a hundred. We have no idea how this happened, for he was not outstandingly clever with his hands, and often dropped things. So, on quiet weekends, Papa went up to Horse Heaven and planted a garden. One Saturday he found, to his dismay, that some creature had broken in and dug up his tubers and eaten them, and trampled down his plants. Inspecting his fences carefully, he found them sound, but at a certain point he discovered a big hollow log capable of admitting an animal thief from outside our fence into the garden. Taking a chair out, at dusk, and sitting patiently, smoking, waiting and watching, Papa observed a neat little black pig emerge from the log and direct himself, grunting happily, toward the rest of the tubers. Papa shooed him away and Piggy departed, annoyed, via his hollow log.

Simple men would have removed the log and ended the trouble. But Papa was never simple. He spent all the next day hunting for, and finally finding, a hollow log with a jog in it, which he carefully substituted for the log through which his night visitor had come to maraud. The new log would deposit Piggy back on his own side of the fence. Again, Papa took out his chair, and sat and smoked and waited for the curtain to go up. At first dark Piggy arrived and traveled through his log. When he realized that he was not in the garden but back where he started from, he shook his head in annoyance and tried again. Something was wrong. After the third frustrating trip through the log, Piggy threw himself on the ground, waved his hoofs in the air and had a temper tantrum. He tried a fourth time, and then, squealing horribly, he seemed to have a complete nervous breakdown.

Then, in pity, Papa removed the log. Enough is enough.

We always had dogs, and usually cats as well. What was interesting, in my childhood, was that everybody knew everybody else's pet; and we were all friends together and we all played together. There was the Bortons' Rufus (a black Clumber spaniel) and later Pooch, the Hornungs' Snowie (a cat), Everett Hood's nanny goat, the Pendletons' Napoleon (a big black rabbit), and somebody's dog named William, who often came over to pass the time of day.

Automobiles had running boards in those days, and Rufus, our dog, rode the running board on short trips. Papa made a little barrier for him there so that he would not be thrown off on curves, as we whizzed along at a fateful twenty miles an hour. On long trips Rufus rode in back with my sister and me, tramping over us from side to side, and slobbering on us. It didn't matter; we loved him and couldn't care less if we got slobbered on. He had one quirk. When we had been away from home on a trip, he always wanted to be let down so that he could ride his running board, in state, back to the house, usually slipping off, with a nonchalant gesture, half a block from home. Some matter of canine pride was involved.

The nanny goat, which pulled my neighbor Everett around the neighborhood in a small wagon, caused me to get a lump on my forehead which I carry to this day, though now it can be seen only in a special light. At one time it was the size of an ostrich egg. Everett was involved in a fight to defend his goat, because there were insensitive persons who claimed that the goat had a bad odor, and this Everett would not allow. He fought, someone was hit, and the victim caromed away at great speed, striking me, an innocent bystander, with his skull. I fell and when lifted up, had the ostrich egg. I wore this protuberance for days, through various changes of color.

I was always searching for cats, and once was told of one I might have if I could catch him in a dark cellar. I went, with a burlap bag, and having no other lure at hand, I took with me a piece of my father's treasured, and odoriferous, Limburger cheese. I snared Herman, who was lovely, a blue Maltese, and from then on, he demanded a daily ration of cheese. Another cat of mine, Tommy, loved corn on the cob, and used to eat it by rolling it toward himself, eating daintily round and round until he had rolled himself into a corner.

I have observed something about all our cats, and have checked it out with other ailurophiles, and my facts can be proved in most cases. Cats have color preferences. Our little cat Demi Tasse, who was, as you might think, small and black, loved turquoise blue and would go to great lengths to be allowed to sleep on a cushion of this color. Whenever he was "lost," my mother would say, "Go look for something turquoise blue and you will find him on it." Once he was found sleeping on the skirt of a big doll, whose dress was turquoise. Once he spent hours on the mantel, where my mother had a vase of blue flowers. My sister's cat Pitty Sing seems to prefer gold, and "makes bread" on all the gold upholstery, unless caught in the act and forcibly removed. The present feline incumbent in my house, a striped gray and white tiger, could sit on orange or blue cushions, but never does. She always heads for something red. If no cushion, then a carpet.

In my happy childhood, cats did not go to school, but many dogs did. One friend, Genevieve, was taken everywhere by her dog, a sort of collie. He perferred to sit beside her in the schoolroom, and, as he was very good, sometimes this was allowed. If not, he sat outside in the hall, close to the door, and accompanied her to the next class. She was, like Saint Margaret of Cortona, never seen without her canine guard. He graduated from grammar school with her, and went on to high school, and for all I know, to college too.

8.

Our town was beleaguered by mosquitoes in the summertime. The tule marshes nearby were their breeding grounds, and it was inevitable that drifters into town and migrant workers who manned the oilfields should bring in malaria. In the early days, Bakersfield was famous for the disease. A joke was told of two Bakersfield cronies. One would say, "Jim, how about goin' fishin' tomorrow?" Answer: "Can't, Tom. Tomorrow is my day for the chills and fever. How about Thursday?" Answer: "Can't Thursday. That's *my* day!"

My father was interested in absolutely everything, and as he had several friends who were doctors, he consulted them and took pains to keep us free from trouble that was avoidable. For example, our town was served by deep well water, perfectly delicious and always icy cold, even in summer, as it came from the tap. But it lacked certain important minerals, and Bakersfield and the valley were (to some degree, still are) a kind of goiter belt. My father bought iodized salt for the table and we had to eat fish at least once a week, whether we wanted to or not. For malaria, he bought a horrible ocher-colored powder, made from chrysanthemums and smelling faintly of the flower, which was said to ward off mosquitoes, and on summer evenings, before we went out to play in the soft darkness, we all had to be covered with it. None of the children on our block got malaria, except one. I did.

I can recall the horrors of the first chill and then the rising fever. This disease is one that lies sleeping in your veins until you experience some change of altitude or manner of living, and then it fells you again. I have had bouts of it in Bakersfield, at the shore, in Boston, in Monterey, California, in Monterrey, Mexico, and in Mexico City. I understand that doctors today do not pretend that they can cure it. They say they "arrest it." In my childhood it was arrested with five-grain tablets of pure quinine sulphate until your ears rang; then the quinine was flushed out of your system with castor oil. The whole process was a preview of Hell, but it seemed to be reasonably effective. Since I developed my chills and fever every summer, I was often shipped off to my grandmother who lived by the sea, in the hope that a change of climate might help me. It always did . . . but only temporarily. Anyone who has had malaria, however, is grateful for the lucunae between bouts.

In those days, when vaccination was used only for smallpox, we children got all sorts of other infectious diseases. These used to sweep through our block, indeed through the whole town, and to add to the discomfort, any household where the doctor diagnosed an infectious illness was quarantined, and a large red or yellow sign was put out in front, to warn away visitors. One year the whole block had whooping cough; since we were all whooping, without exception—teenagers, babies, and in-betweens—our

mothers defied the quarantine signs and let us all play together.
And so we did, stopping to stagger to a tree trunk and cling to it
while we whooped; then the feeble games would go on. But
none of us succumbed or seemed permanently injured.

We all got the measles together, the chicken pox, scarlet fever
and German measles. And mumps. There was one dreadful winter when, first, my little brother came home with mumps. Up
went the quarantine sign, while he had them on one side and
then on the other. Then my sister got them. One side, then the
other. I escaped, but as soon as quarantine was lifted I went
back to school and came home, shortly thereafter, with German
measles. Locked out by the quarantine, poor Papa had to go
back to live at the Club again, while Mama coped with us. Papa
used to come and talk wistfully to Mama through the window.

My sister Barbara and I composed a yell, in honor of our
plagues, which went like this:

> We got measles, we got mumps,
> We got throats with great big lumps,
> We got spots all down our backs,
> Rah rah rah rah, give us the ax!

When, after about five months with scrofulous and spotty
offspring, the final quarantine card was lifted, and my mother
was finally able to open her door and walk out into the street,
she was ready. She had her suitcase packed.

"Fred," she said to Papa, "I've had about all I can stand. I'm
going home to Mama for two weeks." And she departed.

This was less drastic than it sounds, because the faithful Vee
had been with us all through our horrible winter, scolding, coax-
ing, patting and loving us, despite our horrific appearance and
frequent torrents of tears.

In general, I was unlucky with my illnesses. They usually took
me by the throat whenever I was due to shine at some school
festivity (I could recite the entire "Paul Revere's Ride") or to attend a party. But the malaria, which provided me with summers
at Monterey and the chance to be with Grandma, whom I

adored, was to be thanked, for those summers still hold for me many tender memories.

9.

Yellowish pale and trembly from malaria, but able to eat and walk around, I was taken to Monterey, to Grandma. Those journeys were memorable. Papa put us on the train at six in the morning. We had suitcases, favorite toys, and shoeboxes full of lunch—usually chicken legs, hard-boiled eggs and bananas. The train was hot, and the stiff, dusty red plush of the seats got at my legs where the long black stockings and the rubber of my bloomers did not quite meet, but left a little crescent of tender flesh, which itched horribly all day.

At first the trip was thrilling. We made countless expeditions up the aisle to the water cooler for the experience of drinking from paper cups (while they lasted). We awaited the peanut butcher with eagerness. He sold all sorts of lurid magazines, as well as stale candy and dry sandwiches, and he took orders for bottled refreshments, which he delivered warm. Still, it was all new and fascinating at first, and there were always other children and other suffering mothers.

My little sister tormented the conductor by collecting all the little punched tickets, of varying colors, which he had gone about sticking into the tops of seats or into gentlemen's hats. She had to be searched, divested of her spoils, and scolded, four or five times. Trips to the bathroom palled after a while, though at first it had been a thrill to look down through the open toilet at the earth and ties rushing away beneath.

By the time we reached the station where we made the first change of trains, ennui had set in. Yet, there we had to clutch all our belongings and, loaded with boxes and coats, rush headlong across the tracks to where the other train stood, and scramble on, hoping to find seats. Only fifteen minutes were allowed for this change of trains, and it hung over my mother all the way from Bakersfield. I still remember it in my dreams as a place of peril and imminent disaster. I think the name of the station was Goshen.

Then, after a short ride, there was still another change, but more time was allowed at this one. Finally we were on the last of the three trains, and by then most of the small fry had had enough of excitement, spankings and hard-boiled eggs and were laid out, somnolent and limp, along the seats. I nodded and almost slept by then, too, but at last, somewhere toward Aromas, the train made a great turn that carried us nearer the ocean. Someone would always thrust up a window and let in dust and cinders, but also the lovely cool breath of the sea. At Watsonville, Mama would get off the train and buy a bag of crisp apples, delicious beyond compare. Munching and crowding each other for a place at the window, we would begin to revive, and journey's end drew near with the end of the long day.

Cypress trees appearing at the window and then sliding past told us we were near Del Monte, the stop before Monterey. Another ten minutes, and we would all pile out of the train and into the arms of Grandma, who would be waiting, wearing her black tailored suit, her high black laced shoes, her high-necked "waist" with the amethyst pin at the throat, and her black hat with the cherries. It was always just the hour of sunset when we detrained. The bay usually lay still as a piece of stretched silk, reflecting the colors of sunset, and the sounds were the ones we loved—the gulls crying, the rhythmic slapping of the waves on wet sand, and Grandma's soft sweet voice.

Grandma's house was a cottage high on the hill with a view of the whole town and the bay. She had a front garden planted with all her favorite flowers—roses, honeysuckle, amaryllis, pansies, fuchsias, violets, mignonette and heliotrope. In the rear she had neat rows of carrots, onions, beets and lettuce, bushes of tomatoes and string beans, and one large section of potato hills. It was the greatest fun to be allowed to dig potatoes with the pronged garden fork, to gather the lettuce and string beans, and pick the raspberries and loganberries which she had trained over trellises.

Up the road a little way lived the Danas. They had a cow, and I was sent every evening with a scalded lard pail to bring home a quart of milk. The poor cow always cried for two or three days most mournfully when they took away her calf, and you could even see tears in her big soft brown eyes. After a time she would become resigned and stop her sorrowful bellowing. The Danas' cow was the only sad element in the perfect happiness of those days at Grandma's.

Some years later, Papa used to drive us all the way to Monterey in the automobile. Those were excursions fraught with danger and hardship, and they took three days at least. We always started at about four in the morning, so as to be out of the sweltering valley by sunup, if possible. Mama sat in front with Papa, holding the slumbering baby Dick; my sister and I and Rufus were in the back seat with the suitcases, coats and lunch, the water bottles and anything else that had to be packed.

The route lay through the utter desolation of Lost Hills and Hungry Valley, and then along a narrow winding road until we came to Paso Robles. There we always had to sleep overnight before continuing on next day through San Miguel, San Ardo and San Lucas to King City, where we were always taken into a restaurant, the picnic supplies having by then given out, where we all ate prodigiously. Papa inevitably gave the same order—fried eggs and bacon, buttered toast and coffee—no matter what the hour. He said it was almost impossible to spoil fried eggs and toast. Coffee, of course, was always an unknown factor. Papa liked his coffee very strong.

From there we proceeded, faster now, because we had left the blistering hot valleys and were nearing the sea, and everybody became good-tempered and lively.

However, occasionally Papa, who was a pioneer at heart and responded gallantly to challenges, decided to try a new approach. Once we went along a back road to Jolon, staying overnight at a very primitive inn, where, for the first time, despite many unpretentious values in my life, I became acquainted with outside plumbing.

And one dreadful summer, Papa decided that he must negotiate the famous Temblor Grade. This steep narrow mountain road was the cause of many accidents, and from all accounts it was strewn along its length with corpses, skeletons and skulls.

We arrived at the foot of the grade and Papa stopped the car to reconnoiter. There seemed to be a gash in the cliffside that went straight up, with no turn-off or widened space along its length. It was just wide enough to accommodate the car's wheels, with perhaps a few inches left over, and if you started up and met someone coming down, the lower vehicle had to back down, since the other one could never back up the steep grade. And backing, in those early days of driving, was a skill very few had mastered. Even we children began to whimper as we stared up at the Temblor.

"I'll try it first alone," said Papa, and was instantly contradicted.

"You'll do nothing of the kind," announced Mama. "What if you went over the side? What would I do, down here, with all these children? No, we'll all go together."

Papa, who was not a praying man, exhorted us to what was, for him, divine—absolute silence. But I, who had tried out several Sunday schools (shortly before the annual picnic), gave myself to silent prayer. We made the perilous ascent, and nothing started down at us. At last we came out at the top, all together and all whole. We drove thence to a place called La Panza, where we camped that night. (La Panza is a pretty-sounding name but it merely means "guts," and I regret to relate that many other romantic Spanish California names were more practical in their original applications. Thus, *Atascadero* means Hog Wallow, *Manteca* means Lard, and *Los Gatos*, meaning The Cats, originally meant something cats do.)

From there it was another day's drive to Monterey and Grandma.

Often, because of my malaria, I was sent on ahead to get a little pink into my cheeks before the family arrived. Or I would be left with Grandma all summer, and then Mama and Papa, Barbara and Baby Dick would come to spend two weeks, and we would all start home together. I always wept as we left the town, with its rim of pine-clad hills, its blue bay and the cypress-bordered roads. From the very first, Monterey meant only peace and loveliness to me. Barbara, who had been born there, loved it too, and from our grandfather we inherited some Viking blood, which made us need to get to the sea regularly, or be haunted and frustrated.

But also, because of having her to myself almost every year for several quiet months, Grandma came to mean very much to me. She molded my character, such as it is, even more than my busy mother. If I were allowed one word to describe Grandma, it would be "upright." But also she was gentle, soft-spoken and patient, qualities I prize more and more the longer I live.

Our days together in the little white cottage above the town and the bay were quiet. I suppose children nowadays would think them unbearable, for we had no radio, no television, and no automobile. We walked everywhere, we did all our own work (with no washing machine), and we had few visitors, though sometimes we dressed up and made sedate calls.

We had Grandpa with us until I was ten. He was vigorous and strong. He liked to take his cane and walk to New Monterey to play pinochle with friends, or go sailing on the bay in the boat he had built, or attend the sessions of the GAR. He had landed in New York when he was young and, according to his story, had intended only to visit the city and continue on, by sea, to Australia. But he woke up in the Union Army and spent the Civil War years as an infantryman.

After his death, Grandma, after a decorous interval, had many suitors. She was still pretty when she was past sixty. Her complexion was like a young woman's, her eyes blue as morning glories, and the silver streaks in her light-brown braids and around her face were becoming.

The beaux generally arrived on Sunday afternoons, bearing gifts. One brought cans of sardines, for he was manager of one of the canning factories down on Cannery Row. We used to hear the peremptory whistle, calling workers in whenever the sardine fleet came in with a catch; it was always exciting, and then we would see workers hurrying down the street.

Another beau lived some distance down the coast. He came driving a team of horses, which he hitched up nearby, and he brought gifts of sweet corn, and jars of honey. Still a third, a veteran of the Spanish-American War, used to arrive on his steed, a

large white horse, which he would tether to Grandma's gate. He
proffered sophisticated boxes of candy.

Grandma was flirtatious, I thought, and the beaux used to become visibly annoyed when they encountered other suitors in the
parlor, sitting on the delicate chairs with the velvet seats, partak-
ing of Grandma's pie and tea. But Grandma refused all invitations, matrimonial and otherwise.

"There's a time for everything" was her only comment. She
and I had very full days, and it was only on Sunday afternoons
that the beaux intruded.

In the mornings Grandma got up and, according to her creed
(and one followed by my mother), washed, combed her hair,
and put on a fresh starched house dress before setting foot in
the kitchen. Then she had to make a fire in her wood stove. The
house was built over a large basement (where Grandfather
stored his wine); the wood was stacked up there too. There was
a woodbox and a pulley, so that the loaded box could be hoisted
up into a special closet built for it in the kitchen. I filled the
woodbox in the afternoons so that it would be ready for
Grandma in the morning. She started the fire with newspaper
and kindling, and then fed in her sticks of wood. After the old
black stove was purring nicely, she combed my hair into two
tight little yellow braids. We put on our aprons and got to
work. I set the table, taking cream and butter from the safe, a
section of the house which was open to the air, covered only
with wire screening; it was on the north, and things kept there
were always cool. We had no icebox.

Grandma made little dollar-size pancakes, which we ate with
honey or apple sauce, and poured boiling water on the tea in the
pot.

After breakfast she washed dishes in her pantry, and I dried.
She began cooking anything that had to be done on top of the
stove or in the oven. The oven had no temperature gauge;
Grandma simply stuck her hand in, and when it felt right she put
in the cake or pie or whatever she was baking.

I made my bed and dusted the parlor, and then I got to my
"task." Grandma believed that little girls should learn how to do
many ladylike things. Accordingly, I was set to hemstitch a piece

of linen or cotton for dishtowels, and I was told how many inches I must do. Or I was to produce five inches of tatting (hen and chickens was my favorite design), or to crochet an edge on eight inches of handkerchiefs. I was taught how to patch properly and how to darn, threading my stitches through in a neat basket stitch. I also learned how to do acceptable buttonholes.

There was never any question of my going out to play in the garden with the cat, or for a walk, or to the Library (my greatest joy), or reading, until I had done my task to Grandma's satisfaction. And no sloppy work. "If it's worth doing, it's worth doing well," she would pronounce. Many a patch I picked out and did again, and many a buttonhole had to be repeated, on the scrap of cloth Grandma had marked for me.

I had other duties. I blacked the shoes (hers and mine), I went for the milk, I dug potatoes, and I carried messages, because Grandma had no telephone.

On Mondays we washed. Grandma had a clothesline tree, with the lines just the right height for her to lean out of the back porch window and peg clothes onto, giving it a whirl to bring new line into play. On Tuesdays we ironed, with small neat black irons that Grandma heated on top of the stove. She knew when they were right for delicate things or for heavy starched clothes by the way they hissed when she touched a dampened finger to them. I was taught how to do handkerchiefs and straight things first, but later I graduated to petticoats and waists, and finally learned ruffles and pleats. I sometimes lament the "no iron" sign on contemporary clothes, just as I resent packaged cakes and pie crust, for I was taught how to do these things as an artist is taught his craft, and I dislike having my skills duplicated or taken from me.

After our lunch, which usually ended with a wonderful pie or pudding (Grandma was a superb cook), I was free to entertain myself. In a fresh clean dress, and wearing a washable white hat, well starched and ironed and anchored with an elastic band under my chin, I could go to the beach and collect shells or walk along the boardwalk that extended all the way to Del Monte, or go to town along Alvarado Street to Franklin and then up the hill to the Library. There I spent blissful hours, finally choosing a book for myself and one for Grandma.

On Saturday afternoons I went to the movie theater where I watched the development of serial adventures. I saw *The Diamond from the Sky*, with Charlotte Pickford (Mary's sister) and Irving Cummings, and another long serial, involving great danger and excitement, whose name I forget.

I was thus allowed to roam freely, and in those days there seemed to be no danger. Anyhow, nothing untoward ever happened to me, nor was I even frightened.

On days when I stayed home in the afternoons to read my book, or to work on some handmade gifts for my mother, I went, at five, down Cass Street and across the bridge to the bakery shop, where I chose doughnuts or snails for our tea, which we always took just before dark.

Then Grandma, in her bay window in the tall rocker, and I, sitting on a small stool at her feet, watched the night come down. First the delicate gray fog would steal in from the hills across the bay at about the hour the Presidio shut up for the day and took down the flag. We could hear "taps" across the town. Softly the fog would begin to enfold the hills and the houses and hide them from view. The sea would darken, and the sunset, gloriously golden and red, would spread across the sky and then fade. Down on the water, one by one, riding lights could be seen on every little boat, and lights would blossom in windows all over town.

We did not turn our lights on, although Grandma had electricity. (I suspect her bill was about fifty cents a month, we used so little of it.) We sat in the dark and talked, and I told Grandma all my thoughts and dreams and the stories I wanted to write, and she told me all about her girlhood in New York City, the starving time during the Civil War, and her years on the ranch near Soledad.

She had never returned to New York after Grandpa had brought her out to California. Oh, she planned to. One year she sewed all winter, making clothes for herself and Mama, and she had saved money until she had enough for their tickets. The two boys, Edward and Joseph, were to be left behind with Grandpa.

But Mama, who was beautiful, was to be exhibited with pride. The trunk was packed, Mama was buttoned into her blue woolen coat, and Grandma put on her tight brown coat with the little bustle at the back. The trunk was lifted into the back of the wagon, the horses were hitched up, and Grandpa took the reins. They started for the town of Soledad, where they would flag the San Francisco train, and there they would change and begin the long journey to the East.

Mama and Grandma wore their earrings; both had pierced ears. The horses moved along briskly.

But as Grandpa drove, Grandma reflected. Before they reached Soledad, about halfway along the road, she said—and I can almost hear her soft, gentle, but determined voice: "Turn around, Peter."

"Why?"

"I have decided not to go."

Grandpa turned around. Mama was glad; she dried her tears and looked forward to getting back to her dolls and her little dog, Bijah.

The horses were unhitched, the trunk was taken back inside and unpacked. It was nearly time for dinner. Grandma put on her apron. Nothing more was said of the matter. Nobody knows, to this day, what happened, and Grandma never said.

Grandma's father was English-born and she had been brought up in the Episcopal High Church. She knew the mass by heart and could recite all the prayers. But her years at the ranch had got her out of the way of going to church, and both my parents were freethinkers. So we never talked about religion, but we talked about God sometimes, and I knew it was He who put good impulses into my heart and good thoughts into my head, and that He was displeased when I wasn't loving and kind. I also knew He watched over me and took care of me. And I trusted the precepts Grandma gave me.

"Never lie."

"Don't do anything underhanded. Have too much pride."

"Never answer people who insult you, or shout bad or angry words. Shame them with your silence."

"Waste not, want not."

"The Lord hates a coward."

Grandma's oldest son lived in the Philippine Islands. She longed for him, and every day when we heard the train whistle blowing at five o'clock, and knew that the train was then at Del Monte and would come puffing into Monterey in a few minutes, she would say, "Oh, if my Eddie were on that train!" And when she made pies or cakes, she always made an extra, small one, "For Eddie."

We used to wonder sometimes why she loved him so. But later, when I knew him, I found out. He had the same face, the same blue eyes, the same voice that she did. It wasn't that she thought him better or dearer than my beautiful mother or her other son, Joseph, whom she called "Dode." It was just that they were on the same wavelength. She knew when his letters would arrive, and once when he did not write, she knew that something dreadful had happened to him: his young wife had died and he had walked all night in the forest near his plantation and had called out, again and again, "Mother!" She felt his pain across all the miles of ocean.

Her family name was Corbett, and the Corbetts were from Shropshire. But there must have been a touch of the Gaelic somewhere, for she had "the sight," especially about the people she loved.

All through my college years at Stanford I visited her every other weekend. I would wrap my nightgown around my violin in the case, put my toothbrush in the string compartment, and catch the train on Friday afternoons. On Sundays, at three, I took the train back to Palo Alto again. Those weekends, quiet and loved and utterly simple, were my treasures, the best of my college days.

Grandma died, alone in her little house, half dressed, the comb in her hand, her hair down her back. She was getting ready to come to my mother's for Christmas. I was twenty.

I have never ceased to miss her.

10

"Do you take?" we used to ask each other. This was understood: we meant music lessons. For "music," read "piano." Everybody had a piano who possibly could. Families who didn't own pianos rented them. And in every household there were a couple of young ones who "took."

I began to take at age five. My teacher lived only a block away and I had a lesson every week. At home there was a small bench on which to rest my feet, and my teacher had a similar bench for the use of all small fry whose feet dangled from the piano stool.

There were different schools of thought about method. Some teachers were severe, rapped fingers with rulers, and insisted on five-finger exercises and scales. Clementi was heard in homes where the teacher was old-fashioned and strict, and pupils departed from those teachers' houses with eyes red from weeping.

Some other teachers had been seduced by a new method which came over from England and taught a good deal about relaxation. We used a lot of elbow movement outward, and limp flourishes as we lifted hands off the keys.

Whatever the method, every afternoon about three, when we got home from school, until around six, pianos sounded on every block as children "did their hour." On every piano, as on ours, a clock was anxiously watched.

My father cheerfully paid for my lessons. They cost a dollar an hour, but they went as high as a dollar and a half for forty minutes by the time I reached high school and had gone through many methods, from limp to stiff.

My father had only one stipulation with regard to this cultural activity. There was to be no practicing early in the morning, or when he came home from the office—that is, no practicing while he was at home. Court work was hard and he had to have his nerves in good shape. It was assumed that Mama could always lie down with a handkerchief, dabbed in cologne, on her forehead while I practiced.

Alas, Papa could not control the dutiful practicing of Ventura, two houses up, or of Everett, who enthusiastically practiced his trumpet, or Arthur, who worked at his drums. Those agonies simply had to be endured.

I progressed from teacher to teacher, as they got married or moved away or had nervous breakdowns.

One day, as I was listlessly practicing, making mistakes and not correcting them, watching the clock diligently, my father came home early. He listened a while, then said, "Stop that. Now tell me why you have lost interest in your music lessons."

"Papa, I don't want to play the piano! I want to learn to play the violin and work in orchestras!"

"We will stop the piano lessons at once," he answered quietly.

Within two days he came home with a violin, which a friend had helped him pick out from a pawnshop, there being no store that sold musical instruments in Bakersfield at the time. He had found a man who would start me out on the open strings and show me how to use the bow, and I began a devotion to the instrument I have loved ever since.

Now my practice was no longer listless and I did not even watch the clock. I practiced until my arm was tired, and then I stopped and rested. I was often tearful (when I began to study with a demanding teacher), but only because I felt that I was slow and awkward and my plan was to be a great violinist in a short time and be able to play "Humoresque" in public. Despite tears, I was constant and I never gave up.

Meanwhile, my father's reaching mind became intrigued with the lore of violins. He bought books about violins, and after he had learned the history and some of the principles of the instrument, he began buying violins. He bought one from a client which was a reasonably good instrument, and I used it and kept it carefully, wiping away the resin from my bow after each use. Then one day he came home with another one, in a paper sack.

"Funny thing," he told us. "A man went through town yesterday and he was broke, and he tried several places to get money for this violin. Somebody remembered that I had bought one or two, and came to tell me, and I went over to hear this fellow play it. I thought it was beautiful . . . it has a big deep tone, very loud. Play it, Bunkie!"

I took it in my hands. It was (it is, to this day, my favorite fiddle) brownish-yellow in color, larger than standard size by a hair or two, and even under my inexperienced fingers and bow, it sang with a broad deep tone.

"This fellow said he was an Austrian, or a Hungarian, I don't remember," said Papa, "and he said this was a Gypsy fiddle, made for playing out-of-doors. That's why it has this tone. I gave him fifty dollars for it."

Later, when Papa was convinced that I would somehow always play and study the violin, he took me to Los Angeles prepared to buy me the best instrument he could afford. He consulted with musicians from the symphony orchestra there, and they sent him to a luthier named LeCyr, a Frenchman, with instructions to buy a new instrument from him, since Papa couldn't afford one of the authenticated, old "name" violins. "Better a healthy peasant than a sick aristocrat," they all told him. LeCyr's violins were famous for sweet delicate tone, and lovely high registers.

I studied on this violin, took care of it, and appreciated Papa's generous gift; it had cost a lot of money, for those times. But I always came back to my Gypsy fiddle and regularly longed to hear its loud deep voice. I was advised by professional musicians to use the Gypsy fiddle for playing sonatas with piano, because the strength and vibrations of the piano tend to cover any small-toned instrument. Gypsy could always sound out even over the most determined banging. For other chamber music I used the more "violinistic" tone of the LeCyr. But Gypsy was my father's favorite always, and it is mine.

My father, knowing nothing of music except what he could whistle, did me another service, out of kindness and generosity, and because he was intelligent about what education ought to mean, in music as in other subjects.

He bought a phonograph. It was a Victor, but the new model which had superseded the one with the big flower-like horn on top. And he made an arrangement with a local record shop that I was to go and listen to records once a week.

"And you may choose and charge one," he said. "A classical record."

Thus, for several years I had the greatest joy, listening to great music and becoming acquainted, slowly and haphazardly, but with gradually improving taste, with the great literature of sound.

Papa always listened respectfully to my selections. He loved good singing, and we got records by Caruso, Galli-Curci, Martinelli, and Scotti. He was confused by orchestral selections I chose, but as I played them over and over, they gradually became familiar to him, and one of my memories of him is that he would begin to whistle a theme from Beethoven or Mozart before lighting a cigarette and walking to town. I can hear his heels hitting the pavement swiftly, and smell the Egyptian tobacco he liked to smoke.

The great excitement every year was the recital. Every teacher held one. Perhaps one reason I never became very good at either piano or violin was that recitals were for me excruciating agony, and I often managed to change teachers just before I was due to play in one. Psychosomatic medicine may have had something to do with it too, because I remember that I was usually down with measles or malaria or some other plague around recital time.

Besides, I became somewhat commercial early on in my life. Having been released from formal piano study, and being happily involved with my violin, I went back to the piano and taught myself to be a reasonably good sight reader. The result was that at about age thirteen I got my first job, playing the piano at Saturday morning dancing school. I got two dollars for three hours of accompanying the pliés, jetés, battements and so on, and I enjoyed the steadily increasing bankroll very much.

My interest in earning money was detected some years before. At one time, funny papers, as they were called then, carried half a page or so of ads, usually for itching powder, cigars that would blow up, and other things of interest to small fry. My friend Frances (called San) and I studied the ads and one day found one that seemed to offer glowing possibilities. This occurred shortly after we had been disillusioned about the fairies, who used to provide us with cambric tea and cookies about four o'clock, whenever her mother was at home. But one day her mother was out, and the fairies forgot us entirely, and then, in the person of a maid, suggested that there were no cookies but we might like a cold boiled potato each. We didn't want the potato, and the fairies, and we, gave up our association.

San and I saw that if we sent a dollar for blueing packages, and then sold them all, returning two dollars to the company, they would send us each a doll worth five dollars. This was the "prize," and it was the one come-on that got us. We enthusiastically pooled our allowances, and my little sister Barbara's, and sent away for the blueing. When it arrived we were in business.

At once, our separate characters revealed themselves.

San, at the thought of having to go out and sell her blueing to total strangers, developed a terrible headache and the trembles and gave up. She decided to cut her losses and cravenly gave her mother all the blueing as a gift.

My little sister Barbara, a peddler at heart, went out and walked in the middle of the street, piping, "Bluein' for thale! Bluein' for thale!" Nobody seemed to respond to this, so she returned home, with her blueing intact, ready to retire from business, a failure.

But I was tougher. I took her blueing and mine and worked out a sales campaign. I then set out, on foot, for a section of town where nobody knew me; I did not appear for lunch, and by nightfall I had sold all but two packages of blueing.

My father, worried about me when darkness fell, picked up my trail and traced me all the way to Twenty-fourth Street, in increasing horror.

"Oh, so you are the father of that little girl who came by selling blueing! You brute! She told me that you had abandoned the family and she had to sell the blueing in order to get money for herself and her mother to eat!" And a door was slammed in his face.

Further along, he learned that he was a drunken sot who beat my mother. The story changed at each house. At each one I had invented a story to shake the heart, and at each house I sold a package of blueing, ten cents.

When Papa caught up with me, he merely said, "Come along home now," and we walked in silence back to our house.

My father, by skillful cross-examination, found out the whole story of the blueing, of San's resignation, Barbara's failure, and my spectacular success. My mother turned red with rage and sent me out to cut a peach switch, with which she energetically chastised me, scolding all the while that I would tell such lies about my good father. But Papa was amused and philosophical.

"Looks like we'll always have to support Barbara," he said, "but you can stop worrying about Bunkie. She has the makings of a first-rate con woman and swindler."

But from then on, we had to subject all secret plans for commerce to a board, consisting of Mama and Papa, and gradually my feeling for fiction was channeled in other directions.

One, of course, was reading. I was turned loose in my father's library as early as I could read, and by the time I was in sixth grade I had a card in the Children's Library. There I went through all of Louisa May Alcott, with love and tears, and I remember, with equal pleasure, a whole series of "boys' books" by a man named Altsheler, which I also devoured. I soon found my way into more adult fiction, and one late afternoon I walked home alone, slowly, reading *Ramona*. Almost blind with tears as I read that sad romance, I did not see the man who laid a hand on my shoulder.

It was Papa.

"What are you reading?" he asked. I was blocks from home, on my way back from the big library.

"*Ramona*," I sobbed. "Oh Papa, it is terribly sad! The baby dies, and . . ."

"I have a good remedy for such sorrow," he told me, and led me to Coppins, where he ordered an ice-cream soda. It helped.

"When the eyes are smarting with tears you need a counter-irritant," he explained. It was true, and always afterward I had a big apple nearby when I was reading a bittersweet tale.

Actually, the urge to earn extra money was never discouraged by my mother. She hadn't a lazy bone in her body, and she greatly respected gumption. Also having been brought up lacking for nothing, protected and cared for, she was the thrifty one, while Papa, who had worked since he was nine and had put himself through law school, was all generosity and open-handedness. When I was asked to play the piano for night-school classes in dancing, it was Papa who demurred, but it was Mama who saw to it that I had rides to and from the classes, and that I opened a savings account. She was proud of me. Papa worried for fear I might be missing some fun.

"Earning money is fun," Mama said firmly, and I kept my job.

When my brother Dick got a job delivering groceries one summer vacation, and appeared at home wearing an apron which proclaimed right across his stomach, "Good to the last drop," Mama defended him. Papa thought Dick should give up the job and let a boy who needed the money have it. "I can take care of us all," said Papa.

"Boys who needed the money didn't trouble themselves to go out and ask for the job," Mama pointed out. "Don't penalize your son for having some gumption."

Mama believed in energy and activity and in paying your way and doing your part. The popular phrase "to each according to his need" never convinced her. To each according to his willingness and honesty and responsibility suited her better. For the truly incapacitated, however, she was always compassionate and willing to help.

11.

I am aware that my love for my father may blind me to the fact that a record of his life may not be as entrancing to readers as it has been to me. In partial apology, I offer this quotation from a column by Jim Day, which was published in the *Bakersfield Californian* in 1939, many years before my father's death. Words written after someone's demise are fearful and courteous, part of the superstition that one should speak no evil of the dead.

Mr. Day said in part:

> If I were asked to designate what Francis Bacon called "a full man," meaning a man of education and attainments, the association involving Mr. Borton would be

inevitable. He is a man of parts. . . . He is a man of honor with assurance but no complaisance. He is a man of courage yet without effrontery. He is certainly one of the most intellectually honest men I have ever met. The thing about him I admire most, however, is not his virtue alone, but his virtuosity. Not only has he achieved outstanding success in his profession, the law, but he has had time to cultivate an avid mind in a world full of interesting phenomena. I admire him because he has assimilated a tremendous amount of information without having become didactic; because he has learned of the sordid nature of many men, the greed and chicanery of the world, without having become cynical; because he speaks beautiful English; because he is at the top of his profession without arrogance or foolish pride. . . .

and so on. Mr. Day, a much younger man, wrote the above out of a full heart because, to my knowledge, my father never represented him in any lawsuit, and certainly my father never ran for office, nor required his services as public relations manager.

My purpose in setting down what I know and remember of my father is the simple conviction that my father was unusual, because he was serene and contented.

In the same way, I propose later to tell about my mother, who, long before Women's Lib, felt herself to be master of her fate, untouched by longings she couldn't fulfill, and supremely fortunate.

I have often reflected that my own life, rooted in theirs, has been unique for the reason that my parents were happy and united, and felt able to cope with any trouble that might descend upon them. I therefore never felt rebellious, never wanted to "find myself," and had to be literally pushed out of the nest and made to use my wings. In all my life, there were never any two people to whom I would rather turn with trust for guidance.

When we were little, Papa found us infinitely interesting and amusing, as he did all small living creatures, but he always met us on an adult basis when we asked questions.

I remember when I began bringing home report cards that

said "unsatisfactory" in arithmetic. Papa cross-examined me and quickly established the basic fact that I didn't know my multiplication tables. So he took me in hand. We sat in front of the fire and said the tables over, slowly, twice; then he made me think them to myself without speaking. Afterward he had me recite them each evening. I was given a reward for each table learned. My father could whistle like a bird, and I always asked for "Turkey in the Straw." After a week, and seven turkeys in the straw, I was able to handle arithmetic—until I got to high school and came up against algebra and Miss Chubb, and geometry and Mr. Griffith.

At the dinner table, Papa sat with the big Webster's Dictionary on his left hand, and a set of encyclopedias, against the dining-room wall, on his right. The Tiffany lamp, in many colors, hung over our round dining-room table, like a flower. Small fry were permitted to enter the conversation, but only when speaking complete sentences and pronouncing correctly; it was also advisable to know what you were talking about. The dictionary was right there to help, and so was the encyclopedia, and we were referred to them regularly. And no one was allowed to interrupt. This design for gracious dining was not onerous; on the contrary, we all learned to acquire a mass of general information, and an appreciation of good English.

Later, years later, my father told me that he attributed much of his success at cross-examination to his fund of miscellaneous information, plus reliance on his subconscious.

"Everything you ever experience, read, see or hear is stored away for you. If not in your memory, in your subconscious," he told me, long before the rage for transcendental meditation. "Learn to relax and let it float to the surface when you need it. It will be a tremendous help to you in everything you do."

Since he tried cases involving railroads and their operation, mining, cattle raising, the petroleum industry, and many other areas, he was learning all the time, and he told me that this was a great joy. The writing of briefs, then, easily took the place, for him, of the stories and poems he had published in his youth in the *Atlantic Monthly* and other magazines. The law provided him with all the creative expression he needed.

As a young man, Papa had published a quantity of short stories and verses. He had equal success with a number of other young writers beginning at about that time, and he might have gone on to become a professional writer, but law was always his love. And the writing of his briefs gave him great satisfaction. The story went around Bakersfield that he wore out shifts of stenographers when dictating a brief, so intense was his concentration. He would work for eight hours at a time, at white heat. He was always at his best when working against a deadline. One time, his habit of dictating his briefs a day or so before so that there was barely enough time to print it and submit it to the court, got him into a pickle.

He finished his brief, sent the exhausted stenographers home in cabs, and rushed the brief to the printer, emphasizing that it must be ready to be delivered to the judge in twenty-four hours. The poor printer did his best, and used his head. Having no italics, he used blackface type, and Papa had to amend his brief by hand, as follows:

No disrespect is intended, for opposing Council or for the honorable Court, when the expression occurs: Blackface by the Court, or Blackface by Council. This was occasioned by the fact that the printer had no italics.

I wish I had a copy of that now historic brief.

I was moved to write poetry when I was about eight, producing a work of three verses, three lines each, based on the beauty of a frost-covered lawn. I took my poem to my father at once for approbation. He put down his book, read it carefully, and then gave me a lesson on meter and rhyme, found some great collections of poetry for me to browse in, and started me on a love of poetry that has grown with the years.

In those days fathers came home for lunch, and we knew, when Papa just took a cup of tea, that he was trying a case. This was a time when we were all quiet and careful not to disturb him in any way. "Your father is thinking," Mama would say, and we were all deeply respectful of this mystical process. We usually learned all about the case, because Papa was a man who thought aloud. Before his final argument and his summing up of every case, he would work it all out and expound it to Mama over the dinner table. In this way I heard many anecdotes of the courts. Being the eldest, I was impressed, and I remember some of them.

I knew the names of all the local lawyers and the judges, and sometimes I could even appreciate the points of law that Papa found so endlessly fascinating.

In those days a young stripling lawyer settled in town for a few years, and we learned that he had asked each court reporter to phone him at once when Mr. Borton was trying a case, so that he could drop everything, gallop over to court and listen and learn. That young lawyer was Earl Warren, later Chief Justice of the United States.

One time Papa came home chuckling, but he announced that he had lost his case.

"Why?" cried Mama, in consternation. "Well, I'll tell you," Papa answered. "The case was being tried before Judge E., and he was originally from the Deep South—Mississippi or Alabama or Louisiana, I don't remember where. When the lawyer for the plaintiff got up, a young man they brought in from San Francisco, he began, 'Yo honah, when I entud yo faih city, with its splendid streets and handsome homes, and looked upon yo' shinin' white cote house . . .' " and Papa continued in liquid honey-chile accents.

"Then," continued Papa, "I turned to my client, and I said, 'We've lost. The judge hasn't heard that music for forty years.' "

But Papa wasn't always defeated by imports from big-city law offices. On another occasion, the opposing counsel came in early and invited my father to lunch. He was very condescending to the little lawyer from the sticks; he was vain and full of self-confidence. At lunch, where he grandly ordered wine and French dishes, he turned to Papa and said, "It amuses me to be in the land of the Philistines!"

"Well, watch out," said Papa. "You remember that it was in the land of the Philistines that a thousand were slain with the jawbone of an ass!"

When the trial was over and Papa came home, Mama, as usual, was at the door with big question marks in her eyes.

"I slew him," announced Papa, "and with the indicated weapon!"

As a matter of fact, Papa was often solicited by large law firms in the two big California cities, but he preferred Bakersfield, where he had many friends, and where he could take his dog and go hunting in the hills over the weekends. He loved the country and Bakersfield and his home.

Papa loved the law, but not all lawyers. He had an ironic view of what some of them practiced, as witness this verse published in *The Green Bag*, a magazine for lawyers, in the issue of August 1899:

THE FATE OF THE WILL

by Fred Borton

Oh a man there was, and he filled his sack
   (Even as you and I)
With a mine and a mill and a railroad track
(We thought he would leave to his children a stack)
But the lawyers, they knew they would get a whack
   At his wealth in the sweet bye and bye.
Oh the ink we waste and the chink we waste
And the work of our penning hand,
Make sport for the lawyers who never say die
(For now we know that the lawyers are sly)
   And the jury who don't understand.

Oh a widow she was, and she saw her chance
   (Even as you and I)
With her passionate tale of a young romance
(And veil and weeds her cause to enhance),
She led those poor heirs a merry dance.
   (Even as you and I)
Oh the plans we lay and the hands we play
And the trump cards we command,
Are powerless to cope with the widow's tears
(And the lawyer who shouts in the jury's ears)
   And the jury that don't understand.

The judge then scratched his round bald head
  (Even as you and I),
And some fossilized nonsense he solemnly read
From some other old fogies three centuries dead,
Which settled the will, so His Honor said.
  (Even as you and I)
And it isn't the claim, nor the widow's game,
  That kills our conceit so bland
It's the coming to know that our hard work is nil,
For the judge and the lawyers make rags of the will,
  And the jury do not understand.

Papa did not take divorce cases. He disliked the scandalous courtroom revelations, because in those times the divorcing partner had to prove all sorts of vice and crime against the spouse.

Mama once commented acidly, "All these divorces! They are caused by nothing but sex and money!"

Papa's mild answer was, "But so are marriages, Carrie! Marriages, too, are caused by sex and money."

However, he was not blasé about marital difficulties. I think he was modern in that; whenever some client appeared with the story that his wife seemed to have gone crazy and he couldn't stand her any more and he wanted a divorce, Papa always recommended a doctor first.

But he was rather scornful of middle-aged people who were overcome with adolescent dreams of romance. To such stories as, "My wife and I are good friends, but I have to divorce her because I have found my soul mate," or words to that effect, Papa's reply was, "Friendship is a strong basis for marriage. I suggest that you stick with your wife and try to forget the soul mate."

Sometimes he gave very practical advice indeed.

One distracted gentleman came to Papa with the story that his wife had gone with their two children to visit her mother, and would not return to him. The wife, he felt, had been influenced against him by her mother, but he was sure she still loved him.

"Well," Papa advised, "why don't you just kidnap her?"

The idea was attractive, the kidnaped lady was pleased and flattered, the mother-in-law, though she sputtered, could do nothing legally against her son-in-law, and everything was resolved without further ado.

On another occasion Papa acquired a reputation for almost divine wisdom. An elderly client, of foreign origin, came to Papa, very much distressed because a social worker, more busybody than do-gooder, had threatened to deprive him of his favorite son, the youngest of nine children.

Papa heard the story and it made him thoughtful. It seemed odd that the social worker would make such a threat without the ability to carry it out. Under cross-examination, the worried father revealed that he had kept his child home from school to help him on the farm, and this had prompted an investigation. But further questioning brought out the humiliating answer that the client and his wife had never married, and the social worker was going to allege a "disorderly home."

"Good heavens, why didn't you and your woman ever get married?" demanded Papa. "It must be about twenty years you have been living together."

With hanging head, the answer came: "We thought we might have a falling-out."

Realizing that the man would be embarrassed to take out a marriage license in Bakersfield, where he was well known, Papa suggested that he buy his wife a new dress and ring and take her on a honeymoon trip to a distant county, and there get married; that he then frame his marriage license and hang it in the front room; and that he send his child back to school and hire a man to come in and help when there was extra work at the farm.

Much chastened, the client obeyed, and the very next year the income tax landed on everybody with all teeth bared and all claws out. The client was able to take nine deductions for his legitimate children, and he swore that Papa was a prophet and a leader.

Papa was old-fashioned in his tastes, and forgetful about fashions. When we had new dresses, we would pirouette before him, and he would put down his book or paper, look over his glasses, and murmur, "Very nice. Very pretty."

Then he would infuriate us by suddenly taking a good look at us, as we whisked by in some old dress that we had been wearing for two or three years, and say, "That's a pretty dress! Why don't you wear that more often?"

When lipsticks emerged from the murk into respectability, I bought one, a pale rose. I wore it and brought down rage from above on my head. Papa painted his nose rose with the lipstick, and swore he would go to court that way every time I wore it. I always believed everything Papa said, took his threat at face value and went my way unpainted.

Papa hated perfume, sneezed convincingly whenever any one of us dared to use it, and called it, in execrable French, "*Fleur de Floosie.*"

He was proud of my sister's two long braids, each as thick as his wrist, and when, without permission, she chopped them off and came home bobbed, he was crushed. So obviously was he broken in spirit by this treachery of hers that I never cut my braids, and as I passed from braid-loving father to braid-favoring husband, I have my braids to this day—around my head, or coiled on my nape, or on top of my head, but present. For a while I was known as "The girl with the braids." That time has passed, but I still hear an occasional murmur such as, "Here comes that old lady with the braids." Yes, I come, and I shall go, with braids.

It was our happy family custom—after dinner at six o'clock, and when the table had been cleared and my sister and I had washed and dried the dishes—for Papa to read to us for half an hour. This was a winter ritual. We sat around the fire in the fireplace, and we peeled and ate oranges as Papa read, occasionally handing him a juicy segment to keep his throat lubricated.

He read us *Huckleberry Finn* and *Tom Sawyer*, Dickens, poetry (much of Bobbie Burns, one of his great favorites), *Penrod*, in all his adventures, W. W. Jacobs, and a hilarious adventure tale called "Three Men in a Boat." He wasn't trying to educate us. He was just sharing enjoyment.

One time I made for myself a formidable list of classics which I proposed to read during the year. Papa looked it over and approved, but he gave me good advice.

"Start each one, but if it doesn't hold your attention, either you don't understand the style, or it is beyond you in some other way. It won't do you any good to read anything that doesn't interest you, because you won't remember it. Set it aside. But continue to try to read it, and one day it will rush in and fill a great void."

I had reason to remember his words when, after thirty-five years and many false starts, I again began to read *War and Peace*. This time it was the right moment, and at last a void was filled.

One summer day, Papa came home laughing and told us that he had seen a sign in Redlick's department store which proclaimed, "Women's Bathing Suits Half Off."

"And that reminds me," he said. "Go down and buy bathing suits for everybody, Carrie. You must all learn to swim."

"Me too?" quavered Mama.

"Yes, you too," was the firm answer.

As luck would have it, a farmer with a fine orchard, not far out of town, had built a large reservoir and paved it. He built dressing rooms and let people bathe in his reservoir, while the water ran in and out constantly; the used water went to irrigate his orchard. This place was called Robert's Plunge, and it became the joy of our summer days.

Papa arranged to go to his office an hour earlier and to return home at four. As he drove up in the car, we would all be ready and waiting on the front porch.

We could all swim dog fashion, but Papa bought books on swimming and set out to teach us properly. The result was that I learned the trudgeon stroke, which one doesn't see used much any more, but it had special advantages. You lie face down in the water and give a strong pull downward with the left hand, at the same time making a flutter kick. Then you roll over on your right side, pulling strongly downward with the right hand and making a scissors kick. While on your side, you gulp air, which you exhale into the water when returning to the face-downward position. This stroke is not suitable for racing, but it is great for long swims because one doesn't tire so easily. I trudgeoned around and around the pool, perfectly content, not having been constructed for speed swimming anyhow. My sister and brother, under Papa's instructions, learned the crawl and went hurtling through the water like torpedoes. Mama never got any further than a sedate breaststroke, but she was known even to challenge her great friend and rival in the plunge, Mrs. Derby, to races, and even sometimes to win.

One of the nearby farmers who used to drop in to watch the swimmers at their sport, became confidential with Papa. He approved Papa's teaching us all to be self-reliant in the water, and suggested that he could save on doctor's bills for his family by using a fine product he used for his own. "What is that?" asked Papa, always willing to learn. "Hog serium," was the answer. "It cures the hogs and it cured my wife, Elviry, when she was puny. You let me know when you want some."

"I will," agreed Papa. "There's some hog blood around my house, occasionally. Specially at Christmas."

In the fall, when hunting seasons opened, Papa left on Friday afternoons, with his dog, and drove out to the Sicarte Club. This was a club for the hunting of ducks and geese, and was owned and operated by six or seven friends, Papa among them. They had a clubhouse where they bunked at night, a Chinese cook, and a sanquero, who rode the ditches and kept the swamps, where the ducks and geese came to feed, wet and attractive. It was the sanquero who had named the club. The club members spelled the word, as above, but now that I know Spanish, I realize that the Mexican sanquero had told them to name their club the "Grass Club." *Sacate* means grass.

Papa and his dog drove off every Friday, full of energy, and returned, dirty, unshaven and worn out on Sunday afternoon, with their bag of geese and ducks. I remember the kinds of ducks: mallards, canvasbacks, teal. Mama learned a thousand ways to cook them, and we distributed the limp carcasses all over the neighborhood.

Papa quickly recovered and walked swiftly off to the office on Monday morning, but the dog usually lay panting until Friday morning, when it got up, shook itself, wagged its tail and was ready to go again.

Papa was interested in training his dogs properly, so he sent away and got books and followed instructions with care. I used to watch him patiently training his dogs with a turkey wing, teaching them obedience, how to carry the wing softly, without biting, how to deposit it gently at his feet.

At first Rufus, his Clumber spaniel, was the perfect hunting dog, instinctively waiting quietly at Papa's heels while he shot, then swimming in to retrieve fallen birds.

But when Rufus was gone, Papa sent away and bought beautiful hunting dogs. These were called rattailed Irish water spaniels. They looked just like poodles, except that their wool was red and their little mischievous, merry eyes were green. They trained beautifully and were bright, amusing and loving pets, but they couldn't stand our terribly hot summers, and after buying two, Papa desisted. Instead, he went to some Basque friends who were shepherds and bred their own animals to care for the sheep. These dogs were part collie, part short-haired street dog, and, they thought, often part coyote.

Papa said to one of his friends, a successful owner of sheep, "The next time your best bitch whelps, please give me one of the pups. I want a smart dog."

It was done, and Papa brought home a little bundle of golden fluff, with a black nose, black-tipped ears and tail, and we named him Pucci. (I had been reading Italian history.) But the family simply called him Pooch.

Pucci turned out to be as bright and intelligent and obedient as anyone could wish. Papa trained him carefully. Pooch learned the interesting game with the wing at once. As for obedience, he had only to know what you wanted, and he did it. Except that when Papa first took him hunting, Pooch gave way to his instincts, went straight for the chicken yard at the clubhouse and herded all the bewildered chickens into neat huddles, and then turned his attention to the turkeys. Papa couldn't seem to impose the game of the wing at all. Pooch wanted to herd; he was a shepherd dog.

I don't know the present scientific thinking about the inheritance of learned skills, but Pooch was an example of it.

However, being intelligent, when he finally learned that he was to do the wing game with fallen birds that Papa shot, he became the best retriever Papa ever had. And we had, and loved, Pooch for almost twenty years.

Papa was considered to be a man of unshakable dignity, and no doubt that was an asset in his profession. He was never pompous, however, and he had distaste for self-importance.

At one time, together with a number of professional men in the city, he was invited to join a discussion group, which met for supper once a week and talked over world problems and other subjects (never trivial) that interested them. One of the members of the group was Alfred Harrell, owner and publisher of the local newspaper and one of Papa's good friends; other members included lawyers, doctors, ministers, and a priest. The hoi polloi soon learned about these activities and called the group "The Brain Trust," much to Papa's amusement.

Papa enjoyed the cartoon and comic page of the *Californian,* and when he learned that Alley Oop, his favorite, was to be dropped, he wrote, on his letterhead, a firm letter to the paper, which was duly published, much to the consternation of some of the other members of the Brain Trust. The letter said:

> Gentlemen: It has come to my attention that you are about to drop that cultural gem, Alley Oop, from your publication. As that is all I ever read in the paper, kindly cancel my subscription.

Alley Oop was restored and Papa had somewhat pricked the balloon of solemn importance which hung over the sessions of the Brain Trust.

Papa watched the progress of ratification of the Volstead Act with mounting horror. He was not a drinking man, aside from an occasional bottle of Chianti in its little straw coat, but he was a great believer in the rights of the individual, and he was strong in the conviction that morality cannot be legislated into anybody.

When at last California ratified the Act, in 1917, Papa took steps. He went to his friend Dr. Sabichi and asked for a prescription, which said: "A teaspoonful, when in pain." Having struck his blow for freedom, Papa forgot all about it, and throughout Prohibition Mama used tablespoons of his whiskey in her mince pies.

Papa loved bright colors and was capable of going to court in a green shirt, red tie, and navy-blue suit. But Mama always caught him at the door, before his departure, just as he was lighting up his Melachrino cigarette, and checked him, and made certain of reasonable harmony. There was always a good-bye kiss at the door. Once, however, when Papa had, for some reason, forgotten to bestow it, he hastened home from the office to do so.

"Rule of life. First things first," he said. "Never neglect essentials."

But on weekends, when he went hunting with his dog, he wore whatever he happened to fancy, and his fancies were often strange. He loved those high-crowned denim engineer's caps, for instance; indeed, he had a collection of odd headgear which he was allowed to wear only when let loose alone in the mountains by my vigilant mama, who handled the propriety department. In winter he wore mackinaws of wild and wonderful plaids, and sometimes, when it was hot, if he was not hunting, he would tie knots in the corners of a red bandana and wear this improvised cap to protect his bald spot from sunburn.

Attired once in his red shirt and red bandana, he went to a mountain store for new supplies, as he planned to stay over another couple of days, tramping the hills with his dog and his gun. A casual client at the store set eyes on him and said, "Hello, Gyp. How are things?" "Why, they are fine," answered Papa, without a quiver. He had black eyes and hair and a swarthy skin which tanned to look like Spanish leather, and at the moment he also had two days' growth of beard. He accepted, naturally, the fact that, to a stranger, he looked like a Gypsy.

On the Borton side he was descended from the Fenimores and Coopers, and the known ancestor, Ezra Borton, had come to New Jersey from England before 1700. But on his mother's side the family was said to be of Dutch origin, and it is known that Spain held the Low Countries for two centuries. I saw Papa's counterpart often when I traveled in Spain, and it is my belief that in looks he was a throwback to some black-eyed Spaniard, a man with Papa's kind of dignity, integrity and individualism.

Papa was kindly and respectful of every man he met in the

course of his life or his work, and unlike many Southerners who
lived in our town, he called black people by their full names, unless they asked him to do otherwise. In court he was especially
remembered by his friendly way with troubled black witnesses,
who were often afraid of courtroom procedure. Among his
dearest friends were two self-made millionaires, an Italian and a
Russian Jew, both of whom he loved devotedly. One of his best
friends and hunting cronies was a very humble man, not well-
educated and quite poor, who interested Papa with his mountain
lore, and from whom Papa learned. Another friend was a Mexican
cattleman who taught Papa some Spanish and a great deal about
the ranges and the ways of cattle. Papa had no sense of class, not
even the class of monied and non-monied, and his life was the
richer for it.

He had no built-in fear and respect for big organizations and
big companies either; indeed, once he defied the largest oil company operating in our valley.

During the years when my sister and brother and I were in
school, and college had to be thought of and planned for, Papa
accepted retainers from a number of companies who needed
more or less constant legal advice, obligating himself to defend
them whenever they were called into court.

California has a system whereby certain laws to be submitted
to the Legislature must be voted on first by the people in a referendum. If the people reject the proposal, the law may not be
proposed in the form in which it was originally drafted. This is
called the Direct Referendum.

Once, when such a proposal came up for Direct Referendum, a
number of people stopped Papa on the street and asked him if
he thought it would be voted in. He said he hadn't studied the
law, but he supposed it was all right; it had something to do
with regulations about drilling for oil. However, a few days
before election, Papa read the proposed law carefully and
decided that the net result of it would be to prevent small
property owners from drilling for oil, while imposing no such re-
strictions on large holdings of oil-proved property. Accordingly,
he wrote a letter to the newspaper, asking that it be given
publication, in which he explained exactly what he thought the

law would do, and suggesting that the voters of Kern County stand against it. As holder of a few parcels on which, like many other people, he hoped someday might bloom a beautiful derrick and a pump bringing in a certain number of barrels a day, he personally was going to vote against the proposed law.

The ink had scarcely dried on the paper when Papa was blasted with angry phone calls from an officer of a large oil company that was paying him a retainer, and he was roundly scolded (a man receiving two hundred dollars a month from them!) for daring to go against their views and their best business interests.

The phone calls were followed by equally severe and denunciatory telegrams and letters.

Papa replied at once, "As your legal representative, and on retainer to do so, I am obliged to defend your interests in all cases which come before the courts, and I have done so to the best of my ability. As I see it, the retainer was paid in order to assure you of the constant availability of my services, in case of litigation. It did not ever entitle you to my personal opinions and liberty of thought. Since we disagree on the function of the moneys paid me, please cancel our agreement at once, and receive herewith your last retainer."

There was silence for a time, the proposed law was defeated anyway, and in due course the oil company came back to Papa and asked for his services once more. Having made it clear where he stood, Papa again accepted the retainer and won many interesting cases, included a few in which he "wrote the law," as the saying goes about certain procedures in perforating and drilling for oil, among them the famous Whipstocking Decision, which governs rules of perforation with respect to crossing property lines by drilling under the surface.

And though Papa went out hopefully to follow the procedure of drilling for oil whenever any company sank a well anywhere near a parcel of property he owned, he never did "strike oil" (though many others did) and enjoy the euphoria of suddenly finding the gates to gracious living wide open.

Though Papa was never rich, he spent his money as if he were. As we grew older, we children had to learn to keep our hidden longings and desires to ourselves, because, if we voiced them, Papa would rush out and satisfy them as fast as he could. I once thought I would like to have a guitar. Within a day, a fine English guitar, in a leather case, was ready for me, and indeed I cherish it to this day. My little sister, at twelve, fell in love with a black opal ring in a jeweler's window. She was observed to go there directly after school and stare lovingly at it. One horrible day, it was gone from the window, and she tore into the shop to ask where it was.

"Sold," was the answer.

She went home in tears—only to find it beside her plate, marked in Papa's hand, "Pre-Birthday."

Like many professional men, Papa was harassed by people who waylaid him on street corners in order to elicit free advice. One man, in particular, was a constant offender, until even my easygoing father became annoyed. Mama had threatened to walk out if my father vouchsafed any more free counsel.

"What does he think lawyers study for," she demanded, "if not to know how to give wise advice and guide people?"

Papa then dropped the bomb.

"Oh, but he *does* go to lawyers," he told Mama, innocently. "After consulting me, in the street, to find out what to do, he goes and hires a cheap lawyer to argue his case."

At that, my mother blew up, and because of her attitude, Papa carried out the following scenario when next this man cornered him walking home from the office, buttonholed him, and recounted a long series of complaints.

"And what I want to know, Fred," he concluded, "is whether I can sue."

Papa was silent a moment, as if considering.

"Oh yes, you can sue," he answered.

In due course, the litigious gentleman hired a young lawyer straight out of law school, for a miniscule fee, and instructed him to sue. They lost their case. Then the embattled plantiff stormed into Papa's office, full of indignation.

"But Fred, you told me I could sue!" he protested.

"You asked me, and I said you could," answered Papa. "But if

you had come to *me* with your case, I would have told you that
if you sued, you would lose."

That took care of him.

But Papa was easygoing, as I said above. Also, he was un-
failingly courteous, and he had friends in every walk of life.

At one time, some Southern-born gentlemen, in a group, came
to Papa to ask if he thought they could manage to organize a Ku
Klux Klan in the county, "for protection."

Papa appeared to be in deep thought.

"Well, I'll tell you," he said, "if you do, I think you would
have to go unmasked, you know. We did have the vigilantes in
California, in the early days, but everybody knew who they
were. I don't think you could possibly get up any sort of group if
you went around done up in sheets."

That seemed to take all the excitement out of the idea, and to
Papa's relief, it was dropped. A practical man, he knew very well
that a high moral tone would have had no effect whatever on the
Klan-oriented; but exposing themselves to the public gaze was
not to be thought of. They subsided.

My father was an honorable man, and he had ideas about how
honorable men should behave, but he was impatient with plans
to impose moral righteousness on others. These were attitudes
and codes that one imposed on oneself. As for other people, one
took them as they came, admired some, loved many, and pitied
and despised a few.

He was once called into solemn conclave by a group of re-
form-minded citizens who wished to discuss a plan to sterilize
the unfit, with the idea of recommending that it be drafted into
law.

The discussion ranged from the trouble and expense to the
state of caring for the mentally unfit, to the dangers of allowing
criminal types to propagate themselves. From there, the talk
ranged into far-reaching plans for betterment of the races by
careful sterilization of all of the unfit and unpopular.

It was reported to my mother later that Papa listened with interest to all the speakers, but volunteered no comment himself
until he was asked point-blank if he was in favor of thus assur-

ing a strong, healthy, intelligent race, instead of the variety of flawed creatures that cluttered up the earth at the moment.

"I have one question," was Papa's contribution to the discussion. "Who is going to decide who else is to be sterilized?"

This was long before Hitler's ideas about a super race had demonstrated to the world that, inevitably, those who take it upon themselves to decide who is unfit ought to be the first to submit to the knife.

Though Papa had to work hard for everything he had, he never stood in awe of money.

When I went away to college, he gave me a checkbook and made a generous deposit in my account. I was scared and terribly homesick my first year away from home and family; I literally counted the days until the first vacation, which was due around Christmas. I planned to please Papa mightily by showing him how careful I had been with the money. I had kept my check stubs showing what I had paid for tuition, for books, for board and room, for laundry. I had a large balance left; I was proud of myself and expecting praise.

Papa looked over my checkbook carefully and made no sign that he was delighted. Instead, he took me aside and sat me down in his library.

"Honey, I am sending you away to college to be educated," he told me. "Now, education is not a matter of attending classes and doing your homework and reading your assignments. It is a matter of broadening your mind, your capacities, your tastes and your qualities as a person. This cannot always be done inside your family; that's why it is good to go away, get new perspectives, meet new minds.

"The next time you come home from college and show me your checkbook, I want to see that you have made trips up to San Francisco to hear the opera and the symphony and to go to ballet. I want to know that you visited the museums, and that you bought yourself some books not required by the courses you take. And what about violin lessons? Surely you have time to practice? Then get yourself a good teacher, the best you can find, and improve your playing.

"You see, honey," he said, "money, in itself, is not worth a thing. It is only good for what it will buy. The only thing I want you to do with your money is to see that you get value for it . . . see that what you give your money for is worth the time and labor and striving it took to acquire it. A certain balance in the bank is a good thing. But it isn't the best. The best thing is the balance in your mind and your brain, of what money, well-used, can provide you with."

Later on, when I went away to Boston to study music and then to work, he gave me further advice about money, which I have never forgotten. I have occasionally acted against his advice, but whenever I did I regretted it, and I remembered the good sense and humanity of his words.

"Never loan anybody anything whatsoever in the way of money," he told me, "unless it is a business matter: they provide good collateral, they sign notes, and you are willing to go to court to collect if they default.

"If a friend asks for a loan, never make it. Instead, make him a gift . . . as much as you can give without crippling yourself. Then forget it. You'll find that's best."

Yes, I found that was best.

For years after my father's death, my mother kept receiving little notes and checks, sometimes for fairly good-sized amounts, sometimes anonymously, sometimes signed. All said the same thing: "Once long ago when I was in trouble, Mr. Borton helped me out. He never took my note or asked for the money back, but here it is. I guess he knows that I appreciated it."

Loving the law as he did, having devoted his life to it, it never occurred to Papa that Dick might not naturally follow in his footsteps. But after some months at Papa's law college (after Stanford, where he was elected to Phi Beta Kappa), Dick became interested in the stock market. He came home and announced that he was leaving law school and was going to take a job in a San Francisco stockbroker's office. Papa was struck dumb.

Later, talking it over with Mama, Papa tried to get up his courage to play the heavy father, forbid Dick to leave law college, and insist that he forget the job in the stockbroker's.

But Mama had the wisdom of the serpent.

"Don't say a word, Fred" (she told me all this later). "Let him go. Wish him well. Only, simply assume that, since he will be working, his allowance stops."

This was done.

Papa worried and grieved for about nine months. Dick held his job and lived on his salary, and got quite thin and a little shabby.

But Mama's way was best.

Because, before the next term of law school began, Dick asked for and got an audience with Papa.

"Pop," he said, "if you will consider sending me back to law school, I will promise to stay and finish."

"Why, certainly, if that's what you want," Papa answered, and so it was agreed. Dick stayed, graduated from law school, and when he took the State Bar Examination, his grades were the highest of any in the state.

And by the way, it may be a comment on changing times, but what we called our parents may be worth noting.

To me, they were always Mama and Papa, pronounced Momma and Poppa.

But my sister always called them Mother and Dad.

To Dick they were Mom and Pop.

Actually, after passing the Bar Examination, Dick came into my father's firm and began to learn by doing, as the saying goes. He became an expert lawyer, and when, some years ago, a judgeship fell vacant in Bakersfield, he was appointed to the bench by the then Governor, Edmund Brown.

Governor Brown was a politician and a practical man. When the judgeship fell vacant, he sent a questionnaire to members of the Kern County Bar, asking the lawyers to write in the name of the person they would most like to see appointed. The Governor felt that the lawyers themselves would be the best judges of another lawyer's capacity and integrity. The name of Paul Richard Borton was written in by more than ninety members of the Bar, an overwhelming majority.

Of course we were all terribly proud, but Papa, who was gone by then, would have been proudest of all.

Mama told me that one time, after Papa's heart attacks had forced him to leave the office and rest and remain quietly at home, Dick had come in to talk over a very difficult case with him.

They sat out on the screened porch and talked quietly for many hours. When Dick said good-bye and went home, Mama went to Papa and declared, "I'm certainly glad you aren't in the midst of that case and the law business any more!"

"Oh, Carrie," said Papa, "if I only were! If I only were!" And his voice was full of longing.

A great many people, since my father's death, have spoken to me about another of his qualities which was unusual in his time —perhaps unusual in any time. Americans believe they are a democratic people, one that does not limit virtue to class, birth, or education. But that is not entirely true, as any company wife can tell you, one who has been inspected to make sure she comes from the right stock and from a home with manners and ways that "will fit into the company ideal." Despite all our best ideals, we tend to judge people and select our friends from those with the same educational and economic background as ourselves. This is natural, and it is not basically open to criticism. However, my father did not do it. At a time when many prejudices were active, he seemed to exhibit none—except for scoundrels. Among his friends were Supreme Court judges, Basque shepherds, uneducated farm workers, oilfield roustabouts, physicians, reporters, Chinese laundrymen, lawyers, priests, cowhands, bakers, fishermen. The list is long and varied. He found everyone interesting, and he would enjoy a talk or an excursion or a hunting trip with any one of them.

As a public figure, he had to be given a public funeral, so that people could pay their last respects. (Others in our family have avoided these ceremonies, and have chosen strictly private obsequies.) It was suggested to my mother that a young Congregational minister should say the prayers and make the eulogy. This young man came to the house to consult with my mother about what he should say, and after they had talked awhile, he decided that instead of speaking, he would read a poem by Leigh Hunt: "Abou Ben Adhem." The poem tells of an angel who visited earth to list the names of men who loved God, but when he spoke to Abou Ben Adhem, the old man said, "Write me as one that loves his fellow men." The poem concludes with the return of the angel, carrying a list of names of those "whom love of God had blessed, And lo, Ben Adhem's name led all the rest."

When the minister read those words at my father's funeral, with the chapel full of men and women of every walk in life, it touched us children most deeply to hear, after those last words, a soft deep chorus of Negro voices, saying, in unison, "Yes, Lawd! Amen."

12.

Like many beautiful women, Mama was shy. Despite her spectacular good looks as a young woman, and despite the fact that my father fell in love with her when she was fourteen and never looked at another woman in his life, she could still feel jealous. She was enraged at a certain Bakersfield lawyer who stopped her on the street one day to exchange the time of day. My father had just hired an experienced stenographer, of a certain age and eminent homeliness, and only a few weeks before had lost another competent woman, with the same general lack of physical attraction, to the restlessness that overtook many women in those days who longed to get out of the small town and find work in "the city."

"I see you just hired another stenographer for your husband," quipped the joker. "Nothing like being careful."

My mother never spoke to him again.

However, Mama knew the rules about everything, and one of the precepts she subscribed to was, "Assume a virtue if you have it not." So she never phoned Papa at his office, or dropped in on him, or in any way revealed herself as a woman who worked out little tricks and techniques for spying on her husband. There were such women, and Mama despised them.

If I were to choose a word for Mama, from a host of merited adjectives which come to mind, I would select "staunch." She had rigid rules of behavior for herself based on what was decent, correct and dignified, and she had an almost snobbish feeling that one "should always give a good example." She taught us the rules and insisted on them; but I am sure that if any of us had transgressed, Mama would have been a tiger in our defense. Loyalty to her own was complete and unquestioning.

I recall an evening long ago when I must have been about nine, for we had moved into the big two-story house that was "home" to me for over sixty years. I had crept downstairs, barefoot, in my flannel nightgown, to get a glass of water, and I heard Mama and Papa talking in the living room.

"I signed his note," Papa was saying, "and he can't pay it."

"Was it much?" asked Mama in a small voice.

"Yes. If he doesn't pay—and he has only a week more to raise the money—I could sell this house and the car and take our savings and cover it. Or I could go through bankruptcy. Everything is in your name anyhow, so you would be all right."

"What an idea! You will *not* go through bankruptcy!" commanded Mama. "What a thing to think. It would be a disgrace!"

"Well . . . but the alternative . . . and we have to think of the children . . ." began Papa.

"The children are not going to starve, not while I know how to cook beans," proclaimed Mama, our beautiful Mama. "You and I started with nothing and we can do it again. I'm not afraid!"

Papa did not have to sell and he never went through bankruptcy, so I guess his friend somehow found the money to pay the note.

I have never forgotten my first feelings of icy terror, of change and of the unknown, which assailed me when Papa spoke of the awful something called bankruptcy. And I remember the wave of certainty and safety that washed over me at Mama's valiant words. I crept back up to bed and slept soundly, and I don't think I have ever recalled the incident to anyone until this moment.

Another example of Mama's loyalty and courage occurred when my sister Barbara was in college in Los Angeles.

Barbara was not what is called "the college type." She quit college every Friday and came home, and Mama worked on her over the weekend and sent her back every Monday. Meanwhile, Barbara longed passionately for vacations.

But one vacation time when everyone in her sorority house had departed, including the cook, and the housekeeper had a leave of absence, Barbara rang up, tearful and desperate. She was very sick and had a high fever and couldn't get out of bed, and there was no one about even to bring her a cup of tea.

Mama went immediately to pack. The day before, she had had the last of her teeth extracted and she would not get her plates for a month. Toothless and in pain, and horribly conscious that she looked not like herself but like some caricature, she set out, not knowing how she would manage, but only that her child needed her.

Luckily for Mama, her guardian angel guided her toward a little Jewish delicatessen three blocks from the sorority house. The kind proprietor cooked special chicken soup for Mama and Barbara, made soft baked custards and generally clucked over Mama the way Mama clucked over Barbara. In about a week they both wobbled home, to convalesce together.

Mama hid from her friends until she was triumphantly herself again, complete with teeth, but when Barbara needed her, appearance wasn't important.

Mama and her dear friend Hattie knew the life and miracles of everyone on the block, and they were often on the phone together. Our phone was in the dining room, but there was an unwritten law among all the ladies that one didn't make phone calls when the mister was home. Perhaps they feared extensions —who knows? Anyhow, they didn't. But Mama had a regular call from a certain Mrs. M. who didn't know the rules, and who was the amusement of my father and the embarrassment of my mother every time she telephoned. The conversation always went like this:

"Hello. Oh yes, I . . ."

Interruption and long pause while Mrs. M. spoke.

"Well, I . . ."

Long pause.

"No, but . . ."

Interruption and long pause, while my father began to snicker.

"But I . . ."

Long pause.

"Oh. Good-bye."

Mama would return to the table, red in the face and boiling mad.

"Did she have anything to say?" Papa would ask, innocently, helping himself to chops.

Furious, Mama would answer, "Somebody should invent a telephone with a sign on it that tells you who is calling. You do it, Fred."

Mama had an enormous love of life and of all life's good things. She loved good food, the countryside, animals, flowers and trees, and above all else, the sea. Half Danish, some strong Viking strain in her called her to the sea insistently, and she was never so happy as when she was on a boat or seated on the sand near the heaving, restless ocean, with her children around her, breathing in the sharp iodine-scented breath of the water. She blossomed and gained energy whenever she was near the fresh cold sea; she didn't care for hot southern beaches, but reveled in wind, wild gray days and rain. I often wonder how she was able, for so long, to fashion her life around the hot dry sun-drenched summers of our valley.

When my sister and I took a trip with Mama to historic sights in New England she was not well, but she would not put off the longed-for journey. She had frequent headaches, and often in the evenings her feet were so swollen that the design of her shoes showed in the puffed flesh when, with a sigh, she would ease them off. But she would not give up. Every morning when Barbara and I made plans for the day, she would say, "Get me a cup of coffee. Then give me my hat and a couple of aspirins and we're off."

At home, Mama was endlessly busy. I wonder now at the flow of dresses from her sewing machine, the knitted sweaters, scarves and shawls, the crocheted afghans and countless other handmade articles that came from her small hands. She never left anything half done, but always seemed pressed by demons of time to get things finished.

Yet, she didn't overvalue the things she made.

Once she made my sister a beautiful pink dress, with buttonhole embroidery all around the neck and hem. She arrayed Barbara (aged five) in this finery, told her to wait downstairs, and went up to her bedroom to get dressed. They were going to an important function, I forget what. Barbara disobeyed, went out to show Papa her dress, fell into the garage pit, where he repaired his sick automobiles, got covered with grime and thick black grease, and came into the house, wailing, her dress ruined. Mama took one look at it, grasped it by the neck and ripped it off and threw it in the garbage.

This act was most effective, and Barbara did not again disobey orders to sit quietly and wait. But poor child, she was accident-prone and was always in some dire trouble, coming home with torn dresses, a lost shoe, or pieces gouged out of her person. "Bad News Johnson," Mama called her, and got used to Barbara appearing always in a dark funnel-cloud of danger, like a tornado. All this changed when Barbara learned to drive, at age eleven. She became at once the family chauffeur. A splendid driver, bold but skillful, from then on she was able to navigate through life in safety. She was meant to be wheel-borne.

My mother's qualities of fierce loyalty and protection of her family also showed clearly when my father had his massive heart attack. Until his death, ten years later, Mama guarded him from all trouble and worry. She would allow no one into the house who had a cold or coughed or even looked as if he might be about to almost start coming down with one. She cooked Papa's meals, read with him, gave him massages with an electric hand-massage. (This was also greatly enjoyed by Popo, the cat, who, when four o'clock came, arrived promptly to get his massage, immediately after Papa had his.)

And when Papa was gone, Mama did not immediately sell everything and go into a small apartment and plan cruises. "No," she said, to all such suggestions. "I can lay my hand on anything I want, in pitch darkness, in my house, and I shall stay here. Also, I feel your father near, and I like that."

She had a touch of Women's Lib, though—just a touch—for once she said to me, "I loved your father. He was the only man I ever loved, and I wouldn't exchange a moment we had together for anything on this earth. But sometimes, now that I am alone, I wake up and I think, 'I don't have to do one single solitary thing today except what *I* want to do, and it's wonderful.' "

She had a great sense of the practical, and believed firmly that all things work out for the best.

Once she fell down the five steps to our front porch while on her way out to pick up the evening paper. She was alone at the time, but she did not panic. "My glasses hadn't fallen off, I had landed on the grass and didn't hurt much anywhere, and there was the paper," she told me. "So I just lay there and read it until a young man came walking along, and I yelled to him, 'Young man, come over here and up-end me!' "

Mama had some philosophies which were not exactly orthodox, but I often recall them and they seem very sensible to me. One was the manner in which she recommended that gossips be treated: "Gossips do a lot of harm with their tales," she told me. "Always lie to gossips. Then they will spread the story and pretty soon everyone will know enough not to tell them anything. They will be hoist with their own petard."

Mama liked her privacy and was offended by direct personal questions, which she thought were insolent prying and showed bad taste. "As for people who ask personal questions, tell them lies too," she advised me. "Truth is a jewel, like the pearl you don't throw to the swine. Truth is for people you love and trust, who will prize it, not for every Tom, Dick and Harry."

Also, one day, when she was very thoughtful, she said, "When you were born, I lay in bed and thought, 'How wonderful! When my little girl is twenty, I will only be forty-two! What fun we can have!' "

Thinking further ahead, she said, "Be very correct and circumspect and respectful and good until you are forty. From forty to fifty, you can begin to do a few odd and outrageous things. Then, from fifty on, you can live exactly as you please, and everyone will say, 'Oh, yes, she's eccentric,' and pardon you anything."

Mama liked mathematics and was good at it; perhaps because of this gift, she loved card games that brought mathematical powers into play. She was an excellent bridge player and was also good at cribbage, which I am told takes the same sort of mind. (I have never understood it, and at bridge I am treated kindly by my betters.)

But Mama also had a powerful urge to win, and this could be perceived, like a wind from the north, when she sat down and took up her cards. Her face, normally sweet and open, became icy cold, granite-like hard. She was in it to win, and she was *determined* to win. And she *did* win. Even so, the game meant so much that she would even play when she was having a losing streak. Once she was playing with my sister and me and a friend. Mama lost three hands, threw down her cards in a temper and stalked from the room. We looked at each other and started to gather up the cards. Within minutes Mama appeared in the doorway and asked, humbly, "If I play pretty now, will you play with me some more?" We said we would and the game went on.

As a young girl Mama had to hold the horses and drive, because she was not afraid of them, whereas when Grandma got into the buggy, the horses smelled her fear and immediately curvetted and snorted and pranced. This fearlessness was characteristic of Mama all her life. I have often thought that plain courage is probably the keystone of integrity; it is always fear, fear of something or someone, that makes people compromise. Mama never compromised.

Mama hated to be used, and this hatred she summed up in a strong Old West saying: "Don't let anybody play checkers on your shirttail!"

"Have a little Danish sand in your craw," she used to say to admonish me, and "Never give up! Keep going! Keep going!"

When Bakersfield was hit by a constant series of earthquakes in 1965, Mama refused to go and live on the Coast or otherwise change her life in any particular. In fact, I am told that when a sharp quake occurred, she would hang onto a door, eyes brilliant with excitement, and then when it was over, rush to the phone to exult to her friends, "We just had a *good* one! A real ring-tailed sidewinder!"

I realize now that it was my father who was the romantic one, the poetic one. Mama was the brave warrior who set out to conquer life, and did.

She was not religious, though she believed in God and in some cosmic pattern of existence. But "I don't need any heaven," she used to say. "I have my heaven right now. I don't need any future life. I love the one I have. I am not afraid to die."

Given this courage, this disdain even of fearing the unknown, or annihilation, it follows that she was not overcareful of her health, nor did she pay any great attention to medical checkups, vitamins, exercise, diet, or any other modern method of holding off the evil day when one must surrender the body and this life. She preferred to be comfortable and active, and therefore she was reasonably sensible, but the efforts of many people her age to pretend that the years were not passing amused her.

Our family doctor visited her with some regularity after my father's death, and she heeded his advice sporadically. But she was not in awe of medicine, and often expressed amazement at the amount of money spent by young mothers who took their children to the pediatrician every month and were always paying doctor bills, sometimes hundreds of dollars a month.

"I don't think I ever paid out more than a hundred dollars for doctors for you three children in twenty years," she told me. "I relied on bed, camphorated oil, milk toast and castor oil. And look at you. Big and healthy, every one."

Several times, after a visit to take Mama's blood pressure (which was high, but she paid no attention), the doctor said, "I wish you would take off forty pounds, Mrs. Borton."

Mama never replied to this absurd suggestion. She had been forty pounds overweight for about forty years. But one time, when she was well up in her eighties, active, intelligent, managing her own house and taking excellent care of her financial affairs, the doctor was foolish enough to recommend reducing yet once again.

"Doctor," said Mama, fixing him firmly with her bright-green glance, "how many of the patients who would have been eighty-seven, as I am, did you make take off forty pounds? And where are they now?"

She knew very well where they were, for she always read the obituaries first, "to see if my name is there," she used to say.

The doctor didn't bother Mama any more about dieting, and

she continued to put cream on her peaches and butter on her hot biscuits and sugar in her coffee. He contented himself with merely wagging his head and murmuring, "Remarkable person. Remarkable person."

Mama lived to be ninety-three, survived an operation for perforated ulcer at the age of ninety, and was bright and beautiful as a big full-blown pink rose, to the very end.

When she died, we carried out her wishes and gave her ashes to the sea. Far out beyond Monterey Bay, on the open ocean, on the kind of gray misty day she loved best, we floated orchids, camelias, and roses on the heaving swells, then gently lowered the silvery box of ashes into the deep, within sight of the coast and the beaches where she had spent her happiest days.

I often hear her voice, as it came to me over the telephone time after time, as it ended all her letters—and we wrote almost daily for all the years of my life after I left home: "Come flying home into my arms!" and "I love you so much."

She was loyal and loving, like the great heroines of the past. And she was never afraid of anything.

13.

I was the eldest of my parents' three children, so perhaps it was natural that I should be the one who heard and remembered family history and family legends. Having no little sister or brother for almost five years, I was always demanding, "Tell me a story"; and busy parents, tired of inventing, would often begin (as they do everywhere) by telling you about when they were a little girl or boy.

Also, perhaps it was my temperament which made me specially interested in the vague, shimmering images of relatives who had disappeared into the limitless past. I always loved stories, and in the histories of my grandparents and great-grandparents, of my uncles and aunts, there was everything that captures the imagination: romance, mystery, tragedy, comedy.

I don't doubt that every family embodies countless unwritten novels in the memories of its oldest members. I propose to tell about mine because they gave my dreaming childhood much color, and a perception of the vagaries of fate, and because, in hearing about things that happened to people in my family, readers may remember some of the unique and touching experiences that belonged to their own. I hope I can thus stir some memories. These are histories, and the narratives of the great movements of peoples and convulsions of society are nothing but these individual stories melted into a stream that moves forward. History is not greater than any of its tiny parts, for each part is an individual life, lived with all its struggles to learn, to get ahead, to somehow lay hold of the heart's desire.

My great-great grandmother was born somewhere in Germany. There is no one now who can tell me where. Her name was Matilda von Mannheim, and I was given to understand that she was of a distinguished and wealthy family. She must have been strongly romantic (as were so many Germans in the early part of the last century), for she left her wealth and honor behind and eloped to the United States with a penniless young student of chemistry. His name was Seiber, and we were told in our family (perhaps it wasn't true) that he invented the Seidlitz powder (a mildly laxative salt which is mixed in water and drunk while still foaming), and made his fortune.

This romantic pair settled in New York City, and the stories handed down about them are strange indeed. For, it seemed, the romantic Matilda soon weighed well over two hundred pounds, and had to have sofas and chairs specially made to fit her. On the demise of Seiber, she married an elegant Irish gentleman, a doctor, who played the violin and recited poetry. The most startling thing about Great-great Grandmother is that she produced and raised twenty-four living children.

I submit that there are many interesting facts to ponder in this story. For one, what price the slender figure, the months of starvation to achieve it? We were told that she was blond and beautiful, and that the Irish gentleman had strong competition before he won her plump hand. I accept the stories, and I accept the Seidlitz powder fortune. What I find hard to understand is the complete disappearance of Mr. Seiber, the father of the twenty-four children. Nobody ever even remembered his first name. Well.

One of Matilda's children was another Matilda. She was my great-grandmother.

We have pictures of her, a modest, busy, good little body, probably as dear and loving and irritating as anybody's grandmother, but not otherwise outstanding or strange in any way. But she married a strange and interesting man who has gone down into our family legends wrapped in enigma.

His name was John Corbett. He was born in England, in Shropshire, in some little place with the name "Corbett" in it. And we were told he was of an "Army family." Most of the young Corbetts had gone out to India to carry the burden of empire, but John, the youngest, was tubercular and the Army was not for him. In those days it was thought that a long sea voyage was one of the things that might help a tubercular person, so John was shipped off to New York. He felt better on landing, but he was very tall, inordinately thin, and had the curious intensity of people who are burning out their lives in fever. He began working at once and made up his mind to stay. Part of this decision had been taken because he had met Matilda Seiber, a merry little brown wren, and he wanted to marry her. To earn his living, John Corbett polished lenses, and he began also to indulge his artistic gifts by making statuary. At this, it seems, he was very successful. In those days many people ordered statuary: bronze deer, brooding stone angels, prancing horses. All sorts of figures and themes were appropriate for gardens, and there was an endless market for statuary in cemeteries—to adorn the graves, and to remind the living of the immobility of the dead, as motionless, cold and pale as the angel figures above them.

None of this is extraordinary, but what is odd is that he was known to a wide circle as a hypnotist and apparently was remarkably able in this mysterious practice. It was said that he did not have to receive the consent of the hypnotized, but that by merely fixing his eyes upon a person, and pointing a finger at them, he could hypnotize them so that they were completely under his domination. Perhaps, for a man deprived of the feeling of power and prestige that a uniform and an Army title may give, this was an adequate compensation. For what is more powerful than the ability to control a mind, a psyche?

John Corbett amused his neighbors and fellow workers with his powers, and no doubt he basked in the scared admiration he aroused.

But one day, before he had to leave to catch the horsecar for work, one of his children, Ellen, the mischievous one, displeased him in some way, made him late, or spoke in a loud voice (he would not allow strident voices in his house), and he turned on her angrily, pointed at her, and said, "You stand in that corner and don't move." She did, and he departed. But when he returned from his day's labors and descended from the horsecar a block or two from his home, he was met by Matilda, pale and in tears.

"Oh John," she must have said, "do hurry. Ellen has not moved from the corner, she is like a stone, she doesn't hear or see. I am so frightened."

It took John Corbett several hours and all his skill to bring his little daughter out of her trance.

Turning to his wife, he said, "I will never again practice hypnosis on anyone."

Perhaps he never did, but the legends tell us that Ellen was forever after terrified of her father and would not go near him, sit on his lap, or allow him to touch her.

There were five children of that marriage, all with good old English names. They were John, Joseph, Elizabeth, Ellen and Mary. My maternal grandmother was Mary.

I don't know if it is widely known, but during the Civil War some people in the North starved, especially in the large cities. Of course we knew of the suffering of the South. But my grandmother, who was a child during the War, told us that food in New York became so expensive and so scarce that all of the Corbett children were sent out to work for their keep, and they felt lucky to have found places. My two great-uncles worked for a wholesale grocery concern; Aunt Ellen, for a tailor; Aunt Elizabeth, for a florist. Mary, my grandmother, the frail one, worked for a druggist, molding little pills and packing them into boxes and bottles; later, after her terrible accident, she worked as a companion to a wealthy old lady, in the best tradition of modern Gothic romances, which so often start their heroine out as companion in a mysterious house. My grandmother read to, embroidered for, and kept keys to cabinets on her person, for a certain Mrs. Stedman. I saw a picture of Mrs. Stedman, a thin, arrogant-looking old lady with astounding corkscrew curls, but Grandma told me she was very kind and correct, every inch a lady, and while not affectionate, she was nevertheless thoughtful and considerate.

Grandma had appeared in the newspapers some years before in a special way. Sent on a holiday to carry a clam pie to some relatives from the Corbett home on a street in the section now called Harlem, Grandma was run over by a train. In the ensuing melee (the train couldn't have been going very fast) nobody could identify the little heap of bloody clothes, until John Corbett, delivering groceries, came along and identified the clam pie. Poor Grandma was unconscious six days, and it was a nine-day wonder that she lived. She and her family expected her to be an invalid the rest of her life, and she looked the part. Delicate, pale and slim, with large blue eyes and a coronet of golden-brown braids, she was beautiful, and perhaps because she was so evidently not long for this world, my Danish grandfather felt pity and married her. (He had previously married a little Danish girl who was dying of tuberculosis, in order to give her a home and make her last days comfortable.) But Grandma fooled him. She lived to be seventy-five, outliving him by ten years.

On my father's side of the family, there were legends, too. He came of a line, as he used to say, "of eminent preachers, writers and liars." The preachers and writers we have been able to identify. They were of the Fenimore-Cooper clan, and the irascible old James Fenimore Cooper was my father's ancestor (sometime after the first Borton, one Ezra, had immigrated to New Jersey back in 1740 or so). The name Borton is of Norman-French origin, having nothing to do with Burtons, Bordens, or Boltons, and was originally spelled Bourton, or De Bourton. The family gradually moved west and seemed always to be searching for new frontiers. It was a Borton from northern Michigan who met and married my grandmother, my father's mother, who had the charming name of Barbara Barr, and was a handful.

Poor Grandma B. And poor Grandpa B. Their marriage was a terrible mistake, but in those days, if you made a mistake, that was too bad. You had made your bed and you had to lie in it.

Grandma B. was not pretty, but she must have been (in fact, I *know* she was) a charmer. She was tall and slim, with night-black hair and large black eyes, and she was vivacious, capricious and had considerable dramatic talent. She was in her teens in the years just before the Civil War, and she met and charmed a young Southerner who was visiting in Illinois where she lived. They fell madly in love and were making the sort of plans young lovers make, when Fort Sumter was fired on. He felt he must rush home and join his family and comrades in the South, but he promised to write often—every day if he could—and as soon as the trouble was over, which they hoped would be soon, he would come back for her.

So he went away and Grandma waited for his letters, which never came. At first she was worried, then anxious, then disappointed and hurt, and finally furiously angry. And she had a terrible temper.

Deciding that she was a woman scorned, she set out to flirt with the young men in her town of Berlin, Illinois, but there weren't many left. Most of them had gone away to war. But there was William Fenimore Borton, a God-fearing Quaker, who didn't hold with war and killing. She quite turned his head and they were married.

And then, oh poor Grandma, during a lull in the fighting, she received several packets of letters from her Southerner. When Grandma was an old lady, over ninety, and had died napping on her couch with a copy of my first published book in her hand, Mama found the letters. Grandma had kept them all those years.

As for Will Borton, poor Will. I can imagine what his life with the fiery Barbara was like, for on the second call for volunteers from Illinois he joined up, the desperate Quaker, and even went as a sharpshooter. So home life must have been fierce.

Nevertheless, they muddled along together, went out West, and brought four children into the world.

Grandpa Borton taught school, and we still have the bell he used to call his reluctant scholars in to their pine desks. But he died young, when my father was only nine.

Two of the children died in infancy, but Grandma was left with my father, Fred, and with little Nellie.

Nellie tried, in the way young girls always have done, to achieve some glamour by changing her homely name into something evocative. She decided to call herself Nellis. I am like her; I prefer Nellis to Nellie, and I think it sounds romantic and evocative. But our little Nellie taught school in a tiny mountain town, suffered an early illness, refused all painkillers toward the end for fear she might "get the dread habit" of morphine, and died before she was forty. She was short and plump, had big round eyes and a look of innocence even when she was thirty, and she was gentle and obedient. My grandmother, sharply intelligent and fiercely ambitious, was determined that Nellie was to become a brilliant intellectual and marry a rich man. But Nellie was not intellectual; she was only good and willing to please. The rebellious intelligence and driving mind belonged to my father, Little Fred, who was overlooked in Grandma's plans and was used only to help finance Nellie. Yet Papa loved Nellie and he loved his mother too, and forgave her for trying so hard to live another, brighter life, through her daughter.

The Women's Liberation Movement would have helped my grandmother. She would have been able somehow to launch out and make use of her gifts of imposing personality, quick mind, passionate ambition, and personal charm. She was born a hundred years too soon.

Not so, my grandmother Mary Corbett Christensen. Her joy was giving loving service to others, and I don't think she ever gave herself a thought. She didn't even speculate much about our mysterious grandfather. She just loved him.

He was a strange man. I had the privilege of knowing him for ten years, in the time he was retired and lived with Grandma in Monterey, California, in a small house he had built himself. He used to sing the sagas to me in a harsh unmusical voice, in old Danish, and sometimes explained them to me. I remember "The

Death of Baldur the Beautiful," which impressed me more than all the desperate doings of Thor.

As far as we know my grandfather Christensen's story, it was this: He was a mischievous, rebellious boy in old Copenhagen, and was sent to be trained under the most severe master in the city. He learned carpentry and building generally; he also learned how to make fine furniture and inlaid woodwork.

But as he related the modest stories of his boyhood as an apprentice, there were glimpses of another life. He told of the tall golden mirrors in the house at Elsinore, from ceiling to floor, the ballroom under scintillating chandeliers, a fiery old Aunt Katharine (where did I get the impression that she lived in Russia?), and a curious story about a younger sister who, Grandfather said, was a portrait painter. She came home to visit one day, in a carriage with four horses and fur covers, tearfully bade them all farewell and departed for Italy. She was never heard of again.

He had no pictures of his parents, but a few of his sisters: each one named Maria. There were Sofia Maria, Theresa Maria, and Amelia Maria. There was also a brother, who bore the old Danish name of Yens. Then why the curiously European names of the sisters? Another dropped bit of information was that he had an uncle "who had been with Napoleon."

Grandfather had reddish hair and bright-blue eyes. He was not tall, and was rather spare, but very strong. He related that he had been traveling around the world, after having toured Europe, and on the way was wrecked off the coast of Ireland. He managed to get to shore, and in the course of time, took another boat bound for Australia. When it put into New York, he stopped and went ashore to see the sights, and woke up in the Union Army.

Soldiers were shanghaied into the Army during the Civil War, and this may have been what happened to Grandfather. But I have often wondered whether the whole fabric of his adventures might have been woven to hide the truth—that he was a young revolutionary who had been run out of Europe. There had been an uprising against the Crown in Denmark at about that time. Where better could a young exile hide and get his bearings than in the army of another country? And then too, the United States, in the last century, was a refuge for countless young men fleeing from a Europe in upheaval. Well, who knows?

It is true that he served in the Union Army. We have a copy of his honorable discharge, made out in the name of Peter Christensen. I don't know for sure that that was his name; it could be a sort of John Doe for any Scandinavian country.

Grandfather got out of the Army and went to New York. He had nothing but the calico pants he stood in, and a fine case of dysentery. Yet, a few years later, in 1872, he married Grandma. He was then a prosperous contractor and builder, with his own house and crews of men working under him.

Two children were born—a girl, who died in infancy, and a son, named Edward Esbern. Grandfather's illness became chronic, then acute. Doctors recommended a long sea voyage. (This seemed to be the best way to get rid of sick people they didn't know how to cure.) Grandma, her baby and a nurse booked rooms on the steamer, and Grandfather was carried aboard on a stretcher. But by the time they reached Panama he could walk, and he seemed to enjoy the train trip across the isthmus to the waiting ship on the other side. They eventually landed in San Francisco, where they lived for a short time, and where my uncle Joseph was born. Meanwhile, Grandfather, who seemed to have limitless funds, searched the state for a place to live, and eventually bought an isolated ranch in the windy Salinas Valley, near the town called Soledad. There my mother came into the world.

Grandfather occasionally built a house or a school or a hotel. But he did not ranch. He sent to Washington for booklets about what to do, and hired men to do it. Mostly, my mother told me, he sat upstairs in his room and read books; he had volumes in English, Spanish, French and Russian. He kept to himself, and as far as Mama could tell, he maintained no contact whatever with Denmark or his own people.

Except once.

When it became obvious that Mama was going to be very beautiful, he took her to San Francisco to have portrait photographs made, and he sent copies to Denmark. In return, Mama received a pair of gold and coral earrings. But that was the extent of the communication, as far as anyone knew. Grandma, of course, knew no Danish, or any other foreign tongue, and wasn't interested anyway.

There seemed to be money for anything Grandfather considered necessary. Education was necessary, he said, and he sent his sons through college, but also his daughter.

When Mama married and went away, Grandfather put the ranch on the market and, when it was sold, moved to Monterey. Besides his own modest house, he built others to rent; he also built himself a boat, in which he spent many hours sailing in Monterey Bay.

When he knew he was dying, he got up and took his strongbox out of his locked trunk and burned all his papers. Grandma had never seen his papers anyway, and had no idea what was in them. So we never knew. He left a considerable fortune for those days, and it was divided into four parts—a portion for Grandma and for each child—and he left a bequest of over a thousand dollars each to his six grandchildren.

This mysterious grandfather, who could fence and had shown me how, who knew so many languages (and I am witness that his English was unaccented and educated), who seemed to have plentiful money, left us all without a clue as to his identity or his past.

Many years later, a lawyer from Copenhagen traced him to California and came to call on Mama. Mama could tell him nothing about "Peter Christensen," and the lawyer would not reveal the reason for his expensive visit. We presumed that the lawyer then continued on to the Philippine Islands to contact my uncle Edward, the oldest son.

I was agog with curiosity about Grandfather, and when Uncle Ed came back stateside, as he called it, on a visit, I wanted to know all the romance of Grandfather.

"You were the oldest son, Uncle Ed. He must have told you! Who was he?"

But Uncle Ed got the stubborn look I was so often to see on his face. Gentle, kind, but unyielding.

"If he did not want you to know," he said, "you are not to know." And he closed the subject, forever.

To Grandma he was always just "my Peter," and she grieved for him until she died.

As a little girl I often spent summers with her alone, and many a time I heard her say, "There goes old Mr. So and So. He drinks and beats his horse, and there he walks still! Why not him, instead of my Peter?"

Or, "There goes old Mr. So and So. He can hardly see and he forgets his name, and his daughter has to pin it on his coat so people will bring him home when he is lost. And here he is still, and my Peter was taken!"

But the family legends did not cease with Grandfather and his mysteries. There was Uncle Ed himself.

He was another romantic, and in his way, mysterious too. For I think, now that I remember much about him, that to his other activities he probably added intelligence work. There is no other way to explain some of his sudden and secretive comings and goings.

When I was a little girl I often fingered my mother's wedding dress, a beautiful gossamer gown which seemed to be spun from spider-silk.

"It is the piña cloth," I was told. "Your uncle Ed sent it from the Philippines."

Grandma had a doorway hanging made of beads in a design of birds and rushes. Sometimes she let us children snip out bits to make ourselves necklaces. "Your uncle Ed sent it to us from the Philippines."

When I was sixteen, my first dancing dress was made from a bolt of deep pink corded silk that Grandma took from her trunk. "I have been saving this for you," she told me. "Eddie sent it from Manila."

All the glamour of a hero of romance and adventure hung around this legendary uncle of mine. I used to study his picture.

He was tall ("Your uncle Ed stands six feet four in his socks!") and very fair. ("He has the bluest eyes you ever saw, like two pieces of turquoise.")

The dream of my life was to know this uncle, who had gone out to teach in the Philippines in 1901, with the first call for teachers. His reason for going was like everything else about him, romantic. He had been disappointed in love. So he sailed away, putting weeks of lonely ocean between himself and the lady of his heart. But having lost him to the Orient, the lady reconsidered; she followed him a few months later, and they were married. Six months after the wedding, she lay dead of a fever. Uncle Ed never could bear to say her name afterward, nor did he marry again. All her wedding finery, her silks and embroideries, her fans and shawls, he sent back to Grandma.

Uncle Ed remained in the islands, teaching English at first and later acquiring a plantation. He sent back pictures of humpbacked cattle, of rice paddies flooded with workers knee-deep in the water transplanting, of turbaned savages called Moros.

I entered into a correspondence with him as soon as I could write and we exchanged many letters. I wanted him to send me a little Filipino to be my companion and do my chores, to dry the dishes and dust the furniture, and sweep the front walk. He wrote me solemnly offering me choices, sending pictures of small Tagalog maidens, but we never came to any firm arrangement. Their mother wouldn't let them go, or the long sea journey cost too much, or they still had to learn English. Eventually I gave up the idea and stopped saving money for the purchase of my slave, but our correspondence continued.

Then at last he wrote that he was coming stateside to visit.

He was, indeed, all that I had imagined.

He was very tall and elegant in his Chinese-tailored suits of white silk; his eyes were deeply blue in his tanned face. His voice was soft and shy. He came laden with gifts: Peking crystal beads, bolts of hand-embroidered voile in violet and pink, piña cloth, fans of ivory and sandalwood, bottles of *sampaguita* perfume, and of ylang-ylang, loveliest of scents.

As he attended dinner parties, played bridge, traveled about, bought books, talked and visited with bedazzled relatives, it became clear what dear Grandma had never understood, for she had always mourned his absence and wanted him back, and near. He was under a spell. He adored the islands and everything about them—the tropical verdure, the slender dark people, his coconut trees—in short, the life of a planter.

"Why should he come back?" Mama always said. "Here he

would be a simple high school teacher. There he is some kind of Lord-of-the-Manor, with servants and luxuries, a boat for the sea, and wide lands to ride around in."

But there was more than obvious ease and luxury in the life of a planter, as he lived it. He wrote to me more and more often, as I grew up. I learned that he joined The Book-of-the-Month Club, subscribed to important magazines and papers, and read omnivorously. He studied agronomy and plant strains. And he began doing, of his own free will, what many other planters would be forced to do in later years: he looked after his workers. He built them strong clean houses and taught them to use inside plumbing, which at first they had held in such profound respect that they had forbidden their children to sully the shining fixtures. He learned first aid and emergency surgery, for he frequently had to sew up slashed bodies and bind up broken heads. He lectured firmly, in Spanish, English and Tagalog against the use of alcohol, for in one form or another it led to fights and injuries. Occasionally he had to lend a hand at a difficult birth. He taught his people writing and reading and arithmetic, and he regularly sat as judge, in an improvised court, and dispensed justice.

I treasured his letters and the pictures they gave me of his strange exotic life. "Today I shot a crocodile that has been frightening the children in the river. Had to shoot three times to find a vital spot. I wish we could use the meat in some way, but I can't stomach the idea. We will cure the hide, though. I am now driving down piles in the river and will attach strong wire fencing, so as to make a safe place where the little ones can swim." And again, "The people here all sing rhythmic songs as they work. Rather slow rhythms. I wish I could get them interested in fast-stepping jazz! It would help get the crops in."

Another letter spoke of Mr. Micawber, his house snake. "He lies along the rafters, waiting for something to turn up. He is fat and black and shining, and I know he gets enough rats to make it worth his while. I do not pet him, but it is nice to hear him rustling and know he is there."

Uncle Ed began writing that things were changing in the Orient.

"The Japanese are a very proud people and they are growing powerful," he wrote in a letter I received when I was in college. "They will upset the whole balance before too long. They are clever and ingenious, and they will be a great danger. But whatever they may do, it will be as nothing to what the Chinese may be capable of, some distant day when they awaken from sleep, like Gulliver, and begin to throw off their bonds. And the funny thing is, I like the Chinese best. But they will be the most implacable enemies of the West. Right now, thank God, they are still my friends, the most subtle and intelligent, the most honorable people I know."

Once more Uncle Ed came stateside.

"I have seventy thousand cooonut trees," he told us, "and hemp grows between the rows of trees. We grow all our food, raise pigs, cattle and chickens. You can pick orchids off the trees on my land. There is a rose garden in front of my house. If you will come to visit me—say for six months—we will take the boat and cruise south, among the Celebes."

He was a perfectly happy, successful man, and he had received the ultimate accolade. His people on the plantation had an affectionate nickname for him. They called him "Matanda," which in Tagalog means "The Old Man."

How I dreamed of that cruise and longed to accept Uncle Ed's invitation! But it would have been very expensive to get to Manila, and I was the oldest of three children my father had to put through college. It was my cousin Carol who went to the Philippines and visited Uncle Ed and cruised among the romantic islands to the south.

I graduated from the university and in due course got a job and became self-supporting. But our correspondence continued.

My uncle's letters became more and more preoccupied with the changing patterns of feeling in the Orient. There was no airmail in those days, and one letter he wrote me arrived a week after Pearl Harbor had been bombed; that letter had been seven weeks on its way to me. It said in part, "I wonder if our government realizes that the Japanese are not taking orders any more. Certainly our Intelligence has not convinced Washington of what oriental honor, or face, can mean. To demand that the two

Japanese diplomats journey from Tokyo to Washington, there to be hauled on the carpet and scolded like naughty children, is to precipitate serious trouble. I am very much worried. Anything can happen . . ."

And of course it did happen. When Pearl Harbor was attacked, Davao was surprise-bombed the same day. Uncle Ed lay ill in a Davao hospital, recovering from an attack of jaundice, when he heard distant thunder, and later realized that Davao was under attack. He was taken prisoner.

We did not know this. All we knew, as silent week succeeded silent anxious week, was that we could get no word of him. We tried again and again. We wired. We wrote to everyone we knew who might have a way of finding out what had become of him. We contacted the Red Cross. All our efforts came to nothing, and after reading some of the horrors that took place in the islands, we gave him up for lost.

One day late in 1945 my cousin Carol happened to be in San Francisco and she idly scanned the names of prisoners being brought back from the Orient to their homeland. And she saw the name: Edward Esbern Christensen. Our uncle.

She met the ship. At last, down the gangplank tottered a frail tall ghost, in tatters, carrying a splendid new pair of size 14 British-made oxfords.

"Hello, Carol," was his soft greeting. "Anything new?" Carol drove him south at once, to my mother. On the way he weakly explained the shoes.

"We had a little radio at first," he whispered, "and we heard about the march from Bataan. I kept my shoes to march in. They never took them away from me; who would they fit, in Japan?"

Carol helped Uncle Ed, trembling and feeble on his swollen legs, up the five steps of our front porch and rang the bell. My mother came to the door and saw a stooped, white-bearded derelict, a person she did not know. She recognized Carol. Then Uncle Ed said, "Karen?" Mama sobbed. She knew his voice.

He had been a prisoner of war for three years, most of that time at the notorious Santo Tomas prison on the island of Luzon.

He had dwindled from his normal strong, fatless 230 pounds to less than 130. (He might have lasted another week, not more,

the American Army doctors had told him, when he was freed.)
He was wretchedly weak and swollen with beriberi, starved almost to death, his hearing gone, and he could hardly speak. He
was seventy years old and it was a miracle that we had got him
back.

Gone forever, it seemed, was the romantic hero, the successful
planter, the faraway glamourous member of the family. Here instead was a broken man, old and bent, his health gone, his property destroyed, the work of a lifetime blown away. Poor, sick and
defenseless, he had come home to die.

So we thought.

My mother, Uncle Ed's only sister—indeed, his only relative
besides the scattered cousins (for Uncle Joe had died young, in
the flu epidemic, in Mexico City)—began doing what women
have always done for their men. She bought him clothes, washed
and ironed for him, stuffed him with vitamins and medicine. But
mostly, she fed him.

In our house, it has always been the custom for my mother to
serve the family from the dishes set in front of her place. When
she took up her spoon to dish up, Uncle Ed held out his plate
with trembling intensity, a look of desperate fear on his face, as if
he were still afraid the food would be gone before he could get
his share. He ate like the starving man he was.

So a few weeks went by. One day mysterious thumpings were
heard proceeding from Uncle Ed's room. My father glanced in
and then hurried downstairs to report, in amusement, to my
mother: "That old wreck is trying to do some setting up exercises!"

Later, Uncle Ed began walking around the block, and then
dog-trotting, and finally running.

"When I can really run around the block, and not get badly
winded," he told Papa, "I am going to put in for repatriation. I
think I'll be able to make it in another two weeks."

"You want to go back to the islands?" asked my father in astonishment.

"I must."

The day came when Uncle Ed sat down and wrote a letter to

Washington. "The Navy needs hemp," he wrote, "and I know how to grow it. I want to go back to Davao."

In due course he received notice to stand by for a ship that would take him from Los Angeles to Manila.

My mother got his clothes in order and my father sat down and wrote him out a check for five hundred dollars. Uncle Ed's thanks were quiet and heartfelt.

Nevertheless, he had no intention of spending one cent more than he had to of that precious five hundred dollars. Once in Los Angeles, he got himself a job as an office boy(!) in an Army and Navy store. He carried coffee to managers, he posted letters and ran errands. He was nearly seventy-one, and deaf, but he concealed it somehow, and he was spry. His ship put into port and Uncle Ed sailed away with it, back to Manila. From there he went by island boat over the route he had covered so painfully as a prisoner, to Davao, once more. He made his way out to his plantation.

The seventy thousand coconut trees were destroyed, his buildings had been burnt to the ground, his lands were mined, his workers had fled to the hills. The plantation was a total ruin.

Uncle Ed built himself a little hut of nipa palm to shelter in, and he sent out word to the hill people that Matanda was back. Shyly, a few workers came down to see him. Then more and more.

Uncle Ed had provided himself with the United States Government instructions on how to de-mine land. Very carefully and patiently he and some of the men cleaned out the mines. He did not lose a man, though some other planters, more impatient, did.

He had a lot of his five hundred dollars left. He wrote to people who owed him money, reminded them that he was not dead, but in fact alive, and he needed his money. A few paid up. A few others remembered debts and sent in money. He got enough together to buy and set out his coconuts again. Quite a few trees had come up, as volunteers, and he let them stay, but he meticulously set out enough more to make up his seventy thousand.

"They were not in long straight rows, as before," he told me later, when he visited me in Mexico. "But I figured they would make just as good copra." Dreamily he added, "There was nothing so beautiful in the world as a long straight avenue of coconut trees in full bearing . . ."

But coconuts take seven years to come into full production. And the people were hungry. Their rice paddies had been bombed and mined. They were existing on some root vegetables. Uncle Ed had planned to plant hemp between the rows of coconuts after the war was over, but he changed his mind. He planted corn, for it could bring in a crop four or five times in a year, and he recalled that it could be eaten in the form of grits—something not too different from the rice the people were used to. It combines well with a few bananas, or a bit of salt fish.

He planted corn, set up shuckers and driers and grinders, and taught people to eat it. Other planters followed suit, and corn began growing everywhere in the islands.

"We managed," Uncle Ed told me. "With the corn grits as our base and bananas everywhere and deer and wild pigs and birds in the jungle, we could eat. I went hunting every day. We even found a few durians."

The durian, he told me, is a tropical fruit which has a persistent and horrid stench, but if you can manage to get up close enough to eat a piece, you are hooked. Criminals were caught, he told me, by simply posting guards around the durian trees. Loving the fruit as the people did, any felon in hiding would venture out, if he caught a whiff of durian.

Uncle Ed's experiment with corn and the way it solved the problem of an immediately needed basic food, did not go unnoticed. Before he came back stateside again, he was decorated by the Philippine Government for his work in helping rehabilitate the desperate and hungry country.

I had never thought to see him again, after his return to the islands. But after he had restored his plantation by sheer determination, he came stateside yet again. Once more he was tall and straight, and though his hair was perfectly white, his eyes were still a piercing blue behind his glasses. He wore beautifully tailored silk and initialed shirts. All was as before, except that he wore a hearing aid. He was no longer just an adventurer from faraway places. To us, he was a hero.

Secure in my home, where he visited, his seventy thousand

trees in bearing, his people well-fed, he told me he might vote himself a bit more salary next year. He had kept his pay down in the years he was building up the plantation again. And he was at last willing to talk a little about the terrible years in the war-prisoner camp.

"Before we were taken up to Santo Tomas, we were simply under guard in Davao," he said. "We were sent out to forage for ourselves, and I saw that all the others were providing themselves with food, with chickens, grain, anything they could find. So I foraged for something that could easily be carried and that could be traded for something else. I got soap. It kept me partially fed, for a time."

Uncle Ed's great height and his knowledge of oriental psychology helped him. The Japanese amused themselves by ordering him to do ridiculous tasks, which he undertook with gravity and courtesy. They towed him about for fun, as though he were a performing bear. It was only when the war began to go against them that his captors turned taciturn and put him to hard physical labor, instead of dancing or turning somersaults.

"We used to have to line up dozens of times a day and count off, in Japanese, by twenties. They were afraid of losing any of us."

"Count for me."

"I forgot every word the minute we were freed."

"How did you endure the boredom?"

"Well, we had a deck of cards and played bridge, until all the spots were worn away. And we were pretty busy digging graves, there toward the last. And we had your book."

"*My* book?"

"Yes, one of the captured women had a small girl with her, and she had snatched up a couple of books to read to the child in prison. One was your book, *About Bellamy*. We all read it several times. I can recite whole passages from it."

"I loathed it," he told me frankly, "but there was nothing else to read."

"Did you ever despair, Uncle Ed?"

"Those who lost hope were the first ones we buried," he told me.

"I was scared when we were liberated, though," he said, with his quick shy smile. "We were loaded into amphibious jeeps, but I didn't know they could walk on the water, so to speak, and as we headed full speed for the river I thought, My gosh, I have endured these years only to be drowned in a tank!"

He had always made sudden trips stateside, with side trips nobody knew where, and once he had visited me in my home in Mexico, but with strict instructions not to tell anyone that he had been there. I thought that was because he hadn't wanted other relatives to know, because I had always been his favorite niece. Wasn't I the one he sent a copy of *Jurgen*, with all the bad words scratched out? Wasn't I the one he always called Cherryblossom?

But now I think he may have had important duties for which his intelligence, his experience, and his admirable tenacity and secrecy made him invaluable.

The last time I saw him, he said, "There are Communists up in the hills of Mindanao, and once in a while they come down and murder a planter or two. They are called Huks. Don't grieve now, if that happens to me. I have done what I set out to do—twice! Of course, if they had murdered me thirty or even twenty years ago, I would have been seriously annoyed."

Up he went, winging into the blue sky, back to his beloved islands. I never saw him again.

And so ended all the romance, and the legendary, mysterious characters in my history.

Or did it?

What of my nephew Freddie, who roamed Africa, and intends to go back? What of my brother's son John, who won a military decoration in Viet Nam because he disobeyed orders and refused to parade his men at noon into a clearing, thus saving their lives? What of the other nieces and nephews whose lives are now unfolding in a tumultuous world? Perhaps the romance, the adventure, the mystery are there, like seeds in an apple—but I will not live to see it, or hear about it.

14

The movement to liberate women gains momentum every hour, and I watch it with awe and admiration. I also think about the women I have known who had the courage and the wit and ability to liberate themselves, and did. Some of them in the strangest ways: my paternal grandmother, for instance.

When I was in college I visited her on alternate weekends; the other weekends were spent with my maternal grandmother, who was far from any sort of liberation, and only wanted to love and serve.

But Grandma Borton, in her old age, was a free soul if ever there was one. She knew all about proper diet, and approved of it—for other people. For herself, she preferred her regular breakfast of a large wedge of pineapple cake, and a cup of coffee, half cream. For lunch, when she felt like having lunch, she usually made herself cream biscuits, which she lathered with rich butter and jam, and drank more coffee. Once in a while she would walk swiftly uptown and eat frozen strawberries with clotted cream. For the record, and to everyone's confusion, let it be known that she lived to be ninety-three, was slim and quick and tireless, and used to take her glasses off to read the paper. She only wore them for style.

There was a woman who lived on our block who was widowed young and had strong ambitions for her children. It seemed that she would have to find some way to make money in order to finance their educations. So she took courses at night school in stenography, and she 'studied books on management, and she read psychology. She did all this out of sheer determination, because her own education had not gone far; she had married at fourteen and had borne four children. Somewhat defiantly she visited Mama with, instead of her gray hair, a head of bright hennaed waves. In those days (the early twenties) it was pretty bad form to dye one's hair—or at least to admit it.

"I didn't want to," she told my mother. "But it's hard enough being a woman. What you *can't* be is an *old* woman, if you want a decent job."

This pronouncement struck me, even then, as sad and somehow degrading. But in her case it was sheer courage.

She got good jobs and held them, and eventually became a county officer.

And there was an incident involving machismo, at its worst, in our quiet small town. A pretty and popular young woman had broken with an admirer and had gone to a dance with another suitor. The first one, in jealous frenzy, had followed her to the dance and there shot her and then himself. He died at once, but her fate was not so easy. He had severed her backbone, and she lived out her life, into middle age, in a wheelchair, helpless and a burden. I learned that she did all sorts of handwork and would take orders for crocheting, embroidering and hemstitching. I was only a child in grammar school but I felt the waste, the tragedy of this. And all because a man had believed that he had certain rights over her. I brooded over this, and once voiced the heretical opinion that nobody should have any rights over anybody else.

"Well, theoretically, that is so," Papa told me gravely, "but as we all have people and other living creatures which depend on us for life and protection, it must be considered that they have rights. Only, some people don't understand the basis of this . . ."

My mother, despite her complete loyalty to her marriage, had a firm idea of women's rights, and was never overpowered by male arrogance.

We had several walnut trees in our front yard, and sometimes after a rain or a big wind it was a chore to pick up all the nuts. An Englishman, a neighbor who had fallen on evil days, came over after a storm and offered to shake the trees and gather all the nuts, if Mama would give him half. She was glad to agree to this arrangement until he said, playfully, "We have a good saying in England. 'A woman, a dog and a walnut tree, the more you beat 'em, the better they be!'"

Right there he lost his job. Mama bridled, pronounced, "We don't beat dogs, nor even women, in this house! And we will pick up our nuts ourselves!"

When she grew old and it was known that she lived alone, occasionally people tried to take advantage of her. They didn't get far. One gentleman, after a wind and rain storm, drove up early in his car, parked it, and got out with a paper bag. He started to pick up the fallen nuts from Mama's front lawn. She spied him from a window and waited until he had the bag almost full. Then she went out, firmly removed the bag from his startled hand, said, "Thank you for gathering my nuts!" and swept into the house. He returned no more.

But there were others who came and tried to do the same. One even defied Mama. "This is public property, isn't it?" he said, pointing to the small strip of lawn between the sidewalk and the street where there were many nuts.

"Not as long as I pay the taxes on it," snapped Mama. And that settled him.

It will be noted that these transgressors were men, and quite ready to take advantage of an old lady who, they thought, couldn't defend herself.

From then on, whenever there was a storm, Mama was out at the crack of dawn, gathering her nuts, and she would laugh gleefully when the freeloaders drove up with their sacks, got out to look at our lawn, and found it bare.

When she was widowed, more than one clever gentleman called on Mama, hoping to sell her the Brooklyn Bridge, or proposing some other absurdity, but Mama always asked for his credentials and his last bank statement, and none returned.

Besides, Papa knew her intelligence and her sharpness, and was confident nobody would ever swindle his widow.

When he was ill, in the last years before his death, he told me: "I am leaving everything to your mother. She will know how to defend it. Don't be afraid that she might marry again and squander our savings on a second husband. She might enjoy being courted, and she probably will be courted, but she can see through flattery faster than anybody, and she wouldn't give anybody, other than her children, a plugged nickel, no matter how much sweet talk is poured in her ears."

On the matter of widows being swindled, Papa often spoke to us.

"Banks are out to make money," he explained, "but they will pay a fair rate of interest on savings. Anyone who offers more than the going bank rate is offering risk. And if you don't know property values, business methods, and sound investments, you had best leave your money in government bonds and a savings account. Greed is what ruins the widow—greed and flattery. Lonely women respond to the wiles of a handsome young caller, and he awakens greed with his promises of thirteen, fifteen and twenty per cent return on their money."

Papa knew. He had had more than one weeping widow in his office, thoroughly fleeced of what had been left her, and some with angry breach-of-promise suits in their minds.

Papa had some appreciation of women's rights, too, always salted with his sound common sense.

When I married, my young husband asked Papa how much insurance he ought to take out.

"Your wife has a profession," Papa answered. "Let her remain active in it, and then if anything happens to you, she will be safe, and better off than any lump sum of money you could afford to pay for in insurance."

But of course there were, in my time, many instances of women who were exploited, swindled, and generally made fools of by men who were in a position to do it. Most husbands tried to protect them against this.

One man, a friend of my father's, called him urgently one day. He was a young, virile and handsome man, and he said, "Fred, I have to make a will today."

He had had an accident, and blood poisoning had set in. When my father arrived at his house, the telltale red marks were progressing steadily up his arm. Antibiotics had not yet been discovered.

"I'll be dead by tomorrow or next day," he said, "and I must have a water-tight will and trust made out for my wife and my children. Especially for my wife. I'll die contented if I know no crook can ever move in and diddle her out of her inheritance."

All these remembrances, and more, make me wonder if women's rights are basically any more than *general* rights which should protect all citizens. In every case, women were the victims, yes—but the exploitation and evil done against them were rooted in criminal acts, or in the kind of greed and selfishness that all religions have tried to eradicate since time began.

As Papa always said, "Laws can protect, after the fact, and occasionally, before the fact. But they can't extract evil from men's hearts. That's why there have to be laws, as a kind of barrier against rioting evil. While men are wicked, the law will always have to run behind, trying to keep up."

Maybe women can achieve more justice by getting fair treatment on the law books. I hope so. But maybe we had better pray hard all the same, for the Serpent has never been crushed, and will always think of new ways to ruin the weak and the unwary.

Part II

Memories of an Enchanted Youth

Juventud, divine tesoro . . .
Rubén Darío

1.

Reading has always been the chief joy, a never-ending topic of conversation, and often a lifesaver, in my family.

When *Kristin Lavransdatter* was published, my sister got it first. She went around in a daze, occasionally was made to sit and eat, and to go to bed, and was to be found in a corner, out on the lawn, or lying on a couch reading it, until she finished. It is a long book and it took her about ten days. Then I got hold of it. I was *hors de combat* for the next ten days, and somebody else had to set the table, dry dishes, and run errands until I had turned the last page with a great heaving sigh.

Then Mama took the book from my limp hand.

"All right, girls. Take over. Now it is *my* turn." And she didn't stir to do a thing, while Barbara and I cooked, made beds, and took care of the house. She read, in an orgy of imaginative delight, until she had finished it.

And while Papa read to us all every winter evening for an hour or so, when he finished and turned back to his own book, woe betide any lout who interrupted him, or made distracting noises.

We were that kind of a family.

So it is not strange that one of us should try to write, as well. I had produced a poem when I was quite small, and later, while I was staying in Monterey with my grandmother, the blue sea, sparkling with white caps, the cypresses, and the pine-clad hills inspired me again. I labored mightily and brought forth a small mouse of a poem, which, due to Papa's instructions, well-remembered, had rhyme and rhythm. I was deeply pleased with my poem, and I intended it to burst upon a waiting world like a new star. I therefore made a clean copy, in secret, and when sent on an errand into town, I found the office of the *Peninsula Herald* and demanded to see the Editor. I suppose he must have had a slack afternoon, for he received me.

I handed him my poem. So determined was I on publication that I told him he might have it for nothing. I hadn't said a word about this to Grandma, and I still kept my secret. There followed six days of agony, while I waited for my poem to appear in print.

At last! It did, boxed in a fine position, and underneath there was a short explanation. "This poem was written by little Beth Borton, aged eight." I saw nothing odd in that, no hint of apology on the Editor's part. I was eight, and I was little Beth Borton. I sat back and allowed myself to be admired.

Thus vaccinated with printer's ink, I never got over it, and I continued producing works of poetry and prose with regularity.

All through high school I worked at short stories, and as those years coincided with the early years of the movie industry, I also devised and wrote dozens of movie scenarios, which I sent off hopefully to the studios.

(Years later I met a college chum who had a job in the scenario department of one of the big studios. Her task was to winnow out useful ideas from the hundreds of unsolicited scenarios sent in, file them by subject matter, and regretfully return the rejected scenarios. This doesn't prove that anything I wrote might have been taken, but perhaps it may scare some industrious writer away from his typewriter for a few days.)

While I was in high school I wrote another poem, which was accepted and published by the *Literary Digest* and was later set to music by a composer whose name I have forgotten. So again, there arose in me that hope which is a basic ingredient in the making of a professional writer.

It is not merely the wish to see one's creation in print, nor merely the wish to know that it is acceptable. I think, in essence, it is a hungry wish for communication. The person who writes is bedeviled by a constant yearning to reach out and touch many minds, to make contact, to expand his whole sphere of being.

I was fortunate in that I was not ridiculed or shamed out of making my efforts to write. My parents were kindly critical, never mere admirers. And in high school I had the help of a teacher who had published and worked as a journalist. A South African, by the name of Mark Willcox, he encouraged by working with me, and with other students, on an adult level. He taught us the value of form, gave us a feeling for accurate expression and inspired a love of the English language, in its infinite flexibility and expressiveness. He also insisted upon clarity. I am sure that countless teachers all over the United States work in this way with pupils who are ardent enough and industrious enough. I, for one, am forever grateful to their kind.

In my last year in high school, as Editor of our Year Book, it fell to me to deal with printers. This was salutary too, for I learned something about the mechanics of turning manuscript into print. On Cloud Nine, consulting one's inner consciousness and writing out great thoughts, it is easy to forget that on Cloud Eight somebody has to set type, cut paper, ink presses and figure costs. I was a dreamy and imaginative girl, so it was natural, I think, that I planned various careers for myself. Nowadays, young women dream of being models or movie stars or tour directors or pilots or publicity directors. But I concentrated on the arts. I thought of being a splendid violinist, or a ballet dancer, or a caricaturist. I tried all these things. But all the while I knew I was going to write. And my parents knew it.

Therefore, when I went away to college at Stanford University I looked for courses in literature and in writing.

Professor Everett Smith, of the old New York *Sun*, gave a course in journalism which I attended with growing interest.

At the first session of the class he walked in, looked keenly at us all and said, "Anyone who uses the word 'interesting' in a news story will be flunked."

He taught us the basic principles—Who, When, Where, What and Why; the importance of a succinct lead; how to write headlines; how to edit copy. He was invaluable, and a healthy corrective against the pretentious and the pompous. He mowed us down at every session.

But another professor was also one of the great deflators. His name was Grey, and he offered a course in playwriting. I attended this class with high hopes. In the first place it was a roundtable affair and Professor Grey seemed mild and gentle. He explained that there would be no grades, merely a plus or a minus for the course—and this would be decided by the quality, not the quantity, of our work.

"There is no way to teach anybody how to write a play," he explained. "I can give you a few facts about form, what must be accomplished before each curtain, how to manage exits and entrances, and so on, but in the end I must turn you loose to work. That is what you will do. You will write plays. Here in class around the table, we will read each other's plays, and comment on them. We will be our own sounding board. If you write a tragedy and we all laugh, you will have learned something. If you write a comedy and everyone is bored and your dialog is greeted with silence, you will have perceived that something was wrong. That is the only way we can make progress. It is a 'learning by doing' course.

"If you write fifty five-act hilarious tragedies, you will be given a minus for the course. If during the year you write one acceptable scene, which has the anticipated effect upon the audience, I will pass you. Is this clear?"

It seemed clear and it seemed fair. Then.

In the first week and before our next roundtable session, I wrote a one-act play that involved tragedy, a ghost, and some delicate poetic atmosphere. The demonic Professor Grey read my play aloud to the group, and I learned to my horror that he was a gifted mimic and that he could turn any tragic or poetic or passionate line into ridiculous posturing. He read my melancholy play, the audience roared with laughter, and I plodded back to Roble Hall in tears.

However, knowing that one flop was already chalked up against me, it behooved me to try again, and I did. It evoked the same painful result. This went on all year, and though I never intended it, I got the reputation of being an indefatigable writer of rotten one-acters.

There was a certain Mr. Magruder from somewhere in the South, with an accent like slow honey, who wrote a very good play about a black family. Even the horrible Professor Grey couldn't spoil it. We were all moved by it. I was also moved to intense envy.

But Mr. Magruder did not exert himself further. One day Professor Grey asked him why he did not submit another play, and he said candidly that he had no ideas.

"What? No ideas?" cried Professor Grey. "But there's Miss Borton, sitting right beside you! She is *full* of ideas! Have one!" and he pointed to the fecund writer of flops, who had submitted her ninth play.

However, Mr. Magruder did not write again, and I continued disconsolately trying, enduring humiliation whenever one of my efforts was read, with horrid glee, by Professor Grey.

At the end of the course, Professor Grey said, "Will Miss Borton and Mr. Magruder please see me in my office today at four o'clock."

I knew what was going to happen. Mr. Magruder would get the class plus, and I, who richly deserved it, would get the minus.

We were admitted to Professor Grey's office and he said at once, "You two are getting plus for the course. I am flunking the others. They were never really interested anyway.

"Mr. Magruder, you wrote a good play. You have talent and I am obliged to pass you. But I shouldn't, because you are lazy. Writers can't be lazy.

"Miss Borton, you have produced an inordinate amount of terrible stuff, but you are probably the only possible writer in the class. Because you never stopped trying. And that is Rule Number One. Good afternoon."

The dubious honor of that plus had to last me through the rest of my college years. But Professor Grey's Rule Number One has never left me.

2

However, after college, I had no idea how to develop my life into a radiant and glorious one. I had been intensely and miserably homesick in my years away from Mama and Papa, to the point of being actually ill, and I rushed back to the warmth and safety of home every chance I got. Once graduated, I practiced my fiddle, accepted pupils, and tried some writing, but mostly I basked. Wisely, my parents let me alone for a time, and it gradually began to be assumed that I was saving my money to go away for further studies.

I enjoyed my work teaching, and the lovely sameness of my days was marred only by the annual catastrophe of the Recital. The pupils and their parents, and I, the teacher, all lost our heads. Some pupils, with family, arrived at nine in the morning, and sat, frozen with fear and importance until the recital began, at three, refusing sustenance, and gradually becoming glassy-eyed. One child's mother had washed his bow the night before, and had omitted to put any resin on it afterward, so when he started valiantly to saw out his musical offering, nothing whatever happened. Another child, victim of nerves, wept silently throughout her playing of a short piece, and howled the minute the final chord was played on the piano. And one wet her pants and our rug.

When it was all over and chocolate and cookies had been consumed, the last fiddle packed into its little case and all the relatives and friends departed, my mother said firmly, "That's the last one of those!" And I concurred. I also faced the fact that I was going to have to make up my mind what I was going to do, and stop hanging around home where I was happy. In the end, I had, almost literally, to be ejected from the nest.

I finally came to the conclusion that, as I had a start on the violin, I ought to learn more. I suggested to Mama and Papa that I go to Mexico City to study at the Conservatory there, and improve my violin playing and my Spanish at the same time. But some violence broke out in Mexico—not enough to be called a revolution—and Papa put his foot down. We settled for Boston.

Papa and Mama took me and my two violins and my trunk to San Francisco and put me aboard the train to Chicago. I cried all day, but the next day, crossing over the Great Salt Lake, after Ogden, I began to realize that I would have to make an effort to grow up. I began to enjoy the scenery. And I thoroughly enjoyed the train.

I had an upper berth, climbing up every night on a small carpeted ladder, and there, behind my curtain, undressing in various contorted positions I could never undertake now. With my clothes hanging in a small hammock at my side, we hurtled through space. In the morning I climbed down, partially dressed, and joined the parade of frowsy ladies making their way toward the dressing room, where there were three washbowls and a long mirror. In the crowded dressing room, true characters asserted themselves, and one quickly learned to separate the slobs from the tidy, the hogs from the unselfish, and the wheedlers from the self-reliant.

Meals were simply wonderful, and one soon began to wait in salivating eagerness for the sound of the chimes, played by one of the waiters, as he surged through the Pullman cars announcing service. The dining car was all stiff white linen, shining crystal and polished silver, and there was always a fresh rose in each vase on the tables. The food was delicious and the service was deft. The black waiters made us feel like kings and queens, no mean feat. It took grace, gentle manners, some psychology and an enormous willingness to please. It was art, and I never felt anything but admiration and affection for those who served us.

Once in Chicago, the wicked city, where Al Capone reigned, I took a taxi across to another station, expecting at any moment to be assaulted by the Mafia and deprived of my three hundred dollars. There I took another train, called, I think, "The Wolverine," and in another day and a half (making five and a half days and nights, in all), I arrived in Boston, an unexpectedly bleak-looking city, with "cold north" somehow stamped upon its face, as I first looked upon it. I was met by the kind proprietor of the boardinghouse where I was to stay, in Jamaica Plain, and conveyed to it by means of a long trolley ride. At 22 Burroughs

Street I was welcomed by Mrs. Billings, large, beautiful, and motherly. The Billings family occupied two floors of the large duplex. The third floor was rented to three females, one of whom was I. Just across the hall from me (and later a fellow conspirator for hot water for our tub) was another homesick girl, Caroline Allen, just out of Vassar and beginning her first job with the Arnold Arboretum. Caroline, from upper New York State, was ash-blond, willowy and marred in the perfection of her character only by a tendency to make puns. She used to apologize for these, but she was hooked, she couldn't help it, and her friends gradually became hardened to them, as she became hardened to my eternal Kreutzer. We became fast friends. She developed into Dr. Allen, a world authority on laurels, but then she was taking her first steps in her profession, while I was stumbling around trying to find the right slot to fall into, like a ball at roulette.

I spent a year learning solfeggio, harmony, and music history, and all the students at the Boston Conservatory, where I studied, became expert at an assortment of accents: Italian from Mr. Jacchai and Maestro Vito; German from composer Otto Straub, who used to say "Witsa Wertsa" instead of etcetera; Mayfair English from Mr. Somervell, who taught solfeggio; Bostonese from a couple of native-born students; and a rich Mississippi drawl from a girl born in Jackson.

In the Conservatory I made two undying friendships; one was with a little girl from Prince Edward Island, Canada. Rena was shy and dreamy, brown-haired and brown-eyed, and it took her some time to get up enough confidence to speak to me, but we found we had every reason to become close. She was a pianist, and I a violinist; we had our pictures taken together and planned great conquering concert tours.

The other friend was Rose, who had a rich, full voice, and who could have made a great name in opera. But her ambitions were rather toward supporting people she loved, or helping them; she lacked the ruthless urge to go her own way, which makes the artist: She had a delicious sense of humor and no airs; down-to-earth and enormously kind, she often helped pull my feet down to the ground.

We all counted our pennies, shopped in Filene's basement,

and stood in line for "rush seats" to the Friday afternoon symphony. Also, we went to dozens of concerts in Jordan Hall, where many recitalists had to resort to papering the house in order to get an audience.

Our lives were very simple, girlish, and virtuous. I have no doubt that young women today would think us quite old-fashioned.

I awaited my first lesson with the violin teacher to whom I had been assigned. As a child I had studied with a man who played regularly in a theater orchestra, and at college I had studied with Samuel Savannah, in San Francisco, who started me out on open strings again, as I had fallen into bad habits and had nothing even remotely resembling the elegant French style of bowing he used. Later, while teaching in Bakersfield, I had gone every two weeks to Los Angeles to work with a brilliant German violinist named Zoellner, who had put me right back on the open strings, and who advocated a rather stiff, strong, direct German style of bowing. I wondered what Professor Korgueff would do to me.

I might have known.

I waited for him in the audition room at the Conservatory. On the hour, the doorway was completely filled by a six-foot-four Russian, whose high astrakhan cap reached right up to the ceiling. He was wearing a great fur-lined coat which widened him, and he resembled, physically, an enormous bear.

But under the fur cap was a very handsome face, aristocratic and pale. He had ice-green eyes under black brows, and hair going silvery at the temples. Shedding his coat, he revealed a slim and elegant figure, in well-tailored silvery-gray wool, and he was wearing gray spats. He sat down, lighted a long cigar, looked at me thoughtfully, and ordered, in a bass voice: "Begin!"

"Begin what?" I quavered.

He waved the cigar. "Play. Something. Anything."

I unpacked my fiddle, put it under my chin and began to play a Romance by Svendsen. He listened, quietly smoking, and did not interrupt me once. When I stopped, he said,

"All wrong."

I stood silent.

"Give me," he ordered, reaching for my violin. I handed it over, and the first thing he did was detach my shoulder rest and toss it into the wastebasket.

"What shall I use?" I asked.

"Shoulder," he answered. He showed me.

Once more I went back to the open strings. I had to learn a new way to hold my bow, to hold my fiddle, to finger. I was dismayed, but I tried. In time, Korgueff became less forbidding. He called me Lizotchka, and sometimes he bought me tea after our lessons.

During the course of the year he published a remarkable method, which he had invented, for studying double-stops. I purchased a copy of it, though I was a long way from being able to play all the exercises. I asked him to write a dedication on my copy, and he sat down, pen in hand, with a furrowed brow. Being a man of intense integrity, he could not tell a lie, but he was unwilling to hurt my feelings. He finally produced this:

"To Miss Lisa Borton, my first pupil in America, with admiration of person which I hope in time may become admiration of playing. Sergei Korgueff."

Of course I was in love with him. We were all in love with somebody. Dorothy was in love with Nicolas, Rose with her Eugene, Rena had a secret love she told me about sometimes, and I was in love with Korgueff.

He had all the ingredients for a hero of Gothic romance. He was handsome, exotic, distinguished, and unhappy. He knew he was dying (he died after one year in Boston), and it pained him that he must lay his bones in a foreign land. Russians and Mexicans, I think, more than any other nationals, most bitterly feel exiled when away from their own country.

I never told a soul about my love. Not even Rena. But I lived for those lessons, for his occasional smile, for the infrequent word "dushenka," which I thought meant darling. And I cried a lot.

Years later I published a short story, called "First Snow," which was a tribute to him, and a remembrance.

At the end of the year I had made some progress, and even appeared in a Conservatory recital (playing an uninspiring concerto by Sitt), but I was far from anything but a struggling student, and I knew it. So, after a deliriously joyful vacation at home with the family (five days and nights to California, a month there and five days and nights back), I decided to eke out the money my father had given me for my second year, by part-time work, like Rena.

There was, in Jamaica Plain, a little weekly newspaper, one of three neighborhood sheets published in the suburbs, and I went down to the office and applied for a job on the strength of having taken journalism classes in college. To my astonishment, I was accepted at once, for half-time reporting, at ten dollars a week. I was jubilant.

I checked sources of news, found them slim, but learned that organizations sent in little squibs about their activities, and society ladies provided detailed reports of all their social affairs, including menus and descriptions of the fashions worn at their soirées. I at once started to build up a list of sources and found, to my dismay, that undertakers seemed to be the most reliable. "Always somebody passing away," one of them told me, and they usually had full biographical details of the departed. Also, it appeared, the local public was fond of reading about funerals.

I got Caroline to ferret out items of interest from the Arboretum for me, and I visited all the ministers of the churches in our section of Boston. Then I learned, to my delight, that two distinguished and glamourous figures in Boston public life were resident in Jamaica Plain, and I at once tracked them down and demanded interviews. One was Mayor James Curley, a handsome, silver-tongued Irish politician, beloved or loathed—no in-betweens. He never would give my any time, but once I learned that he had had a fistfight on his front lawn with some unreconstructed voter, and I got the story secondhand. And then there was some unpleasantness, and he was defeated or sent to jail, I forget which, at the time. Both disasters overtook him during his career. I remember that on his first public appearance in Boston, after having been released from prison, he opened up that glorious voice and began, "Well, my friends, as I was saying before I was so rudely interrupted . . ."

I longed to interview him personally, for I admired him—his looks, his pluck, and his wily brains.

The other distinguished resident was the brilliant conductor of the Boston Symphony Orchestra, a shy, unapproachable, distant figure whom I had admired from afar with all the other young students who "rushed" to his concerts. His name was Sergei Koussevitsky, but in Boston he used the French form of his name —Serge—which was pronounced by everyone I know just like the woolen material. Serge.

I had begun to learn something of the great repertoire of symphonic classics. Brahms bewildered me at first, but Tchaikovsky spoke directly to my young romantic heart. Only the week before I had heard, for the first time, the great emotional César Franck symphony; I was exalted by it and went around humming the themes and trying to recall the heavenly harmonies.

I found the residence of the great conductor and knocked on the door, though dozens of kindly well-wishers had assured me I was wasting my time; the great conductor *never* gave interviews.

The door was opened by a slim, dark-eyed young man who learned the reason for my call. He started to explain that the Maestro was permanently unavailable for interviews and was probably going to continue by saying that even if he did, he would not be interviewed by a starry-eyed music student working part time for a weekly paper. But I didn't give him time. I looked past him into the hall and saw a tall, regal, blond lady.

"Oh, there is Madame Koussevitsky!" I cried. "I have seen her in the Friday concerts! She looks like my mother!"

The young man at the door was Nicolas Slonimsky, Koussevitsky's secretary, a person I was to see much of and learn much from in years to come. Madame Koussevitsky (I learned later from Nicolas) was very reserved, very austere, a devoted protectress of her husband's time and energy. Yet she looked beyond Nicolas, saw me, and made a sign to him. She said in Russian, "The little girl says I look like her mother. What does she want?"

"She wants to interview the Maestro."

Madame hesitated only a little. Her face softened. "She looks Russian to me. Arrange it. Tea, on Tuesday."

Perhaps I should explain that many Russian refugees in Boston told me that I looked like their people, and I was sometimes spoken to in Russian. No doubt it was because, never having been stylish in my person, I was content to be natural. I always wore my hair in two blond braids around my head, and I often wore Russian blouses, which I liked. Dear Rena, who could sew, made them for me, and often embroidered them, too.

I stood entranced. I knew they were speaking Russian and I loved the sound of it, and wished that I knew what they were saying.

Tuesday came and I had twenty minutes with the Maestro. He was tall, distinguished, and with the kind of Russian face that can look satirical and kindly at the same time. I at once plunged into an appreciation of his art, and I even hummed the themes of the César Franck, which I loved so much. It was incredibly naive, but it seemed to amuse and please the Maestro and he settled down comfortably and told me about his cruises up and down the Volga, conducting orchestras on the boat, and about his practice hours when he studied the double bass, which he made to sound like a deep-voiced and specially beautiful cello.

Several wonderful developments in my life followed this interview.

Most important was a growing friendship with Nicolas Slonimsky, surely one of the world's most fascinating men, and with his beautiful fiancée, Dorothy Adlow, who became my beloved friend, confidante, adviser and protector in a mutual devotion which lasted until her death.

I began to see Nicolas almost daily on the streetcar which bore us from Jamaica Plain to Huntington Avenue, where I attended courses at the Conservatory while he went to Symphony Hall across the street. In those days he usually wore a black suit and overcoat, and a black felt hat, wide-brimmed; he looked very foreign. He amused himself by doing something so exotic that I never quite got over my fearful respect for him. Something of a mathematical genius and also possessing that curious gift which is called perfect pitch, he used to listen for the note sounded by the wheels of the streetcar against the rails. Having identified it, he calculated the speed which produced the sound, also the increasing speed which produced a rising note, or screech; on the basis of this he would turn to me, seated beside him on the straw-covered seat and say, "We will arrive at Symphony Hall at exactly eight thirty-seven," and he was always right.

Besides, he solved problems in higher calculus, to pass the time, whenever he traveled, or had to wait for somebody.

He had other remarkable accomplishments. With a full orchestral score before him, he could instantly reduce it to a piano transcription, reading and translating from every clef and combining the whole. I doubt if there are more than half a dozen people in the world who can do it. He could speak (with characteristic hesitation and a slight stutter) eight languages, and he was an inveterate inventor of complicated jokes.

Quite rightly, I felt as if I had somehow made the acquaintance of a creature from another world.

After Nicolas and Dorothy were married, I was often a thrilled and marveling guest at their home. On one occasion, two other musicians with perfect pitch were at the Slonimskys' for supper: the Italian composer Alfredo Casella, and the Russian composer Vladimir Dukelsky, who wrote popular stuff under the name of Vernon Duke. They set up a contest. All three had to sit in the dark, in the bedroom or hall, with paper and pencil, and write down the chords being played by the amateur helper (me) in the living room. There was no winner. They were all letter-perfect.

Afterward, to Dorothy's annoyance, Nicolas performed the feat of playing the piano from underneath, with hands reversed. Sometimes, in a harsh unmusical voice, Nicolas sang the songs he had composed as settings for *Saturday Evening Post* ads. I remember especially "Babies Cry for It," which Fletcher's Castoria used to blazon on the pages. Nicolas' setting was a triumph of irony and lamentation.

I learned from Dorothy and other friends that Nicolas, who was a superb pianist, had been brought over to the United States by the Eastman School of Music, where, with two other brilliant young men just beginning their careers, they formed the Society of Unrecognized Geniuses. The other two were Paul Horgan, the historian and novelist, and Reuben Mamoulian, the stage director and designer. Gradually the society broke up, as each genius won recognition.

With Dorothy and Nicolas I met other fascinating people, and from all of them I learned. First, from Dorothy, who had been an art major at Radcliffe, and was writing art criticism for the *Christian Science Monitor* and conducting little "Art Tours" in the Boston Museum. She progressed steadily in her career, and was often asked to be a judge at international and national art shows. From Dorothy I learned something about modern art, how to appreciate it, and how to distinguish the pretentious fakes from the genuine artists. Through her I met Mr. Coniff, who opened a studio for making stained-glass windows (an art that had been in decline), and several painters and critics.

Most interesting to me was Isaac Goldberg, for he was a critic and essayist of wide scholarship, a writer, and an authority on Yiddish literature and the Yiddish theater. Both of the latter were entirely new fields of expression to me, and through him I became a respectful student of Hassidic thought and art. At the Goldberg home, where I was fortunate enough to be invited with Dorothy and Nicolas to regular "after Symphony" suppers, I met dozens of the most outstanding musicians, writers and artists of the day, for everyone seemed to know and love the Goldbergs. George Gershwin went there and improvised excitingly on their piano; there I met the fabulous Dr. Abraham Myerson, a towering authority in the field of psychiatry, but who loved to recall his salad days when he had been a streetcar conductor in Boston. Eugene Goossens visited, and Roy Harris, and of course Casella and the dashing Dukelsky. (Dorothy warned me not to become too much interested in his talents and his dark, handsome looks, because he liked only ladies who were well over two hundred pounds, and at that time I couldn't make the weight.) There were musicians from the Symphony: Abdon Laus, the bassoon player, and Richard Burgin, the brilliant concertmaster, and Arthur Fiedler, the viola player, who also conducted the "Pops" in the summertime when the classics gave way to Lehar and Sousa marches, and one could sit at a table and drink lemonade while the concert went on. Dorothy told me, somewhat awed herself, the stories of some of the handsome Fiedler's amours. Then there was Zoltan Haraszti, a Hungarian who wrote impeccable English, and who was curator of rare books at the Boston Public Library. Zoltan looked like a great predatory eagle, but he was the tenderest of men. There were many others who were invited to those Symphony night suppers; many became cherished friends.

Despite my college education, which concentrated on history, attempts at writing and Spanish, I was gauche and provincial. I wonder now why that sophisticated and artistic circle took me in. For take me in they did. Dorothy, so warmly maternal, protected me from myself and covered up my gaffes. I think now that my amazing innocence was what captured their interest. As they say nowadays, "I knew from nothing." As an example, I supposed then that one sexual encounter resulted in instant pregnancy. A friend at college who had announced that she would not marry but intended to sin, worried me a lot.

I was often invited to another intellectual-artistic salon, as well. This was the home of the composition and harmony teacher at the Conservatory, a handsome, romantic, and charming German named Otto Straub, who had been the favorite pupil of Pfitzner, in Germany, a composer whose works are just now beginning to find an appreciative audience in the United States.

Otto was married to a warm and lovely lady, Hilde Lorens, who was hospitable and kind. At their house I ate German roast goose with applesauce on Christmas, and there I met Harlow Shapley, the astronomer from Harvard University, a gentle, unassuming man who loved chamber music, and Miss Cecilia Payne, his assistant, now a world-famous astronomer herself. She had a sly sense of humor, and she used to delight in throwing nosey people off the scent when they approached her and asked her what she did. "I work at night," was usually the laconic answer, and they would slink away to search for more glamourous personalities, thinking she might be a night telephone operator or even a waitress at some all-night restaurant.

At the Straubs' there were wonderful evenings or afternoons of rare chamber music, for Otto was friends with many of the players in the Boston Symphony, and among them they got up quartets and quintets and sextets and octets. Mr. Van der Meer, the superb Dutch horn player, used to play the Brahms horn quartet here, and I heard other groups of woodwinds and brass that were lovely beyond the imaginings of someone who had, hitherto, associated brass instruments only with bands.

Otto Straub was a casualty of the First World War, for he had undergone severe privations in his youth during the war years, and he died, far too young, from their ultimate effects.

3.

Meanwhile, back at the *Jamaica Plain Journal,* curious developments occurred. After a few weeks as reporter, when I collected my princely ten dollars regularly, to my surprise and delight, I was made Editor. But I soon found out that editors have problems reporters never dreamed of.

First, several determined gentlemen arrived at the office, flashed a paper and credentials at me, took out screwdrivers and other implements from their satchels, and proceeded to remove the telephone. I was terrified. Who can run a newspaper without a telephone? The men said this action was for nonpayment of the bill. I drew out my checkbook, paid the bill in full, the screwdrivers came out again, and once more I had a telephone. But I had lowered my wad by thirty dollars, and that was a crisis for me. Still, I reflected, I was now Editor, and I would get a substantial raise. So I reasoned.

Shortly thereafter, two other men arrived, also armed with papers and looking very stern; they said they had come for the typewriter. Again, I paid the bill. After all, the play must go on, and the paper must come out. But I was eating into my salary for weeks to come.

Then a truck drove up, and two gentlemen strode in with the news that they had come to carry away the presses.

I fled in tears to the basement, where the head printer and pressman, Elwyn Long, was in charge. I told him about the telephone and the typewriter, but I knew I would not be able to buy back those presses. We were finished.

Breathing fire, "You let me talk to them!" he shouted, and I remained behind, crouching behind a press while angry words were exchanged. He got rid of the collectors somehow (he had had practice, it turned out), and then he came to me and gave me good advice.

"Let me have the receipts for those bills you paid, Miss Borton," he said. "The publisher gets into these jams once in a while, but he always takes care of things and keeps going. I'll get your money back for you. And from now on, when bill collectors arrive, you send them downstairs to me and I'll take care of them."

He was as good as his word, and we rocked along safely, getting out our little paper on time. Also, Mr. Long took me to his home for Thanksgiving dinner, and his wife, Rose, became a beloved friend.

So a year went by, but I seemed not yet to have made a dent in the publishing world, nor in the great world of musical performance. I had even invested some money in ballet lessons, with the Marinoff Ballet School, but had not been able to keep up with the agile young girls who had been studying ballet since they were small children. I relinquished my dreams, one by one, and I began to reflect that Papa, who had been sending me some money every month, still had two children to put through college. It was not fair for me to continue to be a drain on his resources. I decided that I must become completely self-supporting.

I was the possessor of a Phi Beta Kappa key, earned at Stanford University, but I had been advised to keep it well hidden or boys would never ask me out. Still, Boston was an intellectual city, and the East was considered very scholarly and advanced by the simple Californians, and after consulting Caroline, I hung my key on my bosom and started out looking for a job.

My system was my own and very logical. Raising and lowering my golden key with my agitated breathing, I started at one end of Tremont Street and progressed toward Park, going into each place of business, and offering myself. Raymond Whitcomb, Travel Advisors, didn't want me. Neither did a couple of stores. I came to the Boston *Herald Traveler* building. I went in, asked for the News Room, and was told to take the elevator. There was an atmosphere of frenzied activity there. Men were banging at typewriters, boys were rushing up and down, and occasionally one man would rise from his desk and streak across the room to a telephone booth. I stopped one man who was hurrying past and asked if I might speak to the Editor.

"I'm the Editor," he rasped.

"Do you need another reporter?" I quavered.

"You mean you?" he asked.

"Yes."

"Not until all the men in Boston break both legs," he told me. That made things clear and I went down the elevator and into the next business establishment. I got to Park Street, progressed up it (no luck) and came to Ashburton Place. "Ginn and Company," said the modest plaque. Educational Publishers. I went in. Half an hour later I had a job. The Phi Beta Kappa key did it.

I was hired for the Advertising Department. But first, the Chief of that department told me, I must learn about printing and how the presses worked, so I was to be sent across the river to the Athenaeum Press, at a very modest salary, while I trained. I arranged to begin in six weeks' time, and I used those six weeks to ride joyfully home to California on the train, spend happy days with my family, and then return.

I found the long ride from Jamaica Plain to the Press at Cambridge very onerous; besides, I had to be at work at eight-twenty, and it meant a very early departure. On winter days I froze running the six blocks from Burroughs Street to catch the elevated train which took me into Park, where I could change for Kenmore. Otherwise, it was an hour's ride by surface car to Park, and then I had to change. After getting out at Kenmore Station, there were still five or six blocks to walk to the Press.

So I looked for a room nearer the Press, and I found one, an

adorable room, on Beacon Hill. It was rented to me by Mrs.
Lemmon, wife of a man who worked for the Boston *Globe*. My
room was at 9 Joy Street, the third floor, and I could look straight
down from my windows down Pinckney Street to the Charles
River. On bright days, when it wasn't too cold, I could walk across
the Charles River, and thence to the Press. Later, when I was
moved to Ashburton Place, my room was only a block from work,
and oh joy! Only two blocks from a Waldorf Cafeteria.

For a year I worked at the Press. It was splendid training.
First, I was sent to the Typesetting Department, where the first
thing I had to do was "learn the box." This was a metal shape,
held in the hand, which accepted hand-set type. I learned to
"justify," that is, to space out the type so that the lines were firm
in the box; eventually (so pleased with me was my teacher) I
even learned to set mathematical equations in the box.

While working there, learning the box, and undertaking some
hand-setting, I heard a curious story. There was a Scottish girl
upstairs in the Proofroom who had trained at the Blackstone
Press in Scotland, where much of the printing was done in Latin
and Greek. It seems she knew neither Latin nor Greek, but she
could correct galleys set in those languages, because, through
long experience, she had learned "the right look to them." Final
proofreaders said she seldom let an error get through.

After the box, I was a few weeks in the Linotype and Monotype departments. I liked Linotype the best, where you set type
on a keyboard somewhat like a typewriter, but it was easy to see
that the Monotype machine, which set one letter at a time (not a
whole line or slug), could be corrected more easily. Almost all
the books were set on Monotype, though some still called for
hand-setting, and many of the handsome advertising folders required special type, which had to be set by hand, too.

There followed an unhappy stay in the Binding Department,
where I endeavored to learn how to calculate paging from the
sizes of flat paper, and where I saw, to my distress, more than
one man who had been injured by the knives of the paper cutter,
or hurt by the binding equipment.

Then, having presumably learned enough about the processes

and costs of printing to turn me into an economical worker, I was sent to the Proofroom.

This was a large airy room, full of light, on the roof of the Athenaeum Press, where "first readers" sat at desks in the middle, and "final" and "plate" and "special" readers had booths, caging them in glass except for one side, where they had more privacy, and were able to concentrate without distractions.

The personnel of the Proofroom were imposing. All had doctorates, or at least master's degrees, many had taught, and all were careful—that is to say, meticulous—workers. I lament that due to labor costs, many presses have cut down on proofreading. It was, as practiced at the Athenaeum Press, a work of art and devotion.

The procedure was thus. First, a specialist "prepared the manuscript," correcting typos and other errors, specifying types, and generally envisioning the final appearance of the work.

After the material was set, it was sent up to the Proofroom for "first reading." One person "held the galley" and read from it, while another held a copy and corrected everything he saw that was in error as he went along. After reading a galley in this fashion, the process was reversed, the one "holding," then sitting at the desk to correct, the other reading. A skillful first reader could catch type out of line, missing spaces, and errors in the text, and could thus read from eighteen to thirty galleys a day. One of the special skills was to see that queries, which had been directed to the author by the reader who prepared manuscript, had been taken care of—accepted or slashed out—and great ingenuity was needed when words had to be changed, in order to alter as few lines of type already set as possible.

Then, too, a style sheet had to be followed. Repetition of the same word at the end or the beginning of a line was not permitted, for example, and much ingenuity was needed to figure out ways to correct this when it occurred, without having to reset a whole paragraph.

Authors were then sent the corrected galleys for an okay, and after that, corrected and authorized galleys had to come up for another reading. At that time, the galleys were marked into pages.

Only then did the final or plate reader go into action.

He had to be an authority in the subject, in case some dreadful error of fact or presentation had somehow got by, and also have an eagle eye for anything wrong with the type and the look of the page. When an author got second thoughts about something, or wanted to insert new material, and galleys had gone to be paged and plated, there was a lot of trouble. (Quite rightly, such changes were usually charged to the author, and he had to pay dearly for them.)

When I first stepped into the Proofroom, I was assigned to read simple texts—collections of "readings" of one sort or another; later I was assigned to Spanish texts, since I had studied Spanish through all my high school and college years.

Gradually I was sent around to every reader, as a "first reader," and I began to learn some of the tricks of the trade.

First, you daren't eat any lunch, because after-meal sleepiness was fatal; I soon stopped taking sandwiches with me. Though there were two ladies who brought eggs with them to the Press, secreted them in cups with water at a bend in the steampipes in the pressroom downstairs, and thus had boiled eggs at lunchtime. And there was one lady who did final reading, who gave herself energy by dipping into a can of maple syrup which she hid under her desk.

Remarkable indeed were the readers, many of whom were eccentric in their ways. Most interesting to me was Stephen T. Byington, final reader in Latin and Greek, also in French and other languages, and in philosophy and the most esoteric of the intellectual texts, since Ginn and Company published books for universities, as well as for primary schools and high schools.

Even in freezing weather, Mr. Byington wore flannel bags, a tweed jacket, and no hat. If it was cold enough, he ran most of the way to the North Station, where he took his train. He commuted two hours to work every day from a town in Vermont. I once saw him taking home a large tray of blackberries, which he did in this manner: He would set down the tray, then run fast with his books for about fifty yards; then set down the books, run back for his tray and carry it past the books for some distance; then return for his books, etc. Thus he progressed to the station. We all knew he did this, and it never occurred to any of us that this was odd or that he might have taken a cab. None of us took cabs. We walked and used the subway. Cabs were for plutocrats.

Mr. Byington enjoyed his hours of commuting, for he was engaged on a life work. He was translating the Bible from Greek and Hebrew into colloquial English, and the task excited and satisfied him.

At one point he worried about the expression, in the Old Testament, ". . . and he made the camels to lie down." This seemed to him awkward and redundant. So he took steps. Lawrence of Arabia had been much in the news, and Mr. Byington wrote him a letter, addressing it, "Colonel Lawrence, the Camel Corps, somewhere in Arabia." Months later he got a terse reply as follows: "Dear Byington. We *couch* the camels. Lawrence."

Mr. Byington was handsome. He seemed old to me then because, although he wore a black beard, his hair was gray. He might have been in his late forties. He had piercing dark eyes, and he was graceful and slim, no doubt because of his daily runs to the station.

He was unapproachable, and nobody was allowed to bother him with stupid questions, unless there was an emergency.

However, once I saw him nonplused.

A lady who was in her middle years, also a Ginn employee, though not in the Proofroom, was run over by a truck. The wheels didn't actually go over her, but she was knocked down and tumbled about, to the extent that she was able to collect four hundred dollars for damages, a sum that made it all worthwhile. She earmarked the money for a trip to Europe, and she made careful preparations for this. Shortly before departing, she accosted Mr. Byington in the Proofroom. He rose, with his customary dignified courtesy, and heard her out.

"Please tell me," she said, "how to say, in French, German, Italian and Belgian, 'Certainly not!'" I believe he helped defend possible assaults on her virtue with firm negatives.

There was a plate reader, Miss Margaret Stewart Gordon, an elegant lady of aristocratic Scottish connections, who resented Prohibition, which was raging at the time. Occasionally she would invite me to dine with her at a Greek restaurant where she was known and where one could have a civilized glass of wine with dinner. Only we did not have any glass of wine. The waiter brought us strong coffee in cups, on a tray, with a sugar basin and cream jug conspicuously aboard. He would serve the delicious coffee and solicitously inquire if we would take cream and sugar, to which we always answered, "No, black, please."

Miss Gordon decided that I must have a piano and accordingly sent me one she had in her house. How it was maneuvered up three flights of stairs and into my Joy Street room, I do not know, but one day I found it there. It was an old-fashioned square piano, and I loved it dearly.

On the whole, I was very happy working at the Press in the Proofroom. I earned twenty dollars a week, which I budgeted as follows: seven dollars a week for my room, five dollars a week for my violin lesson, two dollars for transportation, and one dollar for laundry. That left me five dollars to eat with, and I managed. Breakfast was fifteen cents: coffee and a doughnut. And lunch was very often twenty-five cents, consisting of a bowl of soup at the Waldorf or a piece of their justly famous apple pie. Dinner could be managed at Child's, where you could get vegetable stew and a chunk of cornbread for fifty cents. But then, friends invited me regularly. Dorothy was often on the phone with the offer of a bowl of corn chowder, and I had a few beaux, mostly as poor as I, but occasionally they splurged at Durgin and Parks, where we ate enough to hold us for several days at those bountiful tables. I became slim for the first and last time in my life—that is, slim for me. I weighed one hundred and twenty pounds and I thought myself a sylph. The nine-foot-tall ladies, who weigh in, soaking wet, at ninety pounds, so much admired nowadays, had not come into fashion, and there were in my time salesladies who would still show dresses marked sixteen without a sneer.

By this time I had an admirer who wrote music criticism for one of the Boston dailies. There were six newspapers, at that time: the Boston *Herald,* the *Traveler,* the *Globe,* the *American,* the *Transcript,* and the *Christian Science Monitor.* So my life was rounded out with many invitations to concerts, and it happened that I was seen so often at Jordan Hall and Symphony Hall in the evenings, with critics, that it was assumed I was something of a critic too.

One day a piece of news came my way: "Philip Hale, the critic on the *Herald,* is looking for somebody to review the third-string concerts. No pay, but you get your tickets." The words were hardly out of my informant's mouth before I was on my way to the *Herald.*

I found Mr. Hale's office. Of course, I knew about him. He was very erudite and wrote sharp criticism not only of music, but also the theater and books.

I could hardly get inside his cubicle. It was piled high with newspapers, clippings, books, boxes of macaroons, umbrellas and music scores. A distinguished old gentleman sat in a small space he had cleared at a laden table. Silvery hair flowed from under his black derby; under his chin a wide black silk tie was loosely tied into a Bohemian knot. He looked up and I was pierced by shrewd, twinkling bright-blue eyes.

I explained that I wanted to be his third-string reviewer, and he asked me several questions about music which I was able to answer satisfactorily. He seemed most interested in the fact that I was a string player. (I learned later that he thought most string concerts excruciating, and had once written a one-word review of some unfortunate violinist, as follows: "Last night, at Jordan Hall, Mr. Blank gave a recital of violin music." (That was the standard opening. His review followed.) "Why?"

He then pushed his derby back on his forehead and settled down to ask me about my personal history.

"Ah, so you write poetry, eh?"

"Yes. I have had a few verses published."

"Love poems?" His eyes were amused.

I tossed my head.

"Of course!"

"From now on I shall call you Elizabeth Barrett Borton."

Which he did.

4

Mr. Hale sent me to cover the countless recitals of the many "hardy perennials" in Boston's musical world—musicians who gave yearly concerts in order to garner press clippings, occasional engagements, and pupils. Of these, there was a concert almost every night at Jordan Hall, the small, excellent recital hall in the New England Conservatory Building, and sometimes concerts were held at the Flute Players Club, where there were always paintings on display. I remember once being startled at the sight of an entirely naked lady sitting on the grand piano when I entered the Flute Players Club. But wait, it was only a painting, rather carelessly placed.

I loved the concerts, to begin with, and I liked bustling down to the *Herald* office to type out my review and hand it in. It gave me a heady feeling of being a professional newspaperwoman, a dream I still nourished with hope.

Mr. Hale always sent for me by telegram, and as I had by then been transferred to the Advertising Department of Ginn and Company, on Ashburton Place, my apprenticeship at the Press having come to an end, I garnered a certain amount of glamour from my companions.

Mr. Hale worked hard. He got out reviews of the major concerts, prepared notes for the Symphony programs, and wrote almost a full page for the Sunday *Herald*, on drama, music, books, and sometimes interviews. So perhaps it was natural that he sometimes forgot why he sent for me.

He was an erudite and opinionated man. He had studied music in Europe, and was himself an organist. He told me once that he would like to be buried in some church, where his bones could be shaken daily by the great reverberating chords of the organ.

He disliked Brahms, and often said so; he found him turgid, sentimental and thick. He had known Brahms in Europe, and had had some severe altercation with him; gossip said it had been over a woman. But Mr. Hale loved Mozart and the clean, fresh, transparent music of the modern French school then coming into being. Mr. Hale scolded the ladies of the Friday afternoon Symphony who had walked out on *The Afternoon of a Faun,* and set himself the task of teaching Boston music lovers to appreciate contemporary music.

Mozart was his God, and he assured me that Debussy was Mozart's direct descendant.

"However," he warned me, wisely, "be careful. At first, as you hear more and more music, you will begin eliminating all other composers but Mozart, the one sunlit, perfect one. That is natural, to a person with sensitivity. But don't remain alone with Mozart on the mountaintop. He is the apex, but gradually put all the others back into place. Each has his niche, and something to say."

One day I received an important telegram, and I rushed to his office, after my work at Ginn. I got there a little after five; the *Herald* was then just off Tremont Street. He looked at me with some astonishment. He had forgotten why he had ordered me to appear.

"The best macaroons are to be bought in Stearn's basement," he then told me, "and the only honey worth eating is the Hymettus honey, imported from Greece by S. S. Pierce."

He then began loading his green baize bag with books to take home.

"Oh," he said. "I recollect. There's a woman dancing at Symphony Hall who comes with fantastic reviews from Europe. She has been a sensation there, and this is her first American tour. She's a Spaniard, speaks no English, and her French is unintelligible. So nobody has been able to interview her. Didn't you tell me you knew Spanish?"

"Yes!"

"Go and interview her. She is called 'La Argentina,' and she is staying at the Copley." He departed and I made tracks for the Copley.

The lady who received me was dressed with sober Spanish elegance. She wore a perfectly tailored suit in soft olive-green, with a silk blouse to match and low-heeled pumps in leather of the same shade. She wore no jewelry, and her thin strong hands had short clipped nails—the hands of a musician. Her face was extraordinarily expressive, her coloring that prized by most Spaniards. Her hair was a shining dark brown, her skin pale olive, her eyes startlingly green. She had a large nose, a longish face, and a wide mouth with the most enchanting of smiles. I thought her beautiful.

She helped me with my stilted Spanish and spoke with me for about an hour, explaining that her dances were refinements of the dances of Spain, which, she feared, were disappearing.

"Why do you say that?" I asked her.

"Because when a lovely young woman of twenty is hissed in Spain, after dancing, and a stout woman of seventy, performing the same dance, is greeted with hysterical applause, it is evident that the old one knows something the young one cannot understand. So the Spanish dance will disappear."

La Argentina said that though she had been trained in the classical ballet, and at twelve had been premiere danseuse in the Madrid Ballet, she decided not long after that to dedicate her life to collecting and presenting the dances of Spain, so that there might be a record, or at least a memory, of them.

Later, when I saw her dance, I could understand her point of view. She made each dance a precious little gem of drama and movement, and her castanets, played with those strong fingers, spoke, cajoled, persuaded, sighed. She could make them say anything.

When, some years later, I learned of her sudden death from a weakened heart, I felt a personal loss.

Mr. Hale printed my interview in the Sunday section, gave me a by-line, and indicated that the talk had been in Spanish. It was my first by-line. I was beside myself with joy, and bought twenty copies of the paper, to clip and send home.

Meanwhile a young pianist from Spain arrived in Boston, and he spoke only rudimentary English. I was sent to interview him too, and I found him very stimulating. His name was José Iturbi. He told me that when he studies a new piece of music, he never touches the keys of the piano until he has memorized it—every note, tempo indication, and phrase. He studies in bed, he said, with apples and chicken sandwiches nearby, and when he has the music letter-perfect in his mind, he goes to the piano and undertakes a technical analysis.

Mr. Hale gave me another by-line, and I walked on winged feet.

He began sending me to more and more important concerts, and he let me cover the dance recitals as well.

So it was that I went to South Station to report the arrival of a new ballet theater company. It was called the Monte Carlo Ballet, and I was astounded to observe that nearly all the dancers were very young, in their early teens. There was Tamara Toumanova, perhaps fourteen, with her black hair in two little braids tied on top of her head; and Riabouchinsa, graceful and slim as a bird, but still struggling with adolescent acne; and David Lichine, tousle-headed, mischievous. I learned later, as I watched rehearsals and performances backstage, that he published a small company newspaper, in which he made fun of everybody, including himself.

It was strange to see a performance from out front, all the young dancers beautiful as a dream, their youthful bodies trained to grace and precision, offering spectacles that seemed at least half magic—and then to watch them from the wings. From the wings I saw them go to the box of resin and scratch in it like little chickens to make sure they wouldn't slip onstage. And I saw them finish a lovely solo, light as thistledown, leap into the wings, streaming with perspiration, and puffing as if they had run a mile.

Mama Toumanova, as beautiful as her daughter, in spite of being many pounds over two hundred, caught every young dancer in her warm, loving arms, and whispered praise and encouragement. In-between times, she sat and crocheted warm practice tights for all of them, out of thick wool. I learned that, escaping from the Bolsheviks in a boxcar, and praying to God not to be caught, she gave birth to Tamara. The other young dancers had tragic histories; several were orphans who had been gathered up in Paris and trained in the great classic art of their country. This was their first American tour.

Later I had other contacts with great dancers of the day.

Mary Wigman, the German innovator, was one. She believed

in modern expressionism, and was herself an inventor of strange forms, contortions and choreography. She was tall, well-muscled, and robust. Her face, with its aureole of reddish hair which stood out as if alive, resembled that of a female Beethoven in its harshness and rough bone structure. Her contribution to modern dancing was to free it from old forms, and to take it into new and more piercing realms of expression.

Proceeding from Wigman's school of the modern dance, in Germany, were Kreutzberg and Georgi. Kreutzberg was slim, tense, blond, with a shaved skull, and a small, homely face. Georgi, though, had a dark, smoldering beauty, with a sensuous body and a look of languid strength, like a snake or a cat. Together, because of Kreutzberg's incisive and beautiful choreography, and Georgi's perfect balance for his skills, they were a distinguished team.

I went to interview them and found them fascinating. However, Mr. Hale had no room for another interview in his Sunday section, and the interview would be "dead news" in another week.

"I'll tell you what to do," said Mr. Hale. "Rewrite it, blow it up, put in a lot of fancy words, and take it over to Parker of the *Transcript*."

Here I should disgress to explain some of the notorious public rivalry between Hale and Parker. Both were distinguished all-round critics, on powerful papers. But their attitudes toward the English language were opposite. Mr. Hale preferred French clarity and brevity. Mr. Parker rolled around in wonderful words, long sentences, and poetic sensitivity. H. T. Parker was a much younger man than Hale; he looked like a little gnome, and was irascible in his manner, oftener than not. Hale was courtly and handsome, though old. In basic judgments, they were usually in accord, though Parker enjoyed the richly ornamented, romantic music of the German school more than Hale did. (Hale could not abide Wagner and had to steel himself to listen to Richard Strauss.)

Of course I was free to offer my work anywhere; I was not a staff member at the *Herald*. So I wrote my impressions, remembering that the *Transcript* always had more available space than the *Herald,* and I tried to make my piece ornamental and exotic. I was assisted in this aim by the very qualities of the two dancers themselves. Mr. Parker accepted my interview and printed it. But for some obscure reason, I felt faintly treacherous for a few days afterward.

I interviewed Ruth St. Denis for the *Herald,* and found her gentle and unassuming—a quiet elderly lady then—who made little attempt to improve her looks with make-up offstage. Onstage she projected little of the excitement she must have aroused when she began as a young pioneer of modern dance, but her ideas and her choreography came through with much artistry. Ted Shawn, her partner, was younger and a far better dancer, but somehow he was not as likable as she. Or so it seemed to me.

But Mr. Hale gave me many wonderful opportunities to meet and talk with great musicians, as well as hear them in concert.

Rachmaninoff quickly became my favorite pianist, because I had never before heard Chopin played with such virility; the poetic Pole seemed to tempt players to too much rubato, and to melancholy posturing. But Rachmaninoff played Chopin with fire and appreciation. Under his fingers the Ballades became operas performed on the piano, and some of the great Études were played as if chiseled from rock crystal, in such purity and perfection.

"He's an odd-looking man," Mr. Hale had said, preparing me for the first sight of the great Russian. "He ambles onto the stage, with his shaven head and his long-suffering countenance, as if dragging a ball and chain. And once he sits down, he won't get up again. When he finally leaves the stage, no use clapping to get him back. He won't sit down again."

I interviewed Rachmaninoff in his hotel room, where he reminded me suddenly and poignantly of Korgueff. There was the same height, the same sadness, the same deep voice, the Russian accent.

As we talked, Rachmaninoff took a cigarette from his pack, cut it with his knife into four equal sections, and then inserted one quarter section into a small gold holder built like a lorgnette. He smoked this rapidly, and when it was gone, he smoked another section.

"Hot," he said to me, a smile lighting his eyes briefly. "I like smoke hot."

He told me he was glad to give pleasure by playing the piano, but that his life was composition. About Russia, to my question, he answered only, with a wave of the short cigarette, "Do not ask me."

I received the impression of a man carrying some heavy burden, perhaps illness as well as tragedy, who kept himself going by sublimating everything to the composition of music. And I perceived in him a strong mystical strain, which I have continued to discern in every Russian friend I have had through the years. Not for nothing was Russia called "Holy Russia" so long.

However, Mr. Hale was wrong about Rachmaninoff not giving encores. In the several times I heard him in concert at Symphony Hall, he usually bade a sort of adieu to the audience, at last, with his own C Sharp Minor Prelude.

Those were wonderful years in Boston, when Europe sent us so many of her most brilliant musicians—violinists, singers, pianists, and others.

Lucrezia Bori, then somewhat past middle age, was still in wonderful voice, and in person she was an enchantment—the embodiment of what a clever, hard-working Frenchwoman can do to make herself charming. She was exquisitely groomed, down to the last shining black hair, the ultimate eyelash; her dress was apparently simple, but not a line or thread of it could have been changed, and it subtly called the eyes to the piquant, vivacious face.

Altogether different, perhaps because she was so young, was Lily Pons, whom I interviewed immediately after her phenomenal New York debut. Three months after her arrival in America, she came to Boston and I was sent to chat with her at her hotel. She was then protected by a large, elderly, adoring husband named August Mesritz.

Lily Pons had been studying piano in her native city of Cannes, had gone to Paris and there graduated with first prize in piano, at the age of sixteen. But her voice had by then been discovered, and those silvery high voices, which seem to match those of the singing birds, lend themselves to study. After only three years of voice instruction, and one year of singing with provincial French opera companies, she landed in New York— homesick and, because of seasickness, weighing even less than her normal 103 pounds. Within three weeks she had been signed to a five-year contract by the Metropolitan Opera Company, was booked for concerts by the Metropolitan Music Bureau, and was signed by the Victor Company to make recordings—the first artist signed by that company in more than five years.

"She picked three fine plums," said her proud husband.

"No," cried Lily, "Zey fall on my head!"

Tiny (her little foot surely did not measure more than five inches), dressed with French chic in black with touches of green, and wearing a dark-brown fur coat, she was radiantly young, pretty, and happy. Like all beautiful, fortunate young women, she found life endlessly thrilling, and her affection for every living thing spilled over constantly onto the people around her and the animals she acquired. She had a little dog with a "face like a chrysanthemum," and a canary which she brought with her and took everywhere.

"'E seeng mar-velous!"

I learned of her excessive care of her throat, mouth and nose, and of her chest (the preoccupation of all singers), but she seemed to have no worries of any kind. Life stretched before her, at twenty, like an enchanted, endless carpet, covered with the blossoms of homage thrown at her feet.

She pointed to her husband. "'E theenk I must eat more, to get strong, get fat," she told me, black eyes sparkling, "but I theenk maybe American people like me, what you call, skeeny!"

I know that changes take place, that there are emotions, troubles, and disappointments that are a part of every life, but when I first talked to Lily Pons, it was impossible to imagine anything but joy for that radiant small creature.

If Lily Pons seemed to have found for herself a life of perfect happiness, I, in my little niche, seemed to have done the same. I had a beloved, loyal family back in California who wrote me constantly, affectionate friends, and a delightful job, a few beaux, and all the glamour of the world of music was mine for the price of a squib or two.

5

The Advertising Department of Ginn and Company taught me a new skill, which I never really mastered but which I came to respect and love. Besides writing copy, we had to work with typography and type designs, and this whole field opened up vistas of art hitherto unsuspected. The chief of our department, Mr. Robinson, frequently sent one or two of us to exhibits of fine typography, and subscribed to several European and American magazines devoted to the art of type design. I began to perceive that the hand of man is never content with mere function; man will always embellish, refine, perfect. We go through periods of philosophical stripping-down to essentials, resulting in stark and often ugly designs in furniture, clothing, and even lifestyle; but somehow, through it all a few artists emerge who refuse to accept anything less than the truly beautiful. I saw this exemplified in type designs, in examples of typography in bookmaking, even in advertising.

I was fortunate beyond belief in the personnel of that advertising department. It was made up of the fatherly, expert, and wise Mr. Robinson, who was adored by all of us, and six girls. I was the sixth. (Later we had a token man.) We had a secretary, too.

The girls all had different backgrounds and different capacities. Mabel was quiet, gentle, an expert on typography; Marian wrote the important copy for launching serials and new methods; she was the brains behind the advertising that brought about a change in educational methods—history, geography and civics all brought together under the title of Social Sciences. Louise and Mona wrote excellent copy and designed and prepared booklets, on one of which a terrible typo got through the Proofroom somehow: "Reading . . . Made Simplier and Easier."

It became a byword with us, and we always tried, from then on, to make everything Simplier and Easier.

Mabel was small and quiet. Marian had a turned-up nose, owlish brown eyes, and plenty of wit. Louise was of aristocratic Dutch origin; she was tall and blond and elegant, and we all studied her beautifully cut clothes, and the diamond ring on the fifth finger of her right hand, with unenvious admiration. Betty was known to us all as Beautiful Betty; she had curling black hair, dimples, sparkling black eyes, and an enchanting smile, and we all followed the progress of her love affairs with breathless interest. When one beau proposed to marry her and take her out to the Philippines to live, the department was seriously divided, some for, and some against. Finally she married a successful surgeon and went to live in the Midwest.

Mona, tall and willowy, with a luscious low contralto voice and infectious chuckle, was of an old family, and had once been tempted to trace her ancestry with a view to joining the Daughters of the American Revolution. As it turned out, she couldn't; all her people had been staunch Tories, and had violently disapproved of the Revolution.

I was friends with and loved every one of the girls. With Mona I attended physics lectures given by a nephew of the great Darwin. We loved the new windows opening in our minds, and followed the lectures with painstaking care, but I always got lost after about ten minutes, while Mona could sometimes last for fifteen. Still, we felt, the intellectual churning that went on after those lectures made it worthwhile. The lectures were offered free in Boston; all you had to do was sign up for them and list your attendance. Many great minds came to shed their radiance over us.

Marian took me on sales-resistance shopping expeditions on Saturday afternoons. "You buy the first thing you see and it is seldom suitable," was her admonition. So we went shopping, and for each enthusiasm I felt for a hat or a blouse or something else I couldn't really afford, Marian supplied the equal-time answer, pointing out why it wouldn't do. Eventually I left my lonely little room on Joy Street and shared an apartment with Marian.

Our system was superb. There was a big bowl into which we each put ten or twenty dollars at intervals. Either one could purchase food or household things from this bowl. When it was gone, we put in more money, and of course we split the rent and the telephone.

When I went to share the apartment, she gave me her one rule: "No serving liquor to uninvited guests or dropper-inners."

Tea, yes. Or coffee. But no liquor and no food. "Otherwise," she said sagely, "you will soon find you have a gang of freeloaders on your hands, and bang goes the budget."

I had left Ginn and Company and was employed exclusively by the *Herald* when we began to share the apartment. This came about in the following manner.

I had had two interviews published with banner headlines on Mr. Hale's Sunday page, and each one had been praised by him for having been "conducted in Spanish."

Then one day, an unfortunate wretch of a girl was murdered in a Roxbury bakery. She was pinned to the wooden floor with a big knife through her chest. No clues. Police investigated, mystified, etc. But near the body was a scrap of notepaper with a few words of Spanish on it.

Mr. Hale got a note from the Editor who had told me firmly that he would never hire me until all the men in Boston had broken both legs. It read as follows: "Send me that kid that speaks Spanish."

Mr. Hale sent me over to the lion's den of the City Room, where I was detached from the world of art and music and hurtled into a case of murder-reporting.

I wasn't allowed to write any copy. I was just dragged around by the reporters on the story to provide translations in case any more Spanish turned up, but I felt that at last I was right in the middle of life. And in those days, I was.

Reporters were a good deal like they had been portrayed in *The Front Page*. They were brave, resourceful, and tough; they wore broken hats; and they could beat out a story in clear, direct English in ten minutes. No sitting around waiting for inspiration. They were well-informed, clever, flexible, and tireless. And they lived on twenty to thirty dollars a week. This was before the days of the Newspaper Guild.

When the murder case was over, I was "in." But I was the lowest of the low, and had to take stories over the telephone phoned in by out-of-town reporters, rewrite flimsies that had a nut of useful information buried among the publicity, and eventually assigned to that most humble of newspaper jobs—reporting the churches.

I was the only woman on the staff, and far from being discriminated against, I was helped, protected, and saved from foolish mistakes all the time. The reporters, most of them young and very wise, considered me a babe-in-the-woods; they saw me home every night, they showed me where to eat for fifty cents, they leaped to my defense when I was called on the carpet for an error.

Of course I had been briefed by the City Editor, Mr. Minot, when I was hired on the city staff.

"There will be no sitting up on your desk, showing your legs," he ruled. "Never go into the morgue alone. When you have to consult the old clips, I'll go with you, because wolves live in there. Never take a drink from Mr. Drury's bottle; he will invite you to, now and then. And if you go out with any of the boys, you are forbidden to drink. You can have the cherry out of their cocktail. That's all. And I'll check your expense account. Don't let anybody teach you to blow it up, because I will know it."

I was paid twenty-two dollars and a half a week, and the expense account, known as the swindle sheet, provided a dollar or two more. But I made no money on it unless I galloped to some appointment, and then charged a subway fare.

To check my first copy, I was turned over to Mr. Griffin, who, when I first glimpsed him, sat ripping pages from his typewriter, balling them and firing them against the wall. I was scared of him, but he was endlessly kind, and when I was sent on my first real story—covering, with other reporters, the funeral of Calvin Coolidge—Mr. Griffin even invented a story for me to file, in case I got panicky and couldn't think of anything to write.

The ex-President was my first corpse; I had never looked on death, and I expected to be awed and perhaps even frightened. But Mr. Coolidge lay quietly in his coffin, looking somewhat apologetic at causing all the fuss, and what impressed me were his long red eyelashes.

I was not supposed to pay much attention to him anyhow. My assignment was to "cover" Mrs. Coolidge, who stayed firmly at home and refused to be covered by anybody.

I managed to ferret out the name of her doctor, though, and infuriated him by my questions, which he rightly considered to be impertinent, into betraying a certain amount of information. I was able to write a sort of story, and was not entirely disgraced on my first important assignment.

I never actually liked the occasion when, in order to get information, I had to intrude upon private grief or personal trouble. Scoops were important, but were never worth tears, protests and resentment, so I guess I was never a very good reporter, in that sense.

I did achieve one delightful scoop, though, and in spite of the wiles of the protagonist.

It was a bitter cold Sunday morning, and I was not due at the paper until three in the afternoon. I had slept late, as Marian had, as she put it, "packed a steak on her back and gone hiking in the Blue Hills," where at some point she would stop and broil it. I instead intended treating myself to the scrambled eggs at the Statler, which I thought were beyond rubies. The previous Saturday night, I had attended a concert by the Gordon String Quartet, led by Jacques Gordon, brilliant violinist and former concertmaster of the Chicago Symphony Orchestra.

As I walked along Arlington Street, I heard lovely music, excellent violin playing: round, warm tone, exquisite phrasing, true pitch. I looked around. But there was only a beggar standing there on the corner, blind, in shabby clothes, patches over his eyes, and a cigar box, hung around his neck by a cord, for contributions. As I listened to the lovely music floating under the bow, I saw two or three passers-by throw dimes into the cigar box. Sidling closer, I looked hard, and it seemed to me that the blind street fiddler was Jacques Gordon. Unostentatiously dropping a dime into his box, I hurried down the street to the *Herald* office, as fast as I could. I poured out my story to Mr. Minot, who was holding the fort on a dull morning with only one cameraman available.

"All right, you can have a camera. But it leaves me with nobody here if a fire breaks out or there is some other big story breaking. So, if you are wrong, you're fired!"

I wasn't wrong and we got a delightful interview with Gordon, who told me that he liked to prove to himself, once in a while, that many people loved music who couldn't go to concerts.

"Over in Scollay Square," he said, "there were some little ragged urchins, who came up to give me a nickel and ask shyly about the music. That nickel might have meant a bun. I appreciated those coins."

The corollary was sad. "And there are people who might have paid three dollars last night to hear me, who would walk right past today, looking the other way," he said. "It is true, and hard for the musician, that a large part of his audience is always made up of people who merely go to concerts in order to be seen, not really to listen."

Yet, on the whole, as he packed up his fiddle and detached his cigar box, now rattling pleasantly with about a dollar and a half in it, Gordon was happy.

"This dollar and a half," he said, "was my take for about ten minutes of playing. And that isn't bad pay either, when you stop to think about it."

His pleasure in his little masquerade, and the philosophy he engendered, reminded me of a story one of my Russian emigré friends had told me about a Russian who was vacationing in Paris when the Revolution exploded in Russia, and in a twinkling, from a rich man with great estates, he became a man homeless, without a job, with no income, and nothing to call his own but the clothes on his back and a cello he had bought himself a few weeks before.

"For about two weeks," my Russian friend had recounted, "he was desperately unhappy. But then he got a job in a little orchestra, playing his cello, and from then on, he was happier than he had ever been before."

I was young and radiantly healthy in those days, and no doubt it was salutary that I had to cover, in a couple of months, three birthday parties of a special kind. Each old person had reached the age of one hundred, festivities had been arranged for them, and I, with my life before me, was sent to interview those old people, who were about to surrender theirs. One old lady had been an art teacher of some distinction. She spoke well, recalled interesting moments from her life, but had to yell, regularly, with desperation, to an attendant, for "The closet! The closet!" and was hurried off to the bathroom. An old gentleman I was sent to talk to had been made much of by a loving family; he undertook to tell me about a book he was writing. He never got beyond speaking about the reason for his book, and he never progressed beyond the first sentence of his discourse. He would then look around, pitifully, at his family, for help, and they would start him back at the beginning again. After he had made six or seven attempts, I made my farewells. The third person had the look of the very old, and merely mutely sat.

I begged not to be sent to any more such celebrations, for they were heartbreaking. We live longer and retain our faculties to a greater degree, I am now told, for medicine has learned that life should be for the whole person, and not just for a selection of organs which can keep on functioning, whether the personality or the mind has kept up or not.

These desperate old people cured me of a cowardice in a peculiar way. I had been absolutely scared to death of airplanes, but after my interview with the centenarians, I climbed aboard a little plane in Boston and got myself to California in record time —fourteen hours, I think it took. The plane held about twelve seats, one on each side of a narrow aisle, and there was no stewardess, copilot or navigator. There was just a smiling young man in shirtsleeves who undertook to operate the machine; he got us up and he got us down. We came down in Buffalo, in Cheyenne, in Salt Lake City, and some other towns. Eventually, we landed in Los Angeles, where I changed to a much smaller plane, with only five seats, one of which was occupied by the pilot.

I had phoned my family from Los Angeles, and they all came out en masse to the airport to watch me flying in. When the small black flying object appeared against the blue Bakersfield sky, my father said, "She can't be in that thing!" But I was. I tumbled out, dead for sleep, kissed everybody, and fainted, despite the steak I had packed in during a twenty-minute stop in Cheyenne.

However, having been ready to risk early demise rather than live to a hundred, I was sent on other airplane trips by the Editor, who thought me a brave girl. This lasted until I failed him on an important story. It seems there was an attempt, way back in the beginning of air travel, to start up a sleeper service. I was handed my ticket and told to take the sleeper and write up the experience.

The plane, when I climbed aboard, did indeed carry a stewardess, and when it began to get dark we came down for a short stop, while she made up the berths. The lowers were narrow beds, not more than two feet wide, flat on the floor of the plane. The uppers were somehow suspended above the lowers, about two feet above. I had a lower. We were about six brave souls on that flight, and we changed in the washroom. That is, men took off coats and ties and hung them in the washroom, and I took off my dress and hung it up. We all left our shoes with the stewardess. I had had a very tiring week, I guess, because when I crawled into my little berth (like the cradle in which the astronauts rest), I fell asleep and remained that way until the stewardess came and told me to roll out and put on my dress. I had no story to tell. I hadn't even dreamed.

I remember being strongly impressed, though, with the efficiency of the service.

"We are about to come down for breakfast," the stewardess yelled over the roaring of the motor. "What do you want? We will radio down for it."

And sure enough, as we taxied up to a little windswept airport somewhere in Texas, the breakfasts were waiting—ham and eggs, or hot cakes, or whatever had been ordered, and coffee, all smoking hot. We devoured breakfast while the berths were whisked away and chairs fastened in again, and so were on our way.

So, little by little, what with studying background, interviewing, and gaining experience of various orders, I began to find out that although I had considered myself educated when I graduated from college, my education was just beginning.

6.

Fortunately for me, though I was on regular hours and was sent on real stories once in a while (mostly churches, the banquet beat and ladies clubs), I was still on call sometimes for stories about musicians or actors who came to Boston, and was often given Annie Oakleys (free tickets) to a play or the movies in return for a short review.

Thus, with Marian in tow, we once watched a superb interpretation of Hamlet by John Barrymore, performed while he was exceedingly drunk. He staggered a bit, I noticed, but his voice was wonderful, and vibrant with emotion and subtle meanings. But, in the scene where he repulses Ophelia, as I thrilled to the implication that he, Hamlet, loved her but could not bring himself to promise anything, Barrymore took up the end of her floating garment and carefully wiped his nose with it.

We saw performances of Shakespeare fairly often. There were always good audiences, as there were for the perennial *Cyrano de Bergerac,* also a favorite with Boston audiences.

A startling, vivid and dynamic performance of *The Merchant of Venice* was given one year, with the great Russian Jewish actor Maurice Moskowitz as Shylock. I interviewed him in his dressing room after the performance, and learned, from his own lips, why he played Shylock as a vigorous man in early middle age, and not as "old Shylock," bent, white-whiskered, and whining, as I had seen others do.

"I have sound reasons for playing Shylock as I do," he told me, as he took the make-up off, revealing a creamy, rosy face not more than a year or two older than that of the young Shylock he presented on the stage.

Moscowitz commented on Shakespeare in an astute way. I have here quotations from our interview, conducted in 1929.

"Shakespeare was the most eloquent of all spokesmen for the Jews," he said, "because he showed us the Jew as a man, animated by the same feelings as everyone else . . . in short, a human being. Shakespeare does not ridicule Shylock, pity him, or sentimentalize him. I do not play Shylock as a comic character, though for many years he was played in no other vein, and yet Shylock had humor and wit enough, and in the exaggeration of his racial gestures and inflections there is legitimate comedy at times. I do not play him as wholly noble. But he was undoubtedly the only gentleman in the play, the only real man. He was the only personage who was not a parasite, contentedly living off someone else. He was the only man who rose above fate enough to demand his due, against the howling mob and in the face of taunts. He was the only one who knew what he wanted, and tried to get it."

Playing Shylock as tall, strong, handsome, and full of vigor, he defended his conception of the character as follows: "This is the Shylock, young and forceful, who stood to reason according to Jewish law, and according to the lines Shakespeare gave him to say. We know from Tubal that Shylock was very religious, that he went twice a day to synagogue. By Orthodox Jewish law, every male was to marry at the age of eighteen in order to multiply and to spread the seed of Abraham. If a man married and had no children by his wife after ten years, he was required to divorce her and marry again. In other words, the reason for marriage and early marriage was to procreate children. Now we know that Shylock had a daughter of sixteen. So, surely, he might well have been less than forty years old in the play, and that is how I see him, a man in the prime of life."

While Moscowitz was playing Shylock, a character he had studied, pondered over, and deeply felt, another young actor came into Boston with a light play, and graced it with his shy, ingratiating personality and magnificent dancing. His name was Fred Astaire.

I went over to his dressing room to ask him how he felt about playing without the presence of his lovely sister, Adele, by his side; formerly his partner, and a shining star in every play, she had recently married a titled Irishman and retired from the stage.

When I arrived at the theater I found that Astaire was temporarily away, but his valet was there, languidly pressing handkerchiefs and neckties. On the floor, in ranks, were thirty pairs of shoes.

"He practices all the time," the valet told me. "I don't mind. I'd rather work for a dancing man than a singing man. Singing men practice too, and singing men are very tiresome."

Just then Astaire came in, with a kind of shy jauntiness. Gentle and apologetic, he had none of the airs and obvious self-assurance of a stage star. He seemed fragile, weedy. But I had seen him dance, and his speed and agility, all that leaping up and down from desks and tables and chairs to the floor, dancing all the time, could not be rooted in anything but the most extraordinary wiry strength.

With great regularity, Burton Holmes, F. N. Newman, and Branson de Cou gave travel lectures, with colored slides, and in those years (the late twenties and early thirties) world travel had not yet become something everybody did. Reporters, like other citizens, were avid for tickets to those pictures of trips to exotic countries, and we all watched, enchanted by those scenes of China, Singapore, Ethiopia, Ireland, England, Scotland, Austria and Persia.

Perhaps those wonderfully vivid colored slides, taken by experts, projected onto screens, greatly enlarged and charmingly explained, created a paradox for me, because genuine travel, undertaken years later, usually convinced me that most places look like their pictures, and many of them were not as handsome. Certainly, in a comfortable seat in Symphony Hall, looking at scenes of Italy, I was happier and more comfortable than when I tried to unravel the mysteries of Italian plumbing in Padua, and the colored slides of "The Creation" by Michelangelo in the Vatican burst on my delighted eye with more clarity and beauty and perfection than when I stood, with wrenched neck, peering up at them through the darkness in Rome.

One day my editor gave me an assignment to interview a child prodigy, a task I undertook without much enthusiasm. The child was a stout little fellow who played the violin, named Yehudi Menuhin. On the stage, he walked out in black velvet, a solemn child, and played like an adult, a specially gifted and musical adult. The interview was to be a sort of "Meet the Press" affair, and the child was to be presented by his father, Moshe Menuhin, who had not been apart from Yehudi more than five hours in five years. The prospect was not attractive, and I supposed that the little boy, trained to musical perfection by his parent, was probably also trained perfectly to answer the right questions in the right way.

In some ways I was right. The child had been well-trained, but he seemed to me to be normally bright and unpretentious.

For one thing, he made no coy attempts to be "just like other children." He obviously was well ahead of most other children mentally, and his life as a child prodigy, capable of moving great audiences of people and of earning large sums of money, had projected him into early-adult attitudes.

Whereas the average child is one thing at a time, Yehudi was many things. He studied under the supervision of his parents, both brilliant intellectuals; he enjoyed a warm and loving family life; he practiced three hours a day; and he gave twenty concerts a year. An extraordinary life, but then, it was obvious, Yehudi was an extraordinary person. It was only chance that this extraordinary person happened to be, at the time of the press conference, only thirteen years old.

My short personal acquaintance with Yehudi made me realize that, in our specialized age, we have forgotten that remarkable persons are often very versatile; intelligence, when a brain is bursting with it, may spill over into one field or another, spectacularly, but it is a rare genius who is not extremely competent in many fields.

While the young Yehudi was a happy child prodigy, whom I was able to converse with in his childhood, I later met a man, already well past middle age, who had also been a child prodigy but did not remember it, or his childhood years, with much pleasure. He was Norbert Wiener, the brilliant mathematician. Genial and full of vitality, he exuded a love of social contacts and all the major pleasures of a human being, who is of course a social creature. Solitaries are sports in our civilization. Professor Wiener's thought was that the child prodigy is, by his very qualities, removed from the social context which provides us all with joy and pleasure.

At the same time, he outlined a thought which I believe he explained in some of his books, which threw light on the phenomenon of the strong Jewish bent toward intellectual and artistic accomplishment.

"It is assumed that acquired traits are not hereditary," he said one day in a conversation on the lawn of a friend's home. "I dispute that. But, anyhow, intellectual qualities may be bred into a people, just as they may be bred out. Ask any breeder of horses

and dogs if qualities of brain cannot be bred for, just as success-
fully as a color of coat or length of ear. Well, during all the years
of the Middle Ages, Jews by their peculiar social organization,
tight and united within usually hostile surroundings, carried out
a tradition of family planning which put a high value on intellect
and studiousness. The brightest student in the rabbinical schools,
even though penniless, was accepted with pride for the hand of
the daughter of the richest merchant. And the young couple was
exhorted to raise many children.

"Meanwhile, what was happening in the Gentile world? The
brightest young minds were solicited for the Church, or gravi-
tated there of their own accord, because it was the only place
where a poor boy with brains could be certain of possibilities of
prestige and a good life. Celibacy was being greatly admired.

"In other words, broadly speaking, the Jews bred brains in,
while the Gentiles were at pains, in those centuries, to breed
them out."

7.

My life as a reporter carried me into places and situations I
would never have known as an ordinary young woman merely
passing time until "the right man" came along. I visited prisons,
I attended murder trials, I studied mental hospitals, I called on
people in all sorts of trouble.

In other words, I was being trained as a "sob sister," or, as it
was more euphemistically phrased, I covered "the woman's
angle."

Actually, it was a losing campaign from the start. I really had
little heart to intrude on people in grief such as was felt by the
woman whose son was to be executed next day, or the father
who had accidentally run over and killed his small son. I failed
in these things, mostly, I suppose, because I was never convinced that the public had any right to know about private sor-

rows. There is, to this day, great contention among writers in the public press about how much the public is entitled to know. A good argument can be made for those who say that the reportorial eye, detached and descriptive, can teach more than any amount of personal experience can. At the same time, there are those who, like me, can immerse themselves in pain, grief and trouble only through the fictionalized transfiguration of these emotions.

Anyhow, although I strove to handle my assignments well, I was not up to them sometimes, and a kind and perceptive City Editor often relieved me of them.

I had no right to call myself a reporter in the sense, for instance, that Gracie Davidson was. She worked for the Boston *Post*, and she was a whiz. Tall and willowy and blond, with big blue eyes and a lisp, she seemed able to go through keyholes and to persuade the most tightly locked lips to open up and spill their deepest secrets to her. She was known, admiringly, to all the reporters in town as "Grathie."

The result was that I soon got channeled into the slot where I belonged: interviews. Here I had to develop a technique and depend on intuition, and I began to garner the most delightful assignments, interviews with people like Tallulah Bankhead, Jane Cowl, Eva Le Gallienne, and many others.

Jane Cowl came to Boston as Juliet, and though she was, by all calculations, too old for the part at the time, she played it with all the shy passion and trembling generosity of a girl of sixteen.

New England-born, Miss Cowl had strong convictions about those old four-letters words—*work* and *duty*. She believed in both. The idea which caught on so strongly a few years later, that everybody has to fulfill himself and "do his thing" and generally think of no one but himself, she did not accept at all. This seemed odd to me, for the little I had seen of the world of the theater had led me to think that determination, personal ambition and push had to be the prime movers for success in that medium. I said so.

"Oh no," she corrected me, courteously. "That is a calumny spread about the acting profession. What gets actors to the top is work and talent. On the contrary, there is no more generous and open-handed, tolerant, and warm-hearted body of workers in the world than the people of the theater. I think perhaps that is because we know that anyone's success, monetary or critical, is fleeting, and that we are all in a profession dedicated to putting our obligations to the public before our own comfort or convenience."

Eva Le Gallienne, daughter of a writer, spoke of little outside her special realm of interest—acting and the theater. She believed deeply in communing with her audience, and she said this to me, after an extraordinarily successful matinee, in which she played Camille with great tenderness and a sort of worldly sentimentality.

"We all wept together, the little old Boston ladies and I," she said. "It was so sweet to look out into the audience and see row after row of white heads—beautiful old white heads—and with high piled hair and jet combs. They remember the period in which I place my Camille—the period of bustles and leg-o'-mutton sleeves, that worldly, romantic, and extraordinarily feminine age.

"When Camille, in a very sad scene, sits down at her writing desk to bid her lover farewell, we were all weeping. My tears were streaming, and all the dear old ladies were snorting into their handkerchiefs. Then suddenly a wave of feeling swept over us all for the comedy of the communal crying. We all snickered hysterically. Then we braced ourselves and went on with it."

Tallulah Bankhead, when I saw her in her suite at the Ritz, was unexpectedly small, even petite. Perhaps the surprise of her size struck me most forcibly because of the strong bass voice that issued from her throat. I recall very little of what we said except that, even in a hotel room full of other people—visitors, dressers, maids—she held every eye, and everybody else faded into the wallpaper. There is a word for it nowadays: charisma. She had it to an overwhelming degree. She was wearing a simple costume of black velvet trousers and a white satin blouse; her golden hair hung loose around her face, and she had on no make-up. Not strictly beautiful, I suppose, but she had what is more important for an actress—an unforgettable face. All her gestures were wide and exaggerated; she strode around the room with restless energy, giving orders and lavishing endearments on everyone, excluding nobody.

One thing she said that I have never forgotten, though I saved no clipping of the strange, haphazard interview. It was her remark about a little Greek orphan she was supporting, and who wrote to her regularly.

"The poor darling was wounded in the war and lost an eye," boomed Tallulah, "so I promised her a beautiful glass eye as soon as the socket was well enough for her to have one fitted. The child is dark, olive-skinned, with black hair and eyes, but she wrote me that she wanted a *blue* eye! My gosh! They tried to dissuade her, but I said, 'Darling, if you want a blue eye, by gosh, Tallulah will get you one.' And I did."

Tallulah was direct, honest, overwhelming. Interviewing the perfectly lovely Ina Claire later, in a cab, as she sped from her hotel to a performance, I found a lady full of Irish wit and as subtle as a serpent. I couldn't extract an unequivocal opinion from her about anything. But I found her charming, and though she was not young at the time, she was very beautiful. There was not a line in the oval face, which was dominated by large sparkling eyes, and her perfection of looks and grooming was balanced by the irony of her fleeting smile. She was elusive, careful to say nothing that wasn't either meaningless or capable of several interpretations. She had just been bothered to death by reporters who wanted "all the information" about her sudden and short-lived marriage to the movie idol of the moment, John Gilbert, and she was tired of giving out quotes.

Leslie Howard, the English actor whose plane was shot down over the sea by Nazi aviators during the war, played *Berkeley Square* in Boston in 1930. The play dealt with the telescoping of time, with the idea that certain sensitive persons may live in several centuries simultaneously. Priestley, and several other English writers and dramatists played with variants of this idea. The whole concept of time, as we think of it in the Western world, is subject to poetic and scientific experimentation, and the possibilities for drama are, of course, enticing.

Leslie Howard told me that, being English, he was well used

to the idea of ghosts, and rather liked ghosts on the whole. He spoke frankly and with intelligence about many subjects, the English tradition of acting always having been that the good actor is a man capable of reflecting any sort of personality for the stage, and that therefore he must be a man of wide culture and extremely well read. In acting, he told me, he tried to take the word "act" out of his consciousness.

"To be convincing, you must be yourself," he said. "The skilled actor is a person who has trained himself to react sensitively and immediately to any given set of circumstances and situations. In other words, he can feel and project an emotion when he needs to. This is not easy, but it can be learned."

In remembering these distinguished people, cornered as they were by an employee of a large daily newspaper whom perforce they had to be pleasant to, I dare to include them among my lists of friends. The reason is that I have pondered a great deal about what friendship is, and I have come to the conclusion that, in essence, it is communication, in a far more satisfactory form than love.

Like love, friendship depends, in the first instance, on a meeting, on propinquity. In life, for most of us, this is entirely a matter of chance. For the reporter whose job is interviewing unusual and accomplished people, the meeting is arranged by factors that cannot operate in many other professions, and the sudden realization of communication is possible at once, even before long weeks of acquaintance and trust have been built up.

Why, then, did certain of the people I met overwhelm me at once with a warm and genuine feeling of liking and comradeship, while others left me with many printable quotes and a feeling of accomplishment, but with no aura of immediate friendship? Perhaps because one of the reasons certain personalities rise to the top in the entertainment field is a built-in talent for communication, that is, for taking other people at once into the direct circle of their interests and affections. I am sure that at least part of my intuitive feeling about the peculiar powers of communication enjoyed by many public personalities is true. How else explain the adulation accorded certain actors and actresses, singers, preachers, even popular leaders and politicians? They are blessed with the ability to send out waves of friendship that bombard and surround the bedazzled public, which, in turn, responds and communicates.

Telephones, radio and television are marvelous scientific discoveries to facilitate communication. But there are—there always have been—people who could do it without any material help.

The same phenomenon impressed me in Hollywood, where I was sent by my newspaper for five fabulous summers, and where I met and talked to, lunched with, and sometimes even danced with, the mysterious, legendary shadows of the silver screen.

But in the meantime, through friends, I penetrated a life and a way of thinking that were mysterious and unknown to me, but for which I developed a respect and affection that has lasted all my life. This was the life of the Orthodox Jewish colony in Boston.

Years later, Ida Landau in New York, head of the Transworld Feature Syndicate, told me that I knew more Yiddish words and understood more about Jewish traditions than she did. But she was only paying me compliments.

In Bakersfield, when I was a little girl, the Jewish families had no synagogue; they would import a rabbi for the High Holidays, and rent the Lutheran Church to perform their rituals. I was a minor but fascinated part of them because it was I who played, at appropriate moments on my violin, unaccompanied, the Kol Nidre and Eli Eli.

Years later, in Boston, in the home of my beloved friend Dorothy, I met Emmy Hess ben Nathan. Dorothy loved the gentle Jewish traditions, but her circles were brilliantly intellectual and mostly skeptical, and she did not light the menorah, or even observe Jewish dietary laws to any degree. I was often served shrimp salad in her house. Yet she grieved a little for the beauty of the old traditions, and remembered her mother's careful observances with tender love.

Emmy was married to a rabbi, however, an Orthodox Jew, and in her household the old rules were kept.

Emmy was very beautiful. I had seen reproductions of the lovely portrait head of Queen Nefertiti, and had remained speechless before such perfect beauty and grace. Then I saw her, in the flesh, for Emmy, ethereally slender, looked just like her. And the hair concealed under the tall headdress of Nefertiti must have been like Emmy's—night-black, crisply curling, and thick.

Emmy was an artist, trained in Hamburg, and it was not long before she and I began working together. We made a little book of Chinese poems together; I wrote the poems, in loving imitation of the Arthur Waley translations, and Emmy did a wood-carving for the cover, and lovely wood-carved decorative initials for the beginning of each verse.

But this was after we had become fast friends.

Emmy came from a little town in the south of Germany, in the mountains. Her father was the only doctor, and the only Jew, in that town. In Hamburg, studying art, she met Nathan, an Orthodox Jew, born in what was then called Palestine and is now Israel. They fell in love and were married. But deep in her artist's heart, though she was everything a Jewish wife and mother should be, were memories of a *Tannenbaum* strung with Christmas lights, the voices of children singing the old carols, and the glorious chiming of the church bells. Her husband, knowing this, released her to me every Christmas Eve, and in my little room on Joy Street we decorated a Christmas tree, leaned out of my fourth-story window and saw the carolers going by in the snow, and Emmy ate pieces of my Christmas cake, sent in an enormous box crammed with gifts from faraway California.

But in return, I was taken into the warmth of her home on Purim, and even on Rosh Hashanah. On Purim, I went into the little house made in the back yard from laths and decorated with vines and flowers, and we ate Yacovtosh (small cakes made of rich pastry and filled with a sweet made from poppyseed and honey).

And on Friday evening I sat at their table with its snowy cloth, with Nathan ben Nathan, hatted, reclining to one side and reading in Hebrew from the book of prayers. I became part of an even more ancient tradition than ours in our family, and I loved it and felt the pull of the centuries behind it all, the sorrow, the hopes, the patience.

The Ben Nathans were sending money every month to Haifa,

where they were buying an orange orchard. And then, one sad day for me, Nathan ben Nathan sent Emmy and their two beautiful little girls, Judith and Gabrielle, to Haifa to await him. We wrote to each other, and I learned that she suffered trying to learn the difficult Hebrew language; her children, in their school bus, were fired upon by Arab *guerillistas*.

Circumstances intervened, after many years of our correspondence, and I lost track of her address in a move I made from one city to another. I worried and waited for a letter from Emmy to be forwarded to me, to set me right again. But she too had moved, from Haifa to Tel Aviv, and the same unhappy chance had caused her to lose my address. She sent one letter, addressed only to the town where I was living, but I learned of that later. I never received it. But one day, a close friend told me that he was going to Israel, and asked what he could bring us from there.

"The address of Emmy ben Nathan!" I begged. "I know that her husband teaches in Hebrew, that he is a rabbi, and that he lectures in economics. That's all I know."

With those clues, and with the greatest good will, our friend looked for Emmy and found her, and again the monthly letters began to arrive—full of reports of lectures and plays she had seen, of walks along the beach, news of her children. And I send my letters to her. I am invited to visit, and I want to.

"You may be reluctant to come because of the uncertainties, the war footing we are on," she wrote. "But I would hope you could come and be with me in my home and share our life for a while. We live it from day to day, extracting joy from each moment. Anyhow, if tomorrow is for sorrow, tomorrow has not come, and we are here today."

Through Emmy and her Orthodox husband, I met and was able to talk to some members of the mystical Jewish sect of the Hassidim, or Chassidim. The *Ch* is pronounced back in the throat like the Spanish *j*, and can be spelled a number of ways, none of which really indicates the sound.

Sometimes, in large cities, one can see a member of this sect; you can identify the men by their side curls, long beards, sober dark dress and black hats. Though they might be called (as Christian Trappists are), "of the strict observance," and devote hours every day to their required prayers and religious duties, what drew me to them and to an attempt to understand their culture, with its rich literature and poetry, was their mysticism. Always before, the Jewish faith had seemed to me to lack this curious exultation of the spirit, and to be based, instead, on justice, human values, and common sense. Even today I feel that those three great values are not quite enough to live by; there must be some intangibles of the spirit to help one to get away from the realities.

I went to several plays when the great Hebrew Art Theater came to Boston, and listened with awe to the sonorous, masculine sound of the language, and I looked for and saw two great productions of the Orthodox Jewish spirit. One was the play *The Dybbuk*, with the superb actor Maurice Schwartz, which had me shivering at the memory of it for many weeks; the other was a film of a medieval legend, called *The Golem*. This last, with its views of Prague, its mounting terror and wild imagination, was haunting enough, but I watched for its return to little theaters, and saw it twice.

After a time, I even began to feel myself at home among friends of the Orthodox faith, rather than a visiting foreigner, and felt pleased and flattered that I seemed to be one of the company. Until one day, a stranger from New York came up to me at a Jewish party and said, "Who are you? The Bride of Christ in the Ghetto?"

I was startled and offended. But a faint inkling came through to me that, love my friends as I might, I was not one of them. To identify is good, but it is not the best. The best is to love, despite all the differences.

8.

Two personalities I came in contact with through my work had an unforgettable impact upon my life.

One was Mrs. Roosevelt.

I was sent up to Groton, to talk to her and write about her, when she visited that exclusive boys school to attend the graduation of her son Franklin. The younger son, John, was also there at Groton.

As the wife of the President was expected, special arrangements had to be made to give Mrs. Roosevelt a proper reception. I waited for her at the door of the main building. She arrived in a large car driven by a chauffeur, but when she descended she looked disheveled and tired. She was wearing a rather baggy tweed skirt, a sweater and blouse, and an unbecoming hat. I was speechless, for she seemed to me, despite her impressive height and alertness, so unprepossessing.

I spoke, asked her for a few minutes, and was rewarded by a smile that lit up her face and gave it sweetness. She answered all my questions very gravely and kindly, and she quite won me when she turned to John and said, "Hurry now, and get cleaned up. Pa will be here."

The President was Pa. So she must be Ma.

The interview was not exclusive, nor did it record anything important whatever. But I had a glimpse of a woman whose spirit illuminated the shy and unpretty exterior with its warmth and kindness and genuine interest in people and things, and I never again paid much attention to obvious beauty, every hair in place and perfect eyebrows. In a short time, I saw what real beauty is. It was a brief interview, a passing contact.

But with Roland Hayes, the great black singer who brought the Spiritual with all its haunting sorrow and hope into the concert hall, I was privileged to have a more continuing relationship.

I had heard him sing before I was sent to his home to interview him for the paper. He was a householder in Brookline, and thought of Boston and the North as his home, although he had bought a farm in Georgia, his native state, and looked forward to living there during vacations and in retirement.

Small, thin, intense, he had made up in determination and study what he lacked in opportunities in his youth, when the chance of a black man achieving international acclaim as an artist was entirely visionary. But like many another distinguished man, he attributed his success to his mother, to her precepts and to her nobility of character, which taught him courage.

"When I was fifteen," he told me, "I had a vision of what I could accomplish for myself and for my race. I also saw very clearly that there is no person and no thing in the whole world we can depend on, except ourselves.

"It is a hard lesson to learn, but a true one," he said, "that there is really no life at all without giving. In trade, we know that there must be exchange. So it is with anything and everything we do, and with the things of the spirit—as we give, we receive. When winds blow, fresh air rushes in to fill the space where they have been; there is never any emptiness. When we give, we find the mind and heart immediately refilled, like an everlasting well."

Roland Hayes spent eight student years in Boston. As he said, "My mother made her little contribution to education by doing washing for Harvard boys." His struggles were long and constant, but marked by perseverance, and he took any sort of job in order to live, until he was able to offer himself as a trained singer. In England he received his first recognition, when he was asked to sing for the Royal Family at Buckingham Palace. From then on, his career took care of itself.

"Material things can teach us about beauty, but they can hamper," he commented, looking about at some of the beautiful objects in his home.

"Look at that table," he told me. "We call it material, but it is perishable. It will crumble away, whereas the thought that brought it into being is imperishable and will renew itself. We are always knocking up against material things that may distort our values unless we learn to know the concreteness of this age we live in. Even our bodies may hamper our spirits. My eyes that can see only one side of things at a time and my ears that can hear only a certain range of notes and my hands that can touch only a limited number of objects—what are these to depend on? Nothing, in comparison with what an open spirit can do."

His remarkable enunciation in English, French, Russian and

Italian he acquired by spending a few months in each country and "simply keeping my spirit and my ears open."

He was a great benefactor of his race in countless ways, financially and otherwise, but his attitude, while never imitative or obsequious, was never hostile, either. He believed that the black people of the United States were hampered by the culture of the whites, which they tended to imitate, but he felt that the blacks would come into their own kingdom of pride by developing their own living culture from the history and art of their black ancestors.

"This may seem to you a simplistic comment," he told me once in a private talk, "but the gift for entertainment, for service, and for quietly making life pleasant for white people developed because of the original facts of slavery. Proud, hostile, rebellious slaves were not useful, and were simply eliminated. Black children were brought up to be quiet and deft servants, or able to amuse. Though always there have been some people, black and white, who would be, and were, friends. As that proportion increases in the population, our whole country will be enriched."

Roland Hayes was a thoughtful friend. We kept in touch, lunched together sometimes, and occasionally wrote to each other when he was away. I valued those short glimpses of a rich personality. Once, when I was very ill, and still in bed recovering from flu and bronchitis, he rang me up to inquire how I felt, and learning that I was still miserable, he sang to me over the phone a lovely short concert of my favorite songs. I have never forgotten that delicate kindness.

9.

The work of a newspaper office being what it is, I was not reserved exclusively for interviews, though I was often chosen to do them. I put in time on "the banquet beat," and got fat on a constant diet of creamed chicken in patty shells, with green peas, and ice cream, and for an edifying few months I had to do churches, during which time I acquired an idea of what William James calls "The Varieties of Religious Experience."

A few unusual assignments took me out of town to a women's prison, and around to the various mental hospitals in Massachusetts. In one of those hospitals I acquired, through my work, another friend. She was Dr. Ilse Lauber, Austrian-born and trained, a devoted psychiatrist.

This anecdote sounds like many jokes I heard told, but it really happened. On one of my visits to the hospital where Ilse worked, I passed the veranda, where a number of patients sat rocking and chatting. They were friendly to me, interested in my "case," and took me innocently and wholeheartedly into their company. It was a harrowing experience, being thus almost forcibly transported into the distorted world in which these women lived, for they were prey to dreadful fears and convictions, and full of hatred, especially for the doctors. One of them said to me, "They make me go into a treatment room—have they ever done it to you?—and they open up my head and put sand in my brain. It bothers and hurts me all week."

Marian, with whom I was sharing an apartment on Charles Street, used to wait for me with milk toast and hot strong tea whenever I had an assignment to a mental hospital. I heard her telling someone over the phone, "I can't go out on Wednesdays; that's the night I go to bed with Proust." (She was doggedly reading the entire *Remembrance of Things Past* in French.) "And Thursday is out, as poor Bunk has to do one of the loony bins, and she always comes home exhausted and with a raging headache. Friday is the only evening I could make it."

I visited and wrote up five or six mental hospitals that year, and Ilse Lauber taught me as much as I was able to learn about her fledgling profession, with all its yearning hopes and constant frustrations.

She was pretty, a round little wren of a woman with enormous soft brown eyes and waving golden-brown hair. "Ilse," I dared to ask one day, "what drew you into this profession? and why do so many of your confreres in it end up mentally unbalanced themselves? Or am I wrong about this?"

"I think you are wrong. Though perhaps not completely. You

see, Elizabeth, those of us who are drawn to work among the mentally ill are the people with an extra large capacity for empathy. We *feel* their desperate confusion, their bewilderment. And then, perhaps because we enter into their confused and painful life so completely, we become the same."

She was herself constantly frustrated because she wanted a simple thing that the Legislature could not bring itself to give her. She wanted a budget to buy milk for her patients, especially the violent ones, because she thought that a simple glass of hot milk at bedtime, heavily sugared, would help them relax and go to sleep. But it would cost money, and the Legislature felt that money could better be spent on children and useful citizens. I suppose they were right. But Ilse was right, too. Finally, in desperation, she resigned, joined a medical mission to China, and died there not long after, of typhoid.

How happy Ilse would have been, could she have lived to know something of the new biochemical aids for those who are mentally unbalanced. Her little glass of hot milk, so important to her, would fade in importance before the wonderful news that almost no mental patint is considered "incurable" any more, unless there are specific lesions in the brain.

But many things change, and they changed before my eyes when I was a young reporter.

A woman doctor who was named director of a woman's prison seemed startlingly modern when she submitted a budget for cosmetics for women prisoners; she dared to say that being able to use some make-up made her charges less hostile, easier to handle.

But there were old-fashioned, inflexible prison wardens, too. Once, when I went to the Charles Street prison, the warden drew me over to the window and bade me look down into the enclosed exercise patio where the men were walking up and down in their grim, ugly clothes and caps.

"See those fellows down there, miss?" he said. "Every single one is innocent. They are all pure as the lily. They were railroaded into prison. Every one. If you don't believe me, just ask them. They'll tell you."

I had to be careful what I wrote because of the dreadful

threat of libel, and that threat pursued me because I wrote what were called "color" stories, or pieces that attempted to provide atmosphere, or immediacy. Once, when I was sent to write a story about a person who lived on the top floor of an old building, I wrote that I ascended in an ancient, wobbly elevator. A libel suit was clapped on the paper next day, and I had to recant by writing abject apologies, and swear and depose that the elevator was in splendid condition.

The threat of libel could reach absurd proportions. A friend of mine, Moses Smith, of the *American* (a Hearst paper), was summarily fired because he used the word "music lover" in a review. It seems that Mr. Hearst, in a moment perhaps of self-conciousness, had decreed that the word "lover" was never to be used in any of his papers. And Moses Smith, who was a music critic, had broken the august rule.

All the reporters on the *Herald* were required occasionally to "do a Rover." This was a boxed column, on any subject whatsoever, to be written up in a lively, informative way and labeled "The Roving Reporter." I was assigned an occasional Rover and I loved the freedom of subject matter and of treatment, so far from the Who-When-Where-What-Why of the average newspaper story.

But my pride was brought low once when, desperate for a Rover, the Editor took my crowded handbag, passed it over to David Frederick and said, "Do a Rover on Miss Borton's purse, and don't spare the horses." Besides handkerchiefs, money, notes, powder, lipstick, love letters, and a few other items, there were instructions about how to get into my two-way stretch girdle, and this was faithfully reported in the Rover. My face was red for days.

My work took me into a great variety of surroundings, and I saw my friends when I could. Boston is a large city, and I did not (for some time) reflect on the fact that my friends fell into three categories, and that their circles almost never coincided, except casually. I was often with my intellectual and artistic Jewish friends, sometimes with friends from the closed and dignified group of old New England and Boston families (sometimes called "the Brahmins"), and at other times with fun-loving, quick, witty and sensitive Irish friends, who felt hostile toward the Brahmins.

The Brahmins were coldly distant to both the other groups. The Jewish circles were philosophical, in a wry way, about the others. Politically, too, I was caught in the middle of liberal intellectuals—who were in a passion of resentment against the public opinion that allowed Sacco and Vanzetti to be electrocuted, and who paraded all night before the State House on the night of their execution—and my deep feeling for due process of law and respect for judges, which had been bred into me by my lawyer father, who was the soul of integrity. This made it impossible for me to believe at once that corruption and prejudice could prevail against the forms of justice which had been set up in the country. I was bewildered and frightened, and I clung to a wishful belief that the good world I had supposed existed was not as flawed as it seemed.

I learned, very painfully, that underneath the joyous fabric of my life were thousands of suffering, unhappy, resentful and exploited lives. But I was young, and there were long stretches of time when I forgot everything except that I was busy, learning and active, and my excess emotion spilled over into love of the many beautiful, talented and good people who accompanied me along the way.

Then, in 1929, into the radiance and excitement of my life, came trouble. Trouble everywhere. Banks failed. People lost their jobs. Men jumped out of windows. Some sold apples or pencils. My editor called me in and said he thought he could manage to keep me on, but only for half days. I couldn't live on half pay. I was sorry for everybody, but being young, I was especially sorry for myself. I wrote a tearful letter home.

The answer came back at once, from my father, via telegram: "Wiring money for ticket home."

I packed up, said good-byes and went, weeping most of the way.

When I got home, Papa said, "Honey, in hard times lawyers have lots of work, because everybody remembers everybody else who ever owed them money, tempers are short, and people are ready to fight. Now, you relax; I can take care of us all."

After a week or so, Papa came home and said, "Bunkie, you are always trying to write. Now you'll have time to get at it seriously. I have taken an office for you, next door to mine. There's a table, a chair, and a typewriter in there. You'll buy your own paper. You'll go to work with me every day at nine, home for lunch at twelve, back to work at one, and we'll walk home together at five."

So I began work.

For a day or two I sat and stared at the paper in my typewriter, and for a few days more I started things and tore them up. But Papa had made it clear about my hours, and I kept them, and I tried.

After about two weeks my father asked, "How is it going?"

"Well, I started a novel today, Papa!"

"Fine. Just about four thousand, nine hundred and ninety other people started novels today, Bunkie. And about four thousand nine hundred and fifty have more talent than you. But I'll tell you how you can get ahead of almost all of them."

"How?"

"You can finish yours."

I did. It was terrible and I threw it away and started another. In all, I wrote three novels in the year and a half before the Boston *Herald* Editor wrote me again, and said, in effect, "If you want to come back, your job is here waiting for you."

But thanks to my father, I had learned a few lessons about writing, the most important one being that it is subject to two good old four-letter words: *Love* and *Work*. You have to love it enough to work at it.

10.

Business was slow in the summer, and my editor, Mr. Minot, knew that I had family in California, and that a two-week vacation would barely get me there and back, with no time in between. Partly because he thought it might attract readers, and partly out of kindness, he decided to run a summer series of arti-

cles on the movie business and movie stars in Hollywood. I could
write the interviews, and if enough interest was aroused, I could
stay on for the summer, continuing the work until the big fall
season of music, theater and ballet in Boston. I always filled in
my reporting with assignments in those fields, and would be
needed from October on. But it was only early June.

I set out with a high heart, and after a short joyous reunion
with my family in Bakersfield, I took a bus across the mountains,
along the old "Ridge Route" to Los Angeles, and checked into a
small family hotel.

In those days the movie studios had publicity departments
that couldn't do enough for reporters from large metropolitan
daily newspapers.

When I rang up the studios they sent cars and chauffeurs for
me, they set up interviews, they lunched and dined me, and provided me with all the glossy pictures I could use.

In 1929 and 1930, the star system was in its heyday, and everybody in the United States wanted to know "what they were really like."

To some degree, I found out.

My very first interview was with Marie Dressler.

She was overpoweringly sympathetic, kind, and, to use a word
now overworked in its real sense, "professional." She was a
worker, a hard worker, who had risen in her profession because
of courage, determination, and toughness.

"I was down and out a dozen years ago," she told me frankly,
"and I had to let my manager go to my friends, to ask if they
could help. They suggested the movies. But the movies said,
"Sorry. You're old, and we can use just so many character
actresses."

Then she turned that big homely, unforgettable face to me
and replaced the warm smile with a defiant frown, underjaw
thrust out. "But I'll tell you my rule for success," she said.
"Never lose your nerve!"

After *Tillie's Punctured Romance*, when she catapulted into
fame with Charlie Chaplin, she was in demand, and eventually
she achieved the actor's dream—a long series of films in which

she played a character that develops and changes with each situation.

She became the star of *Tugboat Annie* and won awards.

Back of her success, her professional skill, her courage, and her reliability was another quality that she never lost—the philosophy of friendship.

"When you are old, you get over thinking that love is all that counts," she told me. "The world doesn't go around on love between men and women. Lovers get very little done. But friends do. When you are past middle life—and I hope you have the rich experience of love along the way—don't think everything is all over. Don't regret the vanished hors d'oeuvres. When the stuffed turkey is about to come in, flip out your napkin and bite into it! Friends you can gather around you in the later years of life are worth the whole thing, honey. You'll find out."

I found out that even some of the actors and actresses who were criticized for "playing themselves," did not actually do that. The personality so captivating in every role was assumed, like a cloak. These people, perhaps, were the greatest actors of all.

I am thinking now of Maurice Chevalier. I asked for an interview with him, but was denied. He was angry with the studio, for a number of reasons which were explained but which now escape me, and he refused to co-operate in any way. He acted, he fulfilled his contract; beyond that, he would not go one step, and he would not even eat in the commissary with the other actors and actresses. I saw him sitting outside his dressing room, on the small balcony which was attached to it, glumly devouring some sandwiches and chicken. Alone.

Among other things, he had ordered that no one from the press, nor any visitors whatsoever, be allowed on the set where he was working. Yet I had made friends in the front office with an enchanting publicity manager named Virginia, and she simply sneaked me onto his set, with great secrecy, when the lights went up and all the set not being filmed was in darkness. Safely hidden, I saw the great Maurice glowering on the sidelines, made up and in costume, until his cue sounded. Then he leaped into the glare of the lights, and suddenly his person became that of a quivering lover, and he attracted sympathy as easily as a beautiful baby attracts admiring adults. The personality of Gallic charm, with its hint of naughtiness, the outthrust lower lip below the sparkling, merry eyes, the jaunty walk, the Maurice Chevalier of a dozen films, was there before me, and he performed flawlessly, never fluffing a line. The moment he was off camera, he was secretive, resentful, a man who seemed to be in a cold rage.

I never did secure the interview. He returned to France. I may have caught him in a very bad moment, and everybody has them. But one thing was certain—he was an actor of superlative gifts.

Back in the front office with Virginia, selecting glossy still photographs to send in to my paper with my articles, we talked him over, and discussed some of the other actors and actresses as well. The publicity staff had its favorites, as was natural, and before long—as was natural—I had my favorites, too.

There was a tall, dark young man who popped in and out of the front offices teasing the girls, laughing and looking at schedules, and asking if they had thought up a good name for him yet. He spoke in an odd accent, which seemed vaguely English, but was not quite the Mayfair English I had heard a good deal of in Boston. His name was Archie Leach, and he had been signed to do bit roles. He was glad of the money, and unlike many of the other youngsters on temporary contracts to see if they might develop into anything, he didn't buy a big car and fancy clothes and go out gambling. He took good care of his salary and had his eye on the future. They finally got a name for him: Cary Grant. And not long after my first visit to Hollywood, he got his chance. He was, as I said, tall, dark and handsome, and Mae West needed somebody exactly like that for a film she was making. Archie became Cary, and he cannily saw that his contracts kept up with his fame.

Everybody was crazy about him. When he fell in love with the first of the willowy blond ladies he married, a young actress named Virginia Cherrill, all the publicity staff agonized with him until he managed to win her.

There were two reigning stars at Paramount then, and I was scheduled for interviews with both of them. One was a tried and reliable actress, who always turned in a thoroughly good piece of acting, and the other was a bombshell, just over from Europe, and was expected to burst everything wide open. (She did.) The first was Claudette Colbert, and the second was Marlene Dietrich, fresh from her triumph in *The Blue Angel*.

The manner in which they received me—an unimportant, but possibly useful provider of press releases—throws some light on their separate attitudes.

Marlene made me wait, and twice canceled luncheon engagements which the studio had set up for us. Meanwhile, I met a tall young actor who was to play opposite her in one of her first pictures. He was Gary Cooper, who had graduated from Westerns into general leads because of his startling good looks and his general amiability. At the time, he was publicly and privately bemused by a fiery young Mexican actress named Lupe Velez.

Gary, loitering outside his dressing room, strolled over to greet Virginia, my publicity guide, and me, and he offered us both a taste of something Lupe had introduced him to.

"It's powerful," he recommended.

"It burns my throat," objected Virginia.

"That's because you don't know how to drink it," he explained solemnly. "You just lay your head back and let it run down your gullet. That way you don't taste it. It tastes awful."

"You're in the new Dietrich picture, aren't you?" asked Virginia. "What do you think of her?"

Gary rolled his very blue eyes, so bright in his long tanned face.

"She's gotta lotta appeal," he commented at last.

"Yes. But can she act?"

"Lotta appeal," he answered again, refusing further comment.

Finally, I was advised that Marlene was willing to be interviewed one afternoon. I was to wait for her in her dressing room.

After forty minutes, she arrived, accompanied by the director who had found her in Europe, had crashed into love with her, and had brought her to the States and was piloting her through her first pictures at Paramount. His name was Josef von Sternberg. I suspected at once that the "von" had been added by himself. I found him short, hostile, very protective of the beautiful Marlene, and very pretentious about his own gifts as director, which were, to give him credit, exceptional. In the first place, he had a great eye for hidden beauty. The rather rough diamond he polished into the extraordinarily svelte and elegant Marlene of the films, was proof of that. Her natural rough good humor and kindness she saved for her friends; the press was another kettle of fish, in those days. I suppose she was told to be haughty by the man who was determined to make her into the star of the epoch. As he did.

She was dressed entirely in a tailored costume of a deep wine color. Her silk blouse was of that exact shade, as well, as were her shoes, which had short tan buttoned uppers the exact shade of her silk stockings. On her golden hair was carefully arranged a sort of tam-o'-shanter of the same material as her suit. The color, glowing and dark, could not have been better chosen to set off the shining gold hair, the sapphire-blue eyes, the porcelain skin.

She came in, sat down carefully, arranging her beautiful legs in their most favorable position. She gave me front face, three quarters, profile and three quarters again. I sat silent, overcome with admiration. Suddenly raising her eyebrows, she turned to me and said firmly, "I do not like interviews. I do this only because they say I must. In Europe this is not so. One works, one is an actress. One has privacy."

Despite this unpropitious beginning, I started. Her answers were short, taciturn, careful. She seemed to have some slight defect in her speech, because I couldn't understand all her words, and it was not the effect of her really delightful accent. The truth came out. Suddenly she threw aside all her careful modeling poses and turned to me with a distraught expression.

"It is my baby," she said, and homesickness sounded heavily in her voice. "She has lost her first tooth. My husband sent it to me. I have been carrying it around, in my mouth, all day. She is in Germany. I have not seen her in many weeks . . . many weeks."

She stopped and took it out, a tiny pearl-like tooth.

"My baby Maria. My daughter," she said, and put the little tooth back in her own mouth.

Later, I reflected that what Gary Cooper had thought of as a "lotta sex" might indeed come across on the screen as that, but I thought it really was obsessional mother love.

In the front office, they told me that real gold dust was sifted through Marlene's blond hair when she was photographed, and that the thin lifting line of eyebrow, penciled in above her heavy-lidded eyes, was going to change American eyebrow fashions. I saw it happen. But throughout all the ensuing publicity about Marlene, about her overpowering sex appeal, I could think only of that little tooth that she had carried around in her mouth all day.

Claudette Colbert, from France, was perfectly at home in English and in French, and in fact had done some dubbing from one language to the other.

The friendly, helpful Virginia set up an appointment for me to lunch with Claudette in the studio commissary, and I arrived, in good time, wearing my little printed silk with the cape, my wide-brimmed white hat and my white gloves.

"Well, there's a change," said Virginia, when I reported in.

"Claudette is awfully sorry . . ."

I thought, Here we go again. Changing appointments, making me wait.

"Claudette says she is sending her car for you, to take you to her house for lunch."

I was startled and, of course, pleased.

She lived in a pleasant two-story house, comfortable and very tastefully furnished, but not elaborate. And this was the day of movie-star palaces. The chauffeur showed me into the house, and I sat down. In a few minutes lovely Claudette came down the stairs. But what had happened? The pretty face, a perfect oval, dominated by the big velvety dark eyes, was swollen, the eyes almost shut.

"I have a terrible sinus inflammation," she told me, "and it is better for me not to go out. So I do hope you won't mind taking a simple lunch with us here. And now, please meet my mother." The mother, an older version of Claudette, with beautifully coiffed silver hair, made me comfortable, and Claudette, evidently suffering, patiently composed herself to answer all my questions.

What we spoke of was routine material about her career, the necessary change of name because her French name was hard for Americans to spell and pronounce, and other similar matters. But what was remarkable was that here was an actress, dependent to some degree on her beauty for her popularity and acceptance, who was so modest that she received the reporter while miserably ill and deformed by a facial swelling, and that, far from postponing the interview, she bent every effort to make it pleasant. The lunch we were served was very simple, but delicately seasoned, and I left feeling that strange aura of friendship which enveloped me sometimes (not always) when I met the talented people of the screen.

I did not find Charles Laughton exactly *simpático*. He looked just like his pictures—fat, pouty, arrogant. We had one of the studio luncheon engagements, and he ate with precision and speed, pursuing each potato to its final impalement on his fork, with concentrated interest. Very intelligent, he was reasonable enough to know that newspaper interviews had their value, but at the same time, he had been harried too much and was resentful of the sort of personal questions Englishmen nearly always feel are impertinent. Sensing this, and having been briefed on his career anyway, I didn't ask any, but I did want to know how an actor like himself could manage to build up a characterization, when scenes were shot or photographed according to the set available, the time of day and the director's pleasure, rather than consecutively as the story developed.

Laughton himself had just made his first American film, in which he played the part of a jealous husband, opposite the tempestuous Tallulah Bankhead, and his acting was brilliant in its gradual build-up of tension until the final explosion, when the character he played went entirely out of control and precipitated tragedy.

"I do it scientifically," he told me. "I insist on seeing the whole script before I begin work. You might be surprised to know that this is not always easy. As a trained actor, it was horror for me, at first, to think of doing the final scenes in a play before the first scenes, before any chance of build-up. Or in the middle. So I worked out a system of clues for myself, and marked my script with them, informing myself of exactly the amount of relaxation or tension that was needed in the acting and delivery of lines, at that point. Numbers up to ten."

"But how difficult, immediately to assume the tension, the tautness, say, of number seven, just when you come onto the set," I murmured.

He smiled as he speared the last potato.

"I'm an actor," he said, simply. And indeed, the years proved it. Without good looks, or even a physique suggesting strength, and with a good but not exceptional voice, he became one of the most skillful actors in English anywhere, because he was both analytical and a hard worker.

The majority of actors really learned by doing, as the saying goes. They left instructions to the director, and they did their best to obey, to "deliver," as they liked to say at that time. Gary Cooper, when I asked him a question about acting one time, looked around with every evidence of secrecy, to see if anyone was near and then leaned down to whisper, "But I'm not an actor. I just do what the man says. I'm scared that the studio may find out and fire me."

In time, Gary became one of the most subtle and skilled of all Hollywood actors, because he was modest enough to know that he had something to learn, and because he had a large share of that special charisma which endears an image to a public. If you are blessed with charm, as he was, it comes through on film, and charm is, after all, the instinctive ability to please. With that gift, Gary became an actor.

Reporters on the Hollywood scene were used to the fact that many actresses who came through as beautiful on screen, actually were not. They were photogenic, which is not the same. Thus, I was startled when I met Joan Crawford. She was then in the process of being remade for the screen. From a husky girl, with freckles, hoydenish attraction, and a wide mouth which she painted into a little-girl pout, one would not have thought her likely to become a symbol of glamour and beauty. But she did, with help from the studios, and with a lot of determination on her part. She reduced, and it was hard, because she had to reduce muscles by inactivity, and then starve them down. The freckles were easily taken care of with make-up.

The character and interest of a wide flexible mouth suddenly struck the public, and little buttonhole mouths went out forever.

I was interested in a new contract player at Metro, because I had known his cousin when I was in grammar school. Frances Gable, dark-haired and pretty, wore beaver hats (which I envied) and was a close friend of my friend Gladys. Clark Gable was also being made over, and again, the seers who had looked at the bulky young man with the big ears, had seen through to the idol he could (and did) become. I never had a chance to talk with him, though, for one reason or another, but I saw him striding about on the lot, and when they had pinned back his ears and made him grow a mustache, his dark hair and tanned face with the startling gray-blue eyes gave an immediate effect of masculine good looks.

His gravelly voice added to the the general effect of masculine power and virility. With Clark Gable, the era of the pretty boy went out. Actors stopped painting their mouths, and tried for something with the impact of roughness, toughness and American naturalness. Rudolph Valentino was no longer to be imitated, thanks to the popularity of Clark Gable and the actors who followed his lead.

Over at Fox Studios there was a great new singing star whose movies were making millions for the company—though American audiences had heard little of him. I had heard him sing in the various presentations of the Chicago Opera Company, which came reguarly to Boston. He was José Mojica, a Mexican boy who had made his way to the heights through sheer hard work and (he was always the first to say) through the prayers of his beloved mother. He was an only child, and as he grew up, knew poverty and struggles. But he managed to study singing and eventually got a few engagements in Mexico. Then he felt he must try his luck in the United States. Like any other immigrant, without anything but hopes to go on, when he landed in New York he soon found out that he would have to forget his dreams and find something to do in order to eat. He got a job washing dishes in the Waldorf Astoria, and wrote his mother that he "was living in the finest New York hotel," which was true. They let him sleep in a cubbyhole near the linen room, so as to be ready for the night shift washing dishes. But he continued to try out wherever he could and to accept little engagements when he could get them. Once, by chance, the great Mary Garden heard him. She demanded that he be signed to play Pelléas to her Mélisande, and his meteoric career began. He was tall, with a handsome presence and a beautifully trained and controlled voice. Because of his brilliant performances with the Chicago Opera, and because it turned out that he was eminently photogenic, he was persuaded to star in a singing movie, in Spanish, when the talkies came into being. He was an instant success in a series of romantic love stories, in which he wore assorted costumes and played various highminded or mysterious and fascinating heroes. His movies made quantities of money, being distributed all over the Spanish-speaking world.

José Mojica invited me to his home in Santa Monica, which he had built in as exact a replica as he could manage, of his boyhood home in San Gabriel, Mexico. There was his mother, a proud and sedate Mexican lady, deeply pious, presiding over his home. She was treated like a queen by everyone who knew the Mojicas. In the fragrant garden, under a tree, we drank tamarindo water, and ate tostadas spread with refried beans and avocados. Afterward, I listened to Mojica rehearse a concert with his accompanist.

We had many talks, and through them all shone his love for his mother and for his native country, and his gratitude to the United States, which had given him all he had of material worth. But underneath, he was restless, seeking. It became clear what he had been looking for when, after his mother's death, he gave away all his possessions, including a hacienda in San Miguel de Allende, and became a Franciscan monk. Eventually he was ordained, and in the last years of his life he worked hard for his order, giving benefit concerts and directing plays. His was no dramatic decision, to be repented of when poverty, chastity and obedience became onerous. Devoted to his faith and humbly proud of his priesthood, he continued to the very end, thirty years or more. I often used to drop in at the San Francisco Church on Madero Street when I was living in Mexico City, and sometimes I would hear the Rosary sung in his still wonderfully thrilling and perfectly controlled tenor. He always sang there, unannounced, whether there were three or four, or a hundred people, at the Rosary services.

Once I interviewed him at the Franciscan convent in Coyoacán, when he was in Mexico on one of his busy traveling and working schedules. (He had been put in charge of late vocations by his superior in Lima, Peru.) He was staying at the Mexican convent, a sixteenth-century building. The cloisters surrounded a patio, with a fountain and rosebushes. Father Mojica's habit was well worn, his open sandals showing tough, calloused feet. His thick, curly black hair had turned white, and he was a bit more portly than when he had been the star of Spanish talkies in Hollywood. We spoke of the many changes being made in the Church, and I commented on the fact that dozens, even hundreds, of priests were leaving the Church in order to marry, or because they were no longer willing to carry out their vows of obedience to their superiors.

"I think of the Church this way," said Fray José Guadalupe (as he liked to be called): "The Church is a big apple tree. Once in a while God reaches down and gives it a good shake, and all the rotten apples fall off."

As I digested this, he went on: "Actually, it is a good thing when unwilling and rebellious priests leave the Church. The Church is an institution which has had to stand firm through many storms, has had to preserve and protect Christian thought against constant battles and attacks. There is no place in it for disruptive people, for priests who work against the final goals of the Church.

"I believe we are coming into a great age of saints. Saintly souls always emerge during and after an age of troubles, wars, uncertainties and moral disintegrations. After our age, with its morals shifting into selfish gratifications of all kinds, with drug abuse and street violence and an atmosphere of fear and disillusionment everywhere, the saints must appear again with their messages of moral strength and goodness, of purity, peace and hope."

Of course, Hollywood held countless interests for a reporter beyond the presence of the stars, though the actors and actresses in the star system of those days were what fascinated the general public.

I found the directors, the men who envisioned the film as a whole and directed all its parts, of enormous interest, but they were, in the best sense, executives, with gifts of planning and of management. The actors came through to the public in their roles, and were idealized and idolized; the directors put the work of the actors together and presented the plays. But the creative people behind the entire activity were the writers, and they were almost never given any notice by the publicity offices. They sat in their cubbyholes, many of them without secretaries, and slaved to develop dramatic ideas into scenarios that could be filmed, that would present the "personalities" of the reigning stars to their palpitating public in stories that the censors (very important in those days) would pass and that might catch the interest of viewers.

I was interested in the writers and insisted on meeting some of them. Most of them didn't want to be bothered, and either hid, or said they wanted nothing to do with the press, or gave me a few desultory moments. As is well-known now, more than one superb literary talent was lured to Hollywood, as to the gold fields. There they would sit, bored and uneasy while no assignments came their way, or were forced to attend endless "story conferences" during which they were told how to write by people who had never written a line and were not far from illiterate. Faulkner gave up and went home, and was not even missed for months; Scott Fitzgerald broke down and became utterly despondent there.

Once Pierre LaMure, author of *Moulin Rouge,* gave me good advice (which I never had to use, never having had the good luck to sell anything to the movies). "If they buy your story," he said, in his heavily accented English, "take their check, put it in the bank and thank God for your good fortune. But never go to see the film they make of your book. It will break your heart."

I met one young writer who managed to produce, and at the same time keep his head. Perhaps that was because he could see the industry from the inside *and* from the outside, and because he had set his sights high and intended to let nothing deter him. He was John Huston, a writer at Universal, and he was hacking away at several scripts on a good, but not astronomical, salary. He knew the vagaries of the studios because his father, Walter Huston, was a superb actor on constant call, and an intelligent man. But John Huston did his job with verve, and took whatever lumps came his way with cynical amusement. They didn't get far under his skin.

"I aim to go into directing, anyhow," he told me. "That's where you pull the whole thing together. The director is the boss. He can fire a bad actor, and he can make an inept writer do his scenes over. I intend to get into that part of the action before I am much older. If you want to do something first-rate in this world—and I do—you have to maneuver yourself into the position of being the boss. Otherwise, you will never make it."

There were other actors who wanted to direct too, and some of them did. Dick Powell, a singing star who made countless inane little musicals, had ambitions, and in time he became a reliable and competent director.

He told me, on the set where he was acting in yet another sweet little story, that he did this for the money, and that he was just biding his time. "And learning," he added thoughtfully. "You can learn a lot here on the sets, working, if you keep your eyes and ears open."

Many of the actors who skyrocketed into fame and into money lost their perspective and disappeared into nothingness a few years later.

Some of the stars had modesty and wit, and kept their footing in a treacherous business because of sheer level-headedness.

Once, on my second summer assignment in Hollywood, I was strolling on the Metro lot when I heard "Hi, Boston. Come over." It was Robert Montgomery, who flattered me by remembering that I wrote for a Boston paper.

"I know you are just panting for another interview with me," he teased. "Come over to my dressing room." I went, happy to see him. Tall and tanned, he was heavier and healthier than the pale-blond gentleman he played on the screen.

"Now, then," he began. "See that pile of letters on the floor? That's fan mail. Let's read a few of them, shall we?" He picked one up at random and read it aloud.

"Dear Mr. Montgomery," it said, "If you should see Clark Gable there on the lot, would you please ask him to send me an autographed picture? Yours truly, etc., etc." Montgomery burst into rich guffaws.

One day when I was lunching in the commissary at the Metro lot, Spencer Tracy came and sat down beside me and interviewed himself.

He divulged the news that Warren Hymer, "who got one hundred per cent in moron on his report card" (you remember the movie?) was taking a correspondence course in how to be a gangster.

Tracy was a short, broad fellow, with a rather red face and freckles, unruly light-brown hair, and naughty, teasing eyes.

"Hymer is supposed to get his diploma any day now," he said. "He already sent the five-hundred-dollar fee for it."

Spencer started eating my olives.

"I'll miss him when he leaves for Chicago to go into business," mused Tracy. "He's a good guy to have around. Near, so you can kick him. Al Capone is going to let Hymer understudy him. The correspondence school arranged it. They take care of their graduates."

He went on and on, his imagination adding touch after touch to the little conceit that had struck him originally. And his face was mortally sad, despite the olives that he put into it at regular intervals. His weary blue eyes roved about the restaurant as he munched and spun his fancies.

His tweeds were loose, his necktie the same, his shirt rumpled. "Well, drop in again sometime," he said, rising and saluting me, and leaving the table a few minutes before the waiter brought the check.

11.

Those summers in Hollywood were a recurring joy for me. My father, always generous, bought me a little car, a two-seater. These were available at the time, and makers of "compacts" might think about them again. (As I sit and observe lines of traffic on the freeways nowadays, very often I see enormous cars taking up a great deal of space, with only one person in them—the driver. All that power and space wasted. Full cars may be seen, but not often. Why not the small two-seater again?)

I learned to drive the two-seater with great trepidation, and I am here to tell the tale only because there wasn't much traffic in the late twenties and early thirties, especially over that killer of a highway, the "Ridge," which wound over the mountains from Bakersfield to the San Fernando Valley.

Little blinking side lights, to indicate that you were going left or right, had not come into use; we used our hands and arms to signal our intentions.

The current joke was: "If a lady sticks her arm straight out from the car she is driving, it means she is going left, or right, or stopping, or flicking the ash off her cigarette."

Papa was a meticulous driver who never had an accident, or even a scratched fender, in his life, and he taught me to make the signals clearly and in good time: straight out, for left turn; up, for right turn; and down, with the hand moving downward repeatedly, for stopping. He instructed me never to "ride the brake," to go through my gears softly, without grinding, and above all, to keep my mind on what I was doing. Unlike my sister Barbara, who had been driving for years, and who had driven all Papa's cars besides her own Yellow Peril, and whose reflexes were instinctive, I had to try to build up mine, and I wasn't much good at it. Barbara could roar up to a crossing and *know* who was going to come into the highway. I never knew, and was always nervous and worried. And I was inclined to day-dream on a long drive. This caused my father to write out instructions which I had to paste on the glass down low, where they wouldn't interfere with vision but where I would be sure to see them. They were as follows:

Keep your mind on your driving!

On the other hand, poor Papa was so careful with his signals that he nearly wore his arm off the first time he drove the winding Ridge Route with its hundreds of curves. He signaled every turn.

Having the little car, I was able to do my interviews in Hollywood on Tuesday, Wednesday and Thursday, and spend long weekends in Bakersfield with my loving family. Thus it was that the Studios set up five or six interviews a day for me. I happily learned the secrets of the make-up departments, and I talked with photographers, among them the charming and talented Chinese, James Wong Howe, and even did a stint as an extra in a movie being filmed at night. It was an adventure story having to do with sinister goings on in Singapore, and I had the thrill of "signing in," going to the costumer's for my clothes, and being made up, and of standing around in the cold on the set for weary hours while Nujol was sprayed regularly (to make realistic fog) and hordes of extras tried to do the director's bidding. To my surprise, I was cast as a Singapore wench, and my round, innocent face and unsexy walk would, I am sure, have doomed me to starve in such a competitive business in the Orient. Yet I did my best and collected my pay, and was known thenceforth to the publicity manager at Fox, an amiable oldtime newspaperman named Jack Francis, as Singapore Tookums.

Instead of becoming fired up to try to write more scenarios for the movie industry, having penetrated its innards, so to speak, all this discouraged me. I began to perceive what a complicated business it was, how dependent on such fickle matters as public taste (look what happened to Jack Gilbert, whose voice was too high and shrill to keep up with his hero image), and how riddled with a thousand details that depended on human frailty, unpredictable weather, and the public clutch on its seventy-five cents, then the going price for a loge at the movies.

One time, when the studios had planned seven or eight interviews for me in one day (in the hope that one or two of the unknown starlets thus written up might one day "catch on"), a flus-
tered young couple in tennis clothes was propelled toward me.
They were man and wife, English, and they both had small contracts.

The young woman had the pert, delicate, clean beauty of English girls, and a charming manner. Her name was Jill Esmond.

Her husband, not tall, scowling and making no attempt to be
pleasant, had dark-chestnut hair and reddish-brown eyes that
photographed black. He was annoyed. He had been told to get
into tennis clothes for publicity pictures, and then, instead, had
been hounded into a cubicle with this female reporter. He made
it clear that he hadn't much love for Hollywood, and would get
back to England just as fast as he could.

I wrote up the two of them, dutifully, never expecting to hear
much of either one again. I was wrong. The young man's name
was Lawrence Olivier.

I continued to do these summer Hollywood interviews for five
years.

I was determined to write a story or two that wasn't the routine studio-publicity sort of thing, and I inquired around for the
name of an actor who didn't give interviews. W. C. Fields, I was
told. He won't see anybody.

With the connivance of a cameraman, I pretended that I
wanted to learn to juggle, and, thus deceived (but he wasn't deceived for a minute), Mr. Fields received me. He actually gave
me a good lesson, and for a few minutes even I could feel the
rhythmic thrill of the flashing juggler's skill.

Another time when I saw him on the lot, he called out to me,
"Halloooool Can you do the five balls?" He was reclining on a
propped board, one of those inventions that had come into being
for the comfort of female stars who wore elegant gowns that had
to be kept unwrinkled for filming, and therefore they could not
be allowed to sit down in them.

I confessed that I hadn't practiced enough, and he clucked at
me.

"Isn't this the berries?" he asked, indicating his prop board.

"It's to keep my pants pressed. That's a hot one. Me, I used to be a tramp."

"I don't believe you!"

"Oh, yeah. I was. I used to sleep under bridges, and steal pies off windowsills, and cook stew in an old can."

I knew that his first juggling engagements had been performed in tramp costume, and I surmised he was making up a tall story to amuse me.

"I used to see the trains going by, over the bridges," he went on dreamily, "and the people in the dining cars eating beautiful meals, and all the linen and silver and glass. I used to think, 'If I ever make it to the big time, I'm going to go all over the country in trains, and every time I come to a bridge, I'm going to throw out boxes of food to the tramps down below—chicken legs and bottles of beer and bananas and roast beef sandwiches . . .'"

"And did you?" I prompted.

He turned quite red with sudden rage.

"Nooooo! I never threw them anything!" he roared. "Dirty bums!"

That was W. C. Fields. If you ever thought you knew what he was going to say next, you were wrong.

12.

Every summer, around mid-September, I would return to Boston and my job as a general reporter. Because of my Hollywood columns, I was one day called to a publishing house, and a proposition was laid before me. They had a series of books for young girls which had been phenomenally successful. The author had died after the first two books, but the publisher owned the titles and the characters in the tales, and they were continuing the series, with various writers producing the books on contract and to specifications. This series was the Pollyanna books. I was asked to consider writing a Pollyanna book, with the famous philosophy of the Glad Game incorporated into it, and with a Hollywood setting. It did not do my ego too much good to know that the offer had been made to a couple of other writers before my name came up. I said I had to think it over.

In case the reader does not remember, the famous Glad Game in the Pollyanna stories went like this: Pollyanna, a poor child of missionary parents, waited with the greatest anticipation for the "Missionary Barrel" which arrived from the home church around Christmastime, and often contained a few toys as well as second-hand clothing and other things the missionaries might need. But this time there was no toy. However, the Missionary Barrel did contain a pair of crutches. Pollyanna was taught to think, "I'm glad, glad, glad that I don't have to use the crutches." This philosophy was applied to every disappointment and trouble, the idea being always to find something to be glad about.

Among my sophisticated friends, this procedure of always being glad about something was anathema. The climate of thinking was changing; it was generally thought to be much more intelligent to be angry about things. This elevation of anger to a position among the virtues has attracted an amazing number of partisans in recent years.

I wanted to be sophisticated and intellectual, and I feared that my image would be tarnished if I associated myself too openly with the Glad Game. At the same time, I had been bombarding a very patient agent with short stories, and we had not found many publishers. I was dying to be published, to get my foot in the door.

I went with my problems to a wise counselor, a man who was a professional writer: Dr. Isaac Goldberg. He heard me out. Then he said, "Well, there is no real problem. Do you want to be a writer, a professional writer, or not?"

"Oh, yes! More than anything else!"

"Then my advice is, Take every job you are offered, and do it to the best of your ability. Beethoven was not ashamed to work on contract and deliver work that was ordered. Neither was Bach. Or Verdi. Neither was Sir Walter Scott. Or Balzac. This idea that you have to be independent of all pressures, absolutely dedicated only to your own ideas, is fine for private diaries. But the publishing business is just that—a business. If you want to be published, you have to co-operate with the people who are willing to invest in your product, in the hope it may sell and at least get their money back. Up to a point, you have to take orders from them. If you improve yourself, develop into a capable worker, deliver your writing on time, and fulfill your contracts, you may be given more freedom, and eventually have almost as much as you want. But you are just beginning. The publishers are willing to take a chance on you. Grab it, and do as good a job as you possibly can."

I got up to go, my decision having been made. I would accept the contract.

"And another thing," added Dr. Goldberg. "Don't keep anything back, thinking it is too valuable a pearl for this job. Put your best into everything. If you are ever going to be any good, new ideas will come, and you will not find yourself without resources when you need them."

I was extremely grateful to him for his advice, and I still am. It steadied me and kept me on the right road. Not more than a half dozen writers in any epoch are the geniuses to whom everything is given, for whom all rules are lifted. And I always knew that I was not in the genius catagory. I was not even an artist. I thought of myself as a craftsman, and I hoped to be an entertaining one.

I therefore hurried over to Page and Company next day, and signed the contract to write a Pollyanna book with a Hollywood setting. I was to be paid a flat fee of three hundred dollars, no royalty. This was good for me too. I was hired to do a job, not to launch out into the deep, hoping to find a port.

First, I had to reread the previous Pollyannas, get an idea of the characters, their place in time in the stories up to then, and refresh all my ideas about them.

I found, as I read, that it was I who was going back in time. I remembered how I felt when I first read the Pollyanna books as a little girl. And I recalled that the Glad Game had seemed like a fine thing to me then. And I had been, like all the other children reading the books, as highly moral and bigoted as my sophisticated friends deprecated. I had felt that wickedness should not flourish and that good should win and be rewarded. I realized that I hadn't really changed much. So I set to work with enthusiasm to figure out a story for the Pollyanna characters that had been turned over to me.

After all, I said to myself, the Glad Game was just the famous British stiff upper lip, but with a smile on it.

I was, as in so many other developments in my life, extraordinarily fortunate to be given the opportunity to write a book for publication. I was to be paid, a modest sum to be sure, but paid, as I learned. For it was a hard lesson. I had to organize my story, weave in my characters, develop a continuing line of action, and hold to the old firm maxim that a story must have "a beginning, a middle, and an end."

In all, I wrote four stories for the Pollyanna series, and I found (as all writers find, even the really good ones) that, as you learn your skills, your self-criticism increases, with the result that it never becomes easier, but harder, as you continue.

As I reflect now on much of the current writing for children, I wonder if it is wise to assume that they must be hurtled into the "real world" of sex, murder, incest, abortions, and violence in all their reading. It is a rougher, harder world than I knew as a child, and I agree that children must be made as wise as possible by their parents before they are allowed to roam freely in it. But aren't children entitled to escape literature, too? Shouldn't the imagination of what *could* be a beautiful world, be kept, in their stories, in their entertainment? If not, how will they envision it? Man has always dreamed of improvements before he was able to effect them.

I was delighted immeasurably, a few years ago, to learn that a great fantasy, *The High King*, had been chosen for the Newbery Medal—that most honorable prize, awarded annually by secret vote of librarians all over the United States, for the most distinguished contribution to children's literature by an American author.

And an all-time favorite among the Newbery Medal books is that enchanting excursion into the imagination, entitled *A Wrinkle in Time*.

I do feel, strongly, that some of the special gifts of childhood must somehow be preserved, and chief among those is the vaulting imagination, and the child's capacity for love and empathy.

13.

Back in Boston in the fall, winter and spring, I continued my work, enjoying beyond all else the varieties of experience it put in my way. One of the outstanding events of those reporting years for me was the assignment to cover a National Psychiatric Convention. Like many another layman, I had only a faint idea of the explorations across unknown boundaries which were being made by students of the human psyche and the marvelously complicated and wonderful organ which is the human brain. The talks on psychoanalysis were profoundly interesting, and yet I felt most strongly drawn to the work of one of the members at the convention whose talk and illustrating slides showed that actual cellular changes in the brain had taken place in all cases of dementia. (To prove it, he showed slides from brain tissue of countless patients who had died in unrelieved dementia.) The question that immediately presented itself was: Did the disordered mind induce or produce those cellular changes? Or was it the other way round?

Biochemical studies of schizophrenia tend to indicate that no matter what triggers such cellular modifications, the change can be reversed. A thrilling possibility.

At the same time, I was privileged to watch a skillful operation by which a surgeon restored flesh and sensitivity and the ability to work, to a hand that had been stripped of its musculature in an industrial accident. I presume this was the beginning of that branch of surgery which now flourishes, to restore function to injured members.

And an interview with Dr. Minot taught me that pernicious anemia can be combated by feeding an injured liver enormous quantities of—*liver!*

In a way, this was a foreshadowing of the spectacular branch of medicine which includes the transplantation of sound organs into bodies whose organs are failing. Minute particles of skin, dotted upon raw flesh, can take hold and form a new skin covering; minced raw liver can help an injured liver to function again; and the transfusion of new blood can restore healthy circulation. All these processes (phrased here in the most simplistic language), then, must mean that the body can be treated with the similar parts of other bodies.

The thought was startling, exciting, even disquieting. Under certain circumstances, it followed, the spirit could inhabit patchwork bodies for what might be many natural lifetimes. Other people, of course, had the same idea, and a lot of science fiction came into being—that branch of imaginative writing which rests solidly upon some scientific fact or probability. There had been occasional novels of this type; but now, with a public increasingly interested in medical facts and theory, and avid for understandable information about space, natural forces, and the cosmos, an avalanche of such stories appeared. And journalism continued to feed the public hunger for understanding of the great mysteries which had heretofore been left to the specialists. No doubt such superficial reporting did a certain amount of harm, because simplification and popularization can be dangerous. At the same time, truth—even its shadow—is always worth pursuing, whether or not the pursuers have had adequate training. At least, that is what I believe.

Of course, there were vast areas of total ignorance, and still are.

I recall a long correspondence I had with a man who informed me that he had been able to devise an experiment that proved beyond doubt that the speed of light was not a constant, but in fact a variable. His letters were erudite, precise, careful, and to me, it seemed important that he be interviewed and given a chance to prove his point, since I knew that the mathematics of all physics rests upon the premise that the speed of light is indeed a constant.

This matter, and the letters, came to me while I was in California, and the writer demanded a chance to get a hearing. I wrote, advising that I would have to consult with my editors before I could undertake to talk with him, that I was quite ignorant anyhow, and that he had better direct himself to capable scientific reporters, of which there were many.

Then I got a barrage of answers which insisted that he had indeed put his idea before authorities in the field and that he had everywhere been repulsed. The letters began well, but ended up in tirades of abuse against all the outstanding physicists of the day. I asked my father to read the letters, and he advised me not to look up the scientist, whoever he was, because he sounded paranoid. Now, however, forty years later, I have read more than once of certain factors which "bend light" and of occasional fluctuations in the calculated speed of light. My poor mad scientist—whatever became of him? There may be others like him, driven off their base by resistance to ideas that upset too great a body of standard thought.

No doubt wisely, my editor guided me firmly away from all these mind-boggling speculations and sent me out to write up church sermons and ladies-club lunches. He did relax enough to send me to a tremendous mass meeting and rally in behalf of Al Smith when he ran for President, and I came away from that—I, the daughter of staunch Republicans—with stars in my eyes for the Democrats. I thought Al Smith a charmer, Brooklyn accent and all.

But because of this excursion into political reporting, I was allowed to pick up a bunch of due bills and go to Mexico at the time when the revolutionary President, Lázaro Cárdenas, was elected in Mexico. He was feared to be a Red, a dangerous radical. And the country was boiling with picturesque creatures who were also tinted somewhat red, as they painted murals, or composed music, or wrote novels. With the order to interview these people (great confidence was rested in my Spanish), I set off for Mexico.

What happened to me personally, I related at length in a book titled *My Heart Lies South*. I met Mr. Right, that mythical gentleman all Mamas used to tell their daughters to wait for, and he turned out to be a Mexican with black curly hair, a little black mustache, romantic sentiments, and a pleasant baritone voice. We were married a year or so later, and have jogged along in double harness, bilingual and mostly happy, for forty years. To the confusion of the marriage counselors, I must confess that we had little in common when we married but an intense interest in each other. We don't understand each other at all, and never have liked the same things—except our children. But we laugh a lot, and it has been a good marriage, all the same.

I was interested in President Cárdenas as a personality.

As is customary, I waited in a series of anterooms, being passed from one to another, getting nearer and nearer the President. In the same rooms were many other hopefuls who wanted to talk to him.

As it happened, that day I was wearing one of my favorite Russian blouses, in a bright-red silk, and on my blond braids was perched one of those imitation fur hats that are seen in Russian newsreels. And I heard comments in Spanish which, it was supposed, I wouldn't understand.

"Blankety-blank Communist woman, I bet she gets in there first."

Well, I wasn't first, but I did get in.

As I entered the President's office, I saw a tall, dark, middle-aged man dressed in a sober blue business suit, a plain white shirt and modest tie. And I observed that his shoes were large, worn, comfortable, laced shoes that had received many polishings.

He rose, with grave courtesy, shook hands, and waved me to a seat. The office was large but sparsely furnished. There was no carpet on the floor. There was a big desk, but the President had come out from behind it, and we sat talking together some distance away, each of us seated on a plain cane-bottomed chair.

He had not asked to see any questions in advance; he had not set me a fixed time for my questions. Now he sat, courteously awaiting my first words.

He had a long, roughly carved, sad face, with rather stiff upspringing hair, and a thick mustache hiding the long upper lip. The lips were full, but firm, and there was about him a look of patience, of endurance.

I asked the most obvious question first. What would be the outstanding concern of his government?

There was no immediate answer. Rashly, I tried suggesting the trend of his answer. Education? Communications? Civil liberties?

He turned then and looked at me as if wondering whether to answer me or not.

Then he said, "Señorita, of what use is it to a man to be able to read and write, even to enjoy liberty, if he is starving? In a poor country, food is the first concern. You know about our Revolution. Men do not take up arms and risk their lives, unless they have nothing to lose. And when does a man reach that point? When he sees his children hungry. Our Revolution was accomplished and it gave us some machinery. But the work has only begun. And first—yes, first—I would like to see that Mexicans have enough to eat." He went on, "There are parts of my country where people eat lizards and insects, where they are drunk because they have no water and their liquid is the juice of the maguey, which quickly ferments. There are other parts of the country where people go into the jungles and catch monkeys to eat them, because they have nothing else. There are places where children are sent out to the roads, to pick up kernels of corn or barley from the manure of horses that have passed by.

"I am thinking of these people first. Whatever should be done has to be begun, but I cannot hope to finish everything. Yet, the country *could* support people. With many advisors, I must try to figure out how to set in motion some activities that will open up ways to get food and resources and work to the people who are still without hope. Roads? Yes. Education? Yes. Water? Yes. All these things. And many more. Even with good will and the best advice possible, I know that we can only make a beginning."

Later, when the great decree for expropriation of the oil companies, which had not adhered to the Mexican laws governing them, was announced, I could see that he had tried to get to the bottom of the basic problem with his characteristic simplicity. He obviously felt that a country should own and exploit its own resources. As everyone knows, he was well ahead of his times— revolutionary, in the best sense.

Mexicans rate him as one of their greatest Presidents, following the line of Benito Juarez, and often say so. The Western world, now bent on a course which poses liberalism against dictatorships, has begun to realize that he was one of the first to take the stand that the rich and privileged know how to take care of themselves, and can be trusted to do so, but that when the majority have no weapons, economic or civil, the government must take their side, and act for them.

The people I interviewed on that trip to Mexico turned out to be part of a New Wave of the future. I found them all intensely alive, thoughtful, hard-working, and patriotic.

14.

Diego Rivera, though, was a man of his time. In curious ways, he seems now just a little old-fashioned. But, with Picasso, he was one of the first artists in the world to realize the full value of publicity, and he manipulated press stories with extraordinary skill. He was diabolically witty, well-informed and clever.

I was taken to his home and studio in San Angel by Carlos Chavez, a good friend of Diego and of his third wife, Frida Kahlo. I had met Chavez some days before, and we had several talks, which had shown me the depths of his interest in everything basically Mexican in music and in composing. His dream of preparing and conducting a symphony orchestra capable of performing the works of Mexican composers was well under way. Chavez was, and is, a man with a goal and a purpose, and the stamina and energy to keep to it. This he has done over a period of forty years.

Diego Rivera, his wife, and a few other friends were drinking chocolate on the terrace of his home. Juan O'Gorman had built the studio and home in elegant and wealthy San Angel. It was ostentatiously middle-class Mexican, with a fence of organ cactus, and great simplicity in the rooms. Chavez presented me and mentioned my newspaper, and I had my first good look at Diego, who became a friend in ensuing years.

It was a strange, froglike face, with pop eyes and crushed features. The body, too, was strangely proportioned—tall, long-legged, but thick. The hands, though, were fine and sensitive.

"If you are interested in art and beauty, señorita, let me show you something wonderful," said Diego. He led me over to the wall, where he had hung a large advertisement on glossy paper, showing, against a bright-orange background, an array of hardware—knives, screwdrivers, hammers, and the like.

Diego stood in front of it, gloating, having assumed an expression of rapt admiration.

"The most perfect art," he murmured.

Perhaps my own expression did not simulate his enough, for Frida spoke up in a slightly acid tone.

"He loves that. He has been drooling over it for days."

I think that Diego was trying me out. He had had plenty of success making fools of many other Americans, and he tried to keep his hand in.

At one time my friend Peggy O'Gorman, Juan's sister, worked for him for a few months as his secretary. An American lady came to order a water color. Peggy took the order and advised the client that it would cost five hundred dollars and would not be ready for two months. On the morning of the day designated for the painting to be delivered, Peggy reminded Diego that it was due. He had no painting ready.

The client arrived and Peggy showed her into the *sala* downstairs, then hurried up to Diego's studio to notify him that the American lady was waiting below with her check ready.

"Keep her there an hour," was his answer. And he dashed off a water color with all speed.

This anecdote displays his skill and virtuosity, for it was a good water color. But it also displays, I think, his low opinion of many of his clients. A fifteen-minute sketch was good enough for any of them, since he thought none of them knew anything about painting anyhow, and just wanted his name.

Some years later, I was serving as English secretary to Carlos Chavez, when he was Director of the Institute of Bellas Artes, and I had many meetings with Diego, and with other important Mexican artists. Diego came one time, and called a meeting of all the directors of departments of Bellas Artes, to talk over a brilliant idea that had come to him. I was there to take notes, for I provided American newspapers with important news emanating from Bellas Artes.

"The plan is this," propounded Diego. "We will take a poll of all the workers in the factories and in the country to find out what they want us to paint, and then we will obey them. The painter should be at the service of the people!"

There was no discussion, only sycophantic agreement that this was a superb idea. But Diego detected a less than enthusiastic listener.

"Elizabeth," he challenged me. "Don't you think it's a great idea?"

He and David Alfaro Siqueiros had been most excited about the possibilities of the poll. Both looked at me, and I had to answer.

"No," I was compelled to say. "I think the artist should be a leader, not a follower."

Silence.

The discussion took up again, and there was continued excitement. But somehow the idea died out, and the poll was never taken. I was snubbed for a while, but eventually forgiven.

Diego and David Alfaro tried hard to identify themselves with the people, and insofar as they portrayed history and the Mexican struggle for survival, they achieved this. They also contributed through their work to an appreciation of the great art and culture of the Mexican nations of the past, before the Conquest. Part of this was the accepted line of leftist thinking, which endeavored to rewrite history, not from the point of view of the arrogant conquerors, but by making the submerged and exploited peoples the heroes of history. This was, culturally and emotionally, the beginning of all the movements to identify and liberate small ethnic or social groups, which is now at its apogée. This point of view led to much splendid writing and painting; the time was ripe for new ideas, and for reversals of old fixed attitudes.

Orozco, though his murals also portrayed the many tragedies of Mexican history, and the long bloody struggle of the Revolution of 1910, and though he was always referred to, with Diego and David Alfaro, as "one of the three great muralists," was far more independent in his political allegiance. He was profoundly emotional and tragic in his painting, a true revolutionary in the purest sense of the word, but he "belonged" to nobody and to no party.

He was, also, like many great artists in other fields, a man who had overcompensated, for he had difficulties with his eyesight, and perhaps this enforced the pure clean expressive line he developed as his style, using only two or three basic colors—mostly charcoal, earth-brown or copper, and white.

Diego worked from carefully drawn and perfected cartoons which were transferred to the wall, in outline, and then painted in. But many a time I saw Orozco go straight to a wall and start painting—the cartoon in his head.

"What would you do, Maestro, if you wanted to change something?" I once asked.

He turned his ironic smile on me.

"Just tear down the wall," he answered.

Like Rivera and Siqueiros, Orozco liked to shock people, and in fact, the "Great Three" dedicated a good deal of time to this.

Peggy O'Gorman told me that her brother Juan, a very talented young painter and a friend of Justino Fernandez (who later became the final authority on Orozco), was once invited to a banquet where the Great Three and some others were to be present.

According to Peggy, Justino rather treacherously recounted an anecdote against Juan. Rising at the banquet and speaking, Justino turned to Orozco and said, "You know, Maestro, Juan here has told me that your paintings make him sick."

Orozco turned mildly to Juan and asked, "Is this true?"

Red in the face, Juan tried to make his feeling clear.

"I said your painting makes me ill, ill with emotion," he stammered, in explanation.

Orozco rose. "Certainly, Juanito. That's why I paint—to make people feel, to make them grind their teeth and feel ill with emotion and vomit. Come on, Juanito, let's get out of here and go have something together."

All three of the Greats painted a number of superb portraits. David Alfaro's portrait of Carlos Chavez, which hangs in the composer's home, is a great painting. Diego's portrait of Lupe Marin, his second wife, is, in its bold design, a great painting, too. But my personal preference, of all the portraits done by the three, is Orozco's magnificent portrait of Archbishop Martinez, a triumph of distillation of character. One can study it for hours and come away feeling that one has made the acquaintance of a shrewd, brave, intelligent, and ironic man, Mexican to his fingertips.

Curiously, not one of the three Greats was much interested in painting portraits of women. There are a few exceptions, but their best work is seldom easel portraiture of women.

Diego, though, often slipped little portraits into his murals, and once I saw him do this. He was painting the lovely sunlit mural, full of nostalgic details (though he worked in a panoramic view of Mexican history, too), of the Alameda, which adorns the main hall of the Hotel Del Prado, facing the Alameda. Peggy and I had gone in to watch him work, and Peggy saw that he had done little cameo portraits of Lupe Marin, of his daughter Ruth (whom he used to call "Chapopote," meaning "Tar Baby"), of Rosa Rolando Covarrubias, and others.

"Why don't you put me in, too?" wheedled Peggy.

"I will. Stand over there," ordered Diego, and he found a little space where he painted her in, wearing a flowered hat.

Peggy is dead, and I loved her dearly; I often go by the hotel just to look at the little portrait. It showed her gray eyes, her half smile, her air of hauteur, which she often assumed just because it was fun, and I am comforted.

I was present in the lobby of the hotel when the great ceremony of the blessing of the mural by Archbishop Martinez was to take place. The Bishop arrived and went to robe himself in a room provided by the hotel. The lovely mural waited, all tones of gold and leaf green—to my mind, the loveliest of Diego's paintings, in its nostalgia and gentle color. But alas, Diego had painted in a writer, Nigromonte, who had been rabidly anti-Church and who had at one time proclaimed, "God does not exist." Diego had faithfully written this defiant shout, on a tiny bit of white paper, portrayed as a banner in the hand of Nigromonte, though he himself did not exactly share that view.

Archbishop Martinez, resplendent in ceremonial robes, swept out, while the respectful public looked on and waited. (The blessing was to be followed by a banquet.) But (no doubt he had been advised beforehand of where to look) the Archbishop's sharp little black eyes noticed the words, "God does not exist," and he stopped in his tracks. He turned to the owners of the hotel and said, apologetically, "You realize, of course, that I cannot possibly bless a mural which proclaims there is no God!" And he swept out again, got back into his black clerical suit, and departed.

To coin a phrase, All blazes broke loose.

I am sure that Diego, who loved these rows, was pleased as a boy with a frog in his pocket. But the result was not merely exciting new publicity for the painter. Groups of rebellious youths took sides, armed themselves, and fought in the hotel and in front of it. Attempts were made to deface the mural. Organizations which had booked the hotel for conventions became worried and canceled. Agnostic university groups stood patrol in front of the mural. Catholic university boys got in and scratched at the fatal words of Nigromonte. The upshot was that the mural was taken away, covered up, and stored in a forgotten room of the hotel, where it languished for years.

Only since Diego's death, when the unpleasant words were inked out and others, from the same Nigromonte but not inflammatory, painted in, has the beautiful mural been restored to its place.

It is my opinion that someday—when the murals of machinery and workers in blue overalls seem passé and dull—this mural, full of light and endearing details, with its cargo of cameo portraits, will be regarded as Diego's best work.

Frida Kahlo, Diego's third wife, was, in the opinion of many critics, a better easel artist than he. A careful painter, she was a master of brush-stroke techniques, and the sensitive and certain use of color which seems to be innate in Mexicans.

Her work was psychoanalytical in the main, and her subject was herself. She profoundly explored the reasons for her love of Diego, the emotional bonds they shared, and her life of almost constant pain. She had been in an accident, had endured many operations, and was never free from suffering. Yet her beauty, unusual and striking, seemed never to be affected by the way pain had confined her, almost immobilized her.

Her skillful hands were free, and she painted. In self-portrait after self-portrait, you see the thick glossy black hair, bound to her head with colored wools, the heavy dark eyebrows almost meeting above the enigmatic large dark eyes, the faint line of dark hairs which outlined the sensuous upper lip.

I was sometimes embarrassed by the intimacy of the caresses Diego bestowed upon her whenever he was near; she seemed to accept kisses on her neck and shoulders and upper arms without any special response; her expression never changed from its habitual look of controlled thoughtfulness.

She wore loose Mexican dress, mostly the beautiful clothes of the isthmus and of the Indians from the state of Oaxaca. They became her, and they served to hide the apparatuses and harnesses she had to wear.

One of Frida's paintings I most love is a portrait of a deer (with Frida's face) which carries in its body many arrows.

She was not sweet; she was intelligent, sharp, often witty. Peggy ascribed to her the devastating criticism of Diego and Orozco, which, it seems to me, is an almost perfect summation of their work. "Diego," she pronounced, "is a great talent without genius; Orozco is a genius without talent."

Poor Frida. In death, Diego had her body exposed in Bellas Artes. I am sure she would not have wanted this. Also, he draped her coffin with the red flag of Russia, and the symbol of the hammer and sickle. A number of sycophants paraded around her helpless corpse, with left fists raised in the air. It was an unpleasant scene, and the man who was at that time Director of Bellas Artes was promptly fired for having permitted the ritual use of a foreign flag in a Mexican Government institution.

Diego remained vocally and actively a friend of the Soviet Union until his death. Dying of cancer, he went to Russia for their "sleep treatment," in which they kept the sick person almost constantly drowsy or asleep. Apparently this treatment is effective for some illnesses, permitting the tired body to marshal its defenses. Diego came back to Mexico much better and much cheered, but his illness had not been cured, and he died some months later.

Orozco, though popularly supposed to be a Red, was not one in the sense that he gave any allegiance to Russia or to Marxist philosophy. He was perhaps better described as a Mexican leftist, a revolutionary, whose sympathies were with the great horde of Mexican peasants who had suffered from exploitation, in one way or another, under various foreign flags or companies. When he died, it was rumored that he had made confession and received the last rites of the Catholic Church. His will made no pronouncements in favor of any party, foreign or otherwise.

Juan O'Gorman, Peggy's brother, a professional architect, was and is an excellent painter and has many splendid murals to his credit, as well as a considerable body of easel painting. His work is meticulous and carefully detailed. Peggy once said that Juan painted murals in miniature, using magnifying glasses. Not so, but it is true that his work, unlike that of some of the others, is enjoyed even more at close quarters than at a distance.

Juan, though always pronouncing on the side of the least popular philosophy of the moment (some Irish contrariness here), has a streak of practicality not often found in painters. When he was given the commission to decorate, with murals, the library of the National University, he began his work in his usual carefully planned and studied fashion. Having decided to "paint" his mural with a mosaic of many small stones, he went about collecting the stones he would need in natural colors, so that weather could not have a deteriorating effect. These stones then had to be broken and cut to size, and in the quantities needed. Naturally this took a lot of time. It turned out that he was not going to be able to finish the four-sided building before a change of administration in the government. He therefore hastily did a little of each side of the library, his thought being that if he stuck with one side only, the next government might decide to assign the other three sides to other artists, or even leave the building with only one side decorated. With a little bit on each wall, he was safe, and could count on being able to finish all four.

This he did, and the library is an imposing building with its mosaic mural of natural-colored stones. But the university students all call it "The Tattooed Library."

Juan has a large helping of Irish charm, and has the right to call himself "The Gorman," as chief of his family. But he has kept the O'.

A lady once confided to him that she would elope—leaving husband, home and children—with a man who could purr; she thereafter received many phone calls from Juan, during which he purred over the telephone most convincingly. Yet the lady never kept her promise, and Juan himself has been happily married for years to Helen O'Gorman, a well known painter of flowers.

After the disappearance of the Great Three, other Mexican painters came into prominence. Besides Juan O'Gorman, there were Rufino Tamayo, greatly appreciated as a colorist; Rodriguez Lozano (whose pallid, skeletal figures in landscapes have a strong emotional impact); Federico Cantu, who chose religious subjects; Guerrero Galvan, whose children and young women are softly tender and innocent; Gonzalez Camarena, and many others, including a host of women painters of considerable skill. Only one young painter has sunk roots into the Mexican past, where caricature and grotesquerie achieved artistic stylization, and has departed from the traditions of the muralists and the European-type easel painters. This is José Luis Cuevas, whose savage figures and faces leer from countless drawings and paintings now part of museum collections.

There were, in those years, many distinguished Spanish refugees in Mexico, and most of them, favored by the fact that the Mexican Government recognized only their government in exile, and never Franco's, made their way into the arts and sciences, teaching and business, greatly to Mexico's benefit.

Remedios Varo, whose exquisite surrealist paintings are now quoted in the thousands of dollars, had to struggle for a living at first, and she accepted work decorating furniture for a time. With her mane of thick auburn hair, beautiful dark eyes, Spanish aquiline nose, and fragile figure, Remedios had enormous personal charm and was a raconteuse of unusual skill. We often met at parties in the home of her friend, the equally gifted English painter Leonora Carrington, and the Spanish artist Pepe Orna. They had all met in Spain, and had been able to get out of Europe by various strange means. Remedios had left Paris when the German invasion began, making her way somehow to Marseille; there she lived in a hovel while she waited for a ship to America, and it was typical of her that with scarcely enough to eat and everything closely rationed, she should befriend a large dog. Her bread ration went to him every week, and they shared her meat ration, small though it was.

When I first met her she was married to Jean Nicol, who had been a flyer with the French Resistance; later they parted, and Remedios married an Austrian Jew, Walter Gruen, who had escaped the Nazi armies only to be interned under the Pétain French. Somehow he got out of the prison camp and made his way across France and into Spain, disguised as a priest!

Remedios always had cats around her, but she did the opposite of what most cat owners do. Remedios let them out to run and sun themselves all day, but at night she called them in and locked them up. "The night is sinister for cats," she used to say. "Things happen to them—fights and love and accidents." She saw a tree being felled near her home one day, bided her time, and when darkness came she went out, hacked off a heavy branch with many small ones attached, and dragged it up the stairs to her apartment. She set it up in her living room for the delight of her cats, who ran up and down it and sharpened their claws on it.

Mexico was, and still is, alive with painters; dozens of expositions take place every week in the capital, and almost as many in the provincial cities. Also, displays of paintings in open markets, the painters themselves sitting hopefully beside their works, are to be seen in every good-sized town.

Curiously enough, this rush to expression in paint and color is not paralleled by a similar rush to the typewriter. Occasionally prizes are offered for a novel, but there is never an overwhelming submission of manuscripts.

Perhaps preferences in kinds of creative expression appear in cycles. Certainly during the second half of the last century, Mexico enjoyed a great flowering of romantic poets, and some beautiful work was produced.

Even today, it is rare for an original piece of writing by a Mexican to sell more than five hundred copies, and editions of more than a thousand are almost unknown.

The great Mexican novelist of the Revolution, Mariano Azuela, was living in Santa Maria la Redonda, the old part of Mexico City, when I first came to the capital, and I was able to arrange a talk with him. When I asked him what an aspiring young writer should do to prepare himself, his answer was dry and succinct. "Become a doctor," he said. (I knew Mariano Azuela had been a doctor, and had gone through the Revolution practicing his profession with the ragged troops.) He went on to explain, and I thought perhaps he was looking back on that violent, desperate time of his youth with nostalgia, now that he was old and peaceful.

"The doctor sees drama, tragedy, suffering, the things that life is made of. He works amidst grief and fear and desperation. These are things the average, ordinary young person hears about, reads about, but does not experience. Blood? Perhaps you cut your finger, or nick yourself shaving. The doctor may have to take care of the stump severed from a wrist. When the doctor enters a house, nobody is masked. The presence of fear and suffering and death rips the social masks away and leaves sheer character staring out of the faces of men and women.

"And you cannot even write about comedy—which is man's cloak of defense against the savagery of life—until you know what wounds are concealed behind laughter."

The old doctor sat there, shivering a little despite his warm sweater and the gas stove. Oxygen tanks stood nearby, for occasional use. He died not many months after our short talk. His dark eyes stared back into a past that had been tumultuous, full of terror and trouble. From it he had devised his magnificent novels, *Los de Abajo* (in English translation, *The Underdogs*), and many more.

Mexico has had a bloody and desperate past. Perhaps no other nation on this continent has struggled more constantly against foreign oppression, dictatorship and corruption than Mexico, in an effort to achieve some semblance of freedom and democracy. No doubt, that is why the Mexican's greatest gift is his irony, his humor, his sense of caricature. Certainly Mexico has produced some of the greatest caricaturists and political cartoonists that ever lived. One of the great ones was Ernesto Cabral, a shock-headed Veracruzano, whose drawings graced a popular newspaper for many years. When I rang up to ask him for a short interview, he invited me to his studio. He told me that caricature, or the malicious distortion of a portrait to the point that it looks more like the sitter than a straight portrait does, had come down intact to Mexicans from their indigenous forebears. Much of the ancient art is really caricature—exaggerated, stylized, grotesque. To prove it, he seized a piece of Bristol board and, looking at me with his small, bright, amused eyes, did a magnificent caricature of me—all eyes and teeth.

In the fifties I belonged to the very important group called the Association of Foreign Correspondents. This was possible because I could be admitted as an "associate" member. Genuine members were those whose entire living depended upon their work as correspondents for such distant and important news media as *Time* magazine, *The New York Times*, the London *Times*, papers in Tokyo, in South America, in Paris, in Moscow. The kernel of genuine membership was glamourous, in the true and original sense of the word, to all of the rest of us (including Pepe Romero, who got in by reason of representing the *St. Mary's Bugle*). There were exciting people with whom to rub elbows, and once in a while one could squeeze into a little space at a restaurant and overhear marvelous stories. I could not hope to name all the brilliant reporters and writers who graced Mexico City for a few months, or a year or two, in this way. We did see Robert Capa, the magnificent photographer, a few times, before he went to the East (and was killed there); we knew Paul Kennedy, of *The New York Times*, and his wife Diana (now a successful writer of cookery books); the beautiful Flora Lewis; romantic Camille Cianfarra, who left Mexico to become correspondent from Vatican City, and who died tragically in the collision of the *Andrea Doria*.

Dean of all foreign correspondents, for a very long time, was

Arthur Constantine. He could be found every morning at eleven o'clock, consuming a peach melba in the Sanborn's on Madero. (This was after his retirement.) I remember being with the reporters in Monterrey when Henry Wallace visited Mexico. Mr. Constantine, being elected monitor, organized everybody with great skill, allowed each one two or three questions, not repeating those of any one else, and got everybody a story without tiring out the victim.

(The Mexican sense of irony and caricature came in here, for a joke blossomed almost at once about the unfortunate Mr. Wallace. Pronounced carefully and slowly in Mexican phonetics, his name comes out "Váyase," which means, "Go home," or, "Get out.")

Mr. Constantine was very kind to me and gave me tips on stories that I was able to run down and sell to American newspapers. After his retirement, he spent a lot of time trying to work up enthusiasm at the National University for American football. Now, years since his death, it is catching on here, though the great enthusiasm is still soccer.

Once I said to Mr. Constantine that I was delighted with the ambassadorship of Mr. William O'Dwyer, who pleased Mexicans because he was Catholic, had a beautiful young second wife (Sloan Simpson), and spoke Spanish.

Mr. Constantine fixed his icy-blue eyes on me, and scolded.

"American ambassadors are not here to please Mexicans," he told me, "though it is all to the good, if they can. They are primarily here to defend Americans and protect American interests. Never forget that."

I think things have changed since Mr. Constantine pulled my ears; the function of ambassadors has broadened now; often they do much to promote and cement good relations.

Once, Abel Quesada came to speak to the foreign correspondents. He is an able cartoonist, still contributing regularly to the great daily newspaper *Excelsior* in Mexico City. His cartoons are always mildly fantastic, though once in a while he delivers a stinging blow, of great seriousness. His drawing is amiably childish, and he has developed a few recognizable types—the rich Mexican with a large diamond ring in his nose, the poor starving *campesino* (or country man) who is propped up with sticks so that in his weakness he may stand upright, the *Charro Matias,* a kind of *mestizo* in wide *sombrero* and *charro* pants who is always hoping for a quick million, somewhere, somehow, from somebody.

We were on the eve of a national election then, and Quesada commented on it. (He spoke in English, which he knows well.)

"Many of you write for North American papers," he said. "I have always admired much about your country—the iceboxes, the pretty blond girls, the ready-made clothes, the hamburgers. Your country is progressive. But I must say that Mexico is way ahead of you in politics. Right now, not a single one of you knows for sure who your next President will be. You'll never catch a Mexican in that fix."

He was referring of course to the fact that Mexico is governed by "an official party," though there are a few token parties which bloom and die quickly around election time. One always knows who the next President in Mexico will be; he will be the candidate of the official party, the PRI.

More than my contacts with the foreign correspondents were my associations with musicians and composers, because of my years as English secretary to Carlos Chavez, himself a composer of indefatigable activity and constant inspiration.

I learned an odd fact that explained a matter which had puzzled me for some time. How do young musical artists get started playing with great symphony orchestras? Oh, of course some brilliant performer from Europe, who has dazzled critics in a few recitals, can be contracted to play concertos. But what happens to all the earnest young students of piano, violin and cello in the United States? Few can afford to finance themselves in a series of concerts. And yet, with some regularity, new unknown pianists and violinists appear on the programs of the great orchestras.

The ploy was (and is) this. A young artist, without any chance of getting contracts for perhaps four or five years, if then, saves up his money, or collects money from friends and relatives, and commissions a concerto from a well-known contemporary composer—Chavez, or Halffter, or Copland or Britten (to name a few at random)—a composer whose latest work is sure to be solicited by the important orchestras. Having commissioned and paid for the work, the young artist has the exclusive performing rights to it for a fixed number of years. (This is usually established in the contract or the letter of agreement for the commission.)

This procedure works, and it is not to be despised. It was Albert Spalding who commissioned a violin concerto from Sibelius, and who introduced it magnificently.

Yet it is almost the only way the young performer can assure himself a dignified debut.

Once, in talking to Stravinsky, a great friend of Maestro Chavez, who came often to Mexico to conduct his own works with the Mexican National Symphony Orchestra, I asked him how he worked. Did he keep a notebook of themes, or perhaps start improvising and find that some development or emerging theme seemed worth elaborating?

It was the latter—improvising—he told me. Thus, his inspiration came from deep within; the intellectual ordering of the music, orchestration and so on, came later.

In simplistic terms, this is more or less the way most composers work. There is a period when they brood, meditate, or draw upon some inner reserve of invention—in short, a time of creativity. Afterward, there is a long, laborious, and careful time of organizing, plotting, choosing instruments, *working* in the fullest sense of the word. And this work is subject to a most intense self-criticism. Even the original scores of Beethoven, when one examines them, seem to have been studied, changed, revised, corrected, an infinite number of times.

Thus, the composer is a person who combines in his mind several of the most admirable qualities of a human being—creativity, discipline, capacity for intense labor, inventiveness, and self-criticism.

Even more than the writer, who can read bits of his work to friends and learn of its possible impact, the orchestral composer must wait until he can hear his work performed by a full orchestra. How often is this possible? So seldom, indeed, that the future of serious composers is one of the most precarious in any of the creative fields.

Carlos Chavez had to recruit, train, and slave over the creation of a symphony orchestra, in order to be able to give his own, and the works of other contemporary Mexican and foreign composers, a hearing.

The more I had occasion to work with great artists, in every field, the more I became convinced that a capacity for work is a prime requisite for any measure of success. From this thought, I went on to develop a very unpopular theory, which I propounded among my friends and relatives who thought of giving their children music lessons.

"Don't start the lessons while the child is enthusiastic, and stop them the minute he seems to lose interest in practicing," I advised, "because if that is the way you reason, it is better not to start at all."

Actually, this happens in thousands of homes every year, the irate parent declaring to the teacher, "I can't make the child practice. If he doesn't want to, I am wasting my money."

The truth is that no child likes discipline, and music demands it. No matter how musical the child, he will prefer playing with his friends, or talking on the telephone, or anything at all, to the drudgery of music practice. But if the parent will stay firmly with the musical child, help him achieve the discipline of technique and daily practice, then an artist may be developed, if not for public appearances, at least for endless enjoyment in his own home and with other amateur musicians.

I enjoyed very much working with a number of refugee Spaniards—musicians, composers and musicologists who came to Mexico from the Civil War in Spain. Maestros Rodolfo Halffter, Jesus Bal y Gay, and Otto Mayer-Serra were all a great addition to the musical life of the city. Rosita Bal y Gay had been a pupil of De Falla, and became the teacher of many excellent pianists in Mexico during her stay here. Rodolfo Halffter identified with Mexico wholeheartedly, and is still active in the musical life of Mexico City.

There were refugee musicians from other countries of Europe too, in the fifties. The splendid Lener Quartet, which gave unforgettable concerts, and had made recordings of many of the greatest quartets, found itself stranded here, when the war in

Europe involved the country where they had been born (Hun-gary), the country where they were living (England), and the country in which they were booked for a concert tour (the United States.)

Because of their birthplace, they couldn't get visas to the United States; all their money was impounded in English banks; royalties on their records sold in the United States could not be sent to them in Mexico. They were desperate.

Music lovers saw to it that they gave concerts in Mexico, and arrangements were made so that they might teach at the National Conservatory of Music. Mr. Lener was able somehow to get out of the country, but the other three members of the Quartet—Josef Smilovits, second violin; Sandor Roth, viola; and Imre Hartman, cello—trained a whole generation of grateful young Mexican musicians. And all three stayed on in the country that had given them refuge, and shared the rest of their lives with her. Smilovits and Hartman live there still, and Mr. Hartman is still active in teaching.

I had the great privilege of studying with Maestro Roth for some time, and of playing in an amateur orchestra he directed. I was playing in a violin, cello, and piano trio, and the three of us decided to ask Maestro Roth to coach us. He listened gravely as we shot into the first Schubert Trio and crashed our way through it. We finished and sat awaiting his comment.

He could not tell a lie.

"Well," he said. Then, "Mrs. Treviño plays with much enthusiasm."

I knew what that meant and hung my head.

"But come," he said. He stood up and took a pencil for a baton. Under his vigorous direction, we started again. What a difference!

I was thrilled, and arranged to take private lessons as often as I could manage.

Thus it was that I overheard something said to Maestro Roth one day, by an admiring lady, and I heard his reply. It struck me as magnificent, the words of a true artist.

His admirer said, "Oh Maestro, my heart aches for you! An artist like you, and you have to spend your time teaching all these inept young people . . . when you ought to be giving concerts in the greatest halls of the world!"

Maestro Roth bowed.

"Madam," he said, "there is a time in the life of every one of us—artist or artisan or simple citizen—when we should stop and thank God for what we have been given and what we have learned, and start to pass it on."

15.

Once married and settled in Monterrey, with a husband to support me, I decided to cut myself loose from commission writing and try an original story. I sat in my little *despacho*, with my cat Policarpo purring on my lap or stretched out across the table, and I reached back into my memories of music study in Boston, and of ballet study, and plotted a story for young girls.

I used disguised figures from the world of music and theater I had known, and devised a story of a young girl who longed to study ballet but whose father would not let her because his mother, a great ballerina, had been paralyzed after a fall. The father, important in my story, was a Russian musician, a violinist, and also an inventor, a man who hoped one of his inventions might help to further world peace. I called my story *Bellamy's Papa*, but the publisher who accepted it changed the title to *About Bellamy*.

I was delighted. I had published an original! (The very same book that my uncle read, and disparaged, during his imprisonment.) But alas, luck had deserted me. By the time my story appeared (and it was beautifully presented, with charming illustrations), nobody liked the Russians any more; and very soon, indeed, pacifists were suspect, too. My story died on the vine. I moped. I tried journalism again, but once again I was disappointed.

I saw a wonderful dancer, a gypsy, in a little grubby theater in Monterrey. She was electrifying! When she stamped and made a sudden turn, the hairpins flew straight out from her hair. I queried papers and magazines; I wanted to write her up. All of them answered that they had never heard of her and to forget it. She was Carmen Amaya.

Then I saw an astounding young woman fight bulls in the Portuguese fashion, on a splendidly trained horse. She was young, half-American, brave and beautiful as a legend. I queried enthusiastically about her. Conchita Cintron. Again, nobody thought her worth a line.

Only, a little later, the magazines I had queried sent out their own staff writers to do the interviews and stories I had suggested. I gave up.

I took a little job writing a weekly news column for the Laredo *Times*.

When Page and Company wrote to me, proposing yet a fifth Pollyanna, I accepted with humble gratitude.

Then my husband said, "When the check comes (and this time it was going to be five hundred dollars, not three, as previously), take it and go to New York and meet your agent and the editors and publishers. I want you to use the money that way."

And so, with high hopes, I set out. I intended to spend as little of my money as I could manage, so I rode the bus, sitting up night and day. Once in New York, I checked into an inexpensive hotel that catered to Latin Americans, and got on the phone.

I had never met my agent, Virginia Rice, and it was she I rang up first. I explained that I had just arrived, that I proposed to stay three days, and that I had a reticule full of ideas for novels. I wanted to meet editors.

Now that I know something of the activities of editors and publishers in New York, I am amazed and ashamed of my importunate ignorance. Miss Rice seemed stunned. Then she rallied.

"Come to lunch with me," she ordered, "and we'll begin."

I learned later that she rang up Lee Schryver, Fiction Editor of *The Woman's Home Companion*, and said, firmly, "Lee, you owe me a favor. This poor little thing has come all the way from Mexico on a bus, riding night and day, and she wants to meet editors, and she's going to meet one at lunch. *You.* Cancel anything else you have on your calendar and meet us at the Plaza at one."

I was almost giddy with weariness, but very happy to start my campaign in New York. I told Mr. Schryver and Virginia about some of my ideas, and they listened respectfully. Then, over coffee, Mr. Schryver said, "Tell me a little about your life in Mexico."

By then I was homesick, and I began to talk nonstop about my home, my servants, my family.

When he said good-bye, Mr. Schryver said, "Write up some notes about what we have been talking over and send them to me. We might get a nice little article out of them!"

Virginia valiantly set up other meetings, but when I returned to Mexico, again night and day on the bus, it was Mr. Schryver's suggestion that seemed most hopeful to me. I sat right down and wrote it out. It came right back to me, and I was almost tearful as I opened the envelope. But there were magic words scribbled across it in a memo, and Virginia had sent it on to cheer me. The note said, "Tell her to keep going. I think there's a book in this."

I kept going, and the book turned out to be *My Heart Lies South.*

I was able to be in New York for "Pub Day," a most exhilarating and wonderful time. Nothing ever equals the thrill of the first day a book is published. The publishers sent me an orchid, Virginia negotiated a contract by which excerpts were to be published in ten languages in editions of *Reader's Digest*—and, most exciting of all, editors began to call on *me!*

A long excerpt was published in *The Woman's Home Companion,* and the check I received for that bought the house I live in now, though the house was only a small summer cottage then and has been enlarged and renovated for all-year living. Yet I owe it to Virginia and to *My Heart Lies South.*

That book has been in print for over twenty years and only lately was brought out in a new format, with an epilogue.

I think the sudden success of *My Heart Lies South* was due to the simple fact that I threw open the doors of a big Mexican *zaguán,* and let readers see the life that goes on behind the barred windows. And of course the book was informed with my love of my husband's country and of his people.

But most important to me in my life—a life I think of as a pattern of friendships—was meeting and getting to know Virginia Rice. She was a successful and dedicated literary agent, and I owe much to her wisdom about my work, but above all, she was a wonderful friend. In ensuing years we became devoted companions, often traveled together and visited each other's homes. She had a great capacity for love and a magnificent sense of humor; when I remember our times together, I can recall so much that we laughed at together. We cried together too, over some plays that moved us. But our friendship was a joyous one, through many years of association.

Once, when an excerpt from my book *Where the Heart Is* was bought by *The Saturday Evening Post,* Virginia wired me: "WONDERFUL NEWS SATEVEPOST HAS BOUGHT EXCERPT FROM WHERE THE HEART IS I WENT RIGHT OUT AND BOUGHT A CHOCOLATE BAR AND ATE IT LOVE VIRGINIA."

Virginia celebrated with a chocolate bar.

Loving Virginia as I did, it was a special joy for me that the book I dedicated to her won the Newbery Award: *I, Juan de Pareja.*

After I had got my foot in the door with *My Heart Lies South,* I wrote a series of juvenile stories, all but one of which are still in print, and I had the great pleasure of seeing every single short story I wrote for children eventually reprinted in a collection or an anthology.

Some friends protested the classification "Juvenile," because, they said, they loved my stories and they certainly felt mature enough.

I had to explain that the classifications are somewhat rigid, having to do with age and interest groups. In an attempt to be witty, I said to my friends that nowadays anything not actually pornographic is classified as juvenile. But my wisecrack was thrown back in my teeth when one of my adult novels, one I had labored over with great care, was chosen for a juvenile book club. I was glad of the choice and subsided with a red face, never again to be guilty of acidulous remarks.

Anyway, if I am to be classified as juvenile and innocuous forever, then so be it. Long ago I promised my mother that I would never write anything she would be ashamed to read.

And my mother brought up her family to respect a closed bathroom door and a closed bedroom door. It was not a matter of Puritanism, for my parents were freethinkers of the truest kind. It was considered a matter of simple good manners.

EPILOGUE

Many people have appeared in my life, contacted me briefly or for longer periods, awakened in me feelings of warmth and admiration, respect, and affection. I have, in the manner of tho most odious name-droppers, spoken of those whose images or reputations are widely known. But there were, of course, countless others who meant as much to me, personally, though their fame (except locally, or within their families) was nil.

Why should I suppose that any of these anecdotes and remembrances might interest a reader?

I think, as I look back over what I have told in this volume, that the important thing I want to emphasize is that there is still much goodness, generosity, and kindness all around us, that friendship is still the greatest treasure God has offered us for the taking, during our lives, and that, as they say in Spanish, "Amor con amor se paga." Love is repaid by love.

I think too that in an age of general despondency, when I find so many young people cynical, or ready to abandon life for dreams, narcotics, and various forms of self-destruction, it is important to realize that there is still, hovering over and around us all, like a cloud, a strange thing which we might as well call Luck. Certainly my own life has been lucky and fortunate beyond expression. And there is a Chinese saying worth pondering here: "One must be happy to be lucky."

I have been happy. I am grateful for the life I have lived. I wish happiness, like a smile, were something I could bestow.

Note to the reader: My husband felt that this little poem I wrote for friends and sent at Christmas, in 1970, sums up my philosophy and hopes. I offer it here, as a farewell, to all who have followed the course of my modest memoirs up to now.

> Nothing endures. No creature.
> This we know.
> How many are my darlings,
>   so loved, so dear,
> That have slid down into the deeps of memory . . .
> Father so wise,
> Grandmother all goodness,
> Uncle who followed the sun around the world,
> Beloved friends who shared their thoughts,
> Small furry beings who taught me
>   what true love is.
>
> So hard, so many, the terrible Good-byes.
>
> Farewell to shores where I was happy,
> To rooms that offered haven,
> To homely inanimates, yet cherished . . .
> A piece of hand-knit wool,
> A scrap of lace made by loved fingers,
> A vase that held a ray of light, like a jewel.
>
> All, all gone.
> And some (Forgive!) forgotten.
>
> But then comes Christmas, and the Star!
>
> O Blessed Star that showed the Way,
> the Way through which all,
> all that was loved
> is ours forever.

Tears, pain, and partings, first.
The Cross.
But afterward,
All joy repossessed.